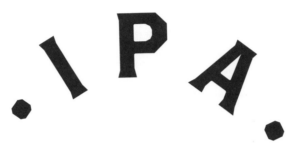

A LEGEND IN OUR TIME

·IPA·

A LEGEND IN OUR TIME

ROGER PROTZ

PAVILION

Page 2 Cans were derided for years as a poor way to package beer, but, with improved technology, a growing number of brewers are canning IPAs and other beers. Beer in cans avoid the off-flavour known as 'light struck' that can affect bottled beers.

First published in the United Kingdom in 2017 by

Pavilion

43 Great Ormond Street

London

WC1N 3HZ

Copyright © Pavilion Books Company Ltd 2017

Text copyright © Roger Protz 2017

ISBN 978-1-91121-632-2

A CIP catalogue record for this book is available from the British Library.

10 9 8 7 6 5 4 3 2 1

Reproduction by Mission, Hong Kong

Printed and bound by 1010 Printing International Ltd, China

This book can be ordered direct from the publisher

at www.pavilionbooks.com

Contents

WHY IPA?..06

(01) RESTORED TO GLORY 12

(02) THE BEER OF THE RAJ 20

(03) HOW IPA IS BREWED 54

(04) CLASSIC IPAS 82

(05) THE GREAT REVIVAL 102
United States   105
England   161
Scotland   214
Wales   222
Ireland   228
Canada   232
Belgium and the Netherlands   238
France   246
Italy   252
Switzerland   258
Germany   261
Scandinavia   268
Australia   272
New Zealand   278
China and Japan   283

(06) NEW BEERS ON THE BLOCK 290
Black IPAs   292
Fruit IPAs   298

GLOSSARY   304
RESOURCES   310
ACKNOWLEDGEMENTS   313
INDEX   316

Why IPA?

The rebirth of India Pale Ale – IPA – flows from the remarkable and seemingly unstoppable worldwide craft beer revolution. In both hemispheres and in every continent, young brewers, with passion, reverence and commitment, are bringing flavour back to beer after decades of domination by global giants and their bland products. Craft brewers have innovated with both skill and imagination, bringing drinkers such new styles as golden ales, oak-aged beers and beers brewed with spices, fruit, coffee and chocolate.

But they have also, with restless enthusiasm, dug deep into old recipe books to bring back rare or forgotten styles. These include IPA. The style's phenomenal rise in popularity is due to the fact that, when brewed to its true, original form, it meets the demands of modern drinkers for exceptionally hoppy beers. The IPAs brewed in 18th- and 19th-century England for the Raj in India were packed with hops – double the quantity used for domestic beers. As well as giving bitterness to beer, the acids, resins and tannins in the hop plant helped keep IPA free from bacteria on the long and arduous journey to India, with wide variations in temperature and tempestuous seas.

IPA has become the template for modern brewers who fashion what they term 'hop-forward beers'. Both brewers and dedicated drinkers are as knowledgeable about hops as a wine-maker is about grape varieties and new hops have been designed to help meet the almost insatiable clamour for fresh aromas and flavour in beer.

In the United States, where the combination of hot sun and abundant rain in the Pacific North-west produces hops bursting with citrus flavours, new varieties such as the Amarillo and the Citra have deepened the character of American interpretations of IPA: Citra wears its heart on its sleeve and delivers an immense aroma and flavour of lychee, peach and gooseberry. English hop growers no longer rest on the sturdy laurels of the Fuggle and the Golding, with their piny, spicy and peppery notes, and have developed new, bolder hops with more of a citrus kick, including an English version of the American Cascade. New Zealand hops are especially highly prized and have enabled craft brewers there and in Australia to develop vibrant versions of IPA, reminding us that after the style had captured India in the 19th century it went on to find new acclaim both down under and in the United States.

Such is the fervour for IPA that brewers have burst out from the confines of the original style to develop new versions. Today there are double and imperial IPAs, some with impressive strengths of 12 per cent ABV. Both in the US and Britain, a number of brewers produce black IPAs: this has caused some controversy, as it's a major departure from the roots of the style. But there's no doubt that the addition of dark malts brings a new dimension to the flavour of the beer. The most recent innovation in the US is fruit IPAs that use grapefruit, watermelon and tangerine. English brewers, recalling that while IPA went one way to India, tea made the return journey, produce Earl Grey IPAs with the addition of bergamot, a citrus fruit.

A divide has opened up in the United States. What are dubbed 'West Coast IPAs' are renowned for their intense hop character, with up to and even beyond 100 units of bitterness. It's debatable just how much bitterness the average palate can tolerate and the answer has come from drinkers. The result is that even the most ardent users of hops are now rowing back on their use and are producing 'session IPAs' that can be consumed without drinkers requiring a tongue transplant.

The taste of modern IPAs prompted the question: what were the beers made for the Raj in India in Victorian England like? I couldn't summon up a time machine but I could engage with brewers with interest in the subject. UBREW in South London is a specialist brewery that allows small brewers and home-brewers to use their equipment to make beer. The owners generously agreed to produce an IPA to a recipe based on those used by Bass in Burton-on-Trent in the 19th century. The production of what we called Catalyst IPA was straightforward and didn't depart from modern procedures (see page 16). But when we decided to age the beer in wood for three months, to replicate the length of a sea journey from London to India, previous perceptions were abandoned. The beer took on a funky and slightly acidic aroma and flavour, the result of the action of wild yeasts trapped deep in the wood. The main wild yeast is called *Brettanomyces*: it means 'British fungus' and it gives a character to beer that brewers call 'horse blanket'.

While Catalyst was aging in its cask, the historian Ron Pattinson came up with the revelation that the Burton brewers had left casks standing in their yards for up to a year before they were despatched to India and would have picked up a powerful funky, acidic note as a result of wild yeast activity. He proved his case by brewing in collaboration with the Goose Island Beer Company in the United States a Stock Ale, a forerunner of IPA, which was aged in wood for twelve months. The result was startling. The beer was tart and mouth-puckering, not dissimilar to the famous lambic beers in Belgium that are produced by spontaneous fermentation by wild yeasts. There is little doubt that the original beers brewed for India were very different to mainstream IPAs today. But brewers have risen to the challenge and already 'sour IPAs' are being added to the pantheon.

As well as sampling a large number of beers for this book, I have had the pleasure of talking to brewers in many parts of the world and have been bowled over by their enthusiasm for the subject. Milan Beer Week proved equally invigorating. Who would have expected such an event in a country bursting with fine wines? But beer is the drink of the moment there, with the number of breweries expected to pass 1,000 within a few years. Several of them are producing IPAs and it was good to find that Italian brewers are not ignoring the English legacy and going completely down the American route where both flavour and hops are concerned. That is not to disparage the role of American brewers in leading the revival but it has been disappointing to find beer-makers in Australia and New Zealand importing, at considerable cost, American hops when they have superb supplies in their respective backyards.

With so many IPAs being made today, who to include and who to leave out? My task was made easier by the help of good friends in the beer-writing fraternity. In the United States, Julie Johnson, Daniel Bradford and John Holl, past and present editors

Buying beer

It's always fun to taste beers fresh from the brewery at the taproom or in a brewpub. A beer festival or a good pub will have a range of beers drawn from cask or keg. In the UK and Ireland, some beers are available in draught form only – these are indicated in the text. Otherwise, you should be able to buy the beers in this book from specialist bottle shops and online retailers.

It's particularly important that hoppy beers are drunk fresh and full of the hop character their brewer intended, so always check the 'best before' date on the bottle or can. Don't turn your nose up at canned beer: canning technology has improved dramatically in recent years and many brewers now prefer cans to bottles, because the can protects beer against light, which may cause the hop oils to deteriorate.

---

of *All About Beer* magazine, were generous with their time and recommendations, as was Garrett Oliver, the most famous of the craft brewers in the country and also a fine writer. He was prepared to step beyond his own IPA at Brooklyn Brewery and suggest rival brewers' versions. Stephen Beaumont in Canada and Matthew Kirkegaard in Canada and Australia recommended beers from their respective countries while Maurizio Maestrelli and Joe Stange were generous with their time in Italy and Germany. I had the good fortune to visit Berlin just as Stone Brewing from California was opening a vast brewery and restaurant complex in the city to bring IPA to German drinkers more used to lager and wheat beers.

Many other countries have joined the act. Scandinavia has chosen a fascinating route, with several 'breweries' there, notably Mikkeller in Copenhagen, not owning their own plants but making beer all round the world in collaboration with other producers and coining a new term: 'gypsy brewers'. Belgium, which has sufficient great beers to satisfy most drinkers, is making IPAs, and France, the Netherlands and Switzerland have joined the ranks. Even the Far East has weighed in, with versions of the style being made in China and Japan.

When I started writing about beer, the world of brewing was staid and conservative. Most British brewers produced just mild and bitter while the rest of the world made lager, either brilliant versions or dull fizzy water. Even in Belgium, with its treasure trove of great beers, most drinkers plumped for what they call Pils. But now the beer world churns and turns, aflame with argument and debate, a ruthless analysis of style and ingredients, and a determination to make beers packed with flavour. IPA has clambered out of the grave and is alive, well and stimulating drinkers around the world. Imperial, double, black and fruit ... where will the bandwagon head next? Nobody knows, but the trip will be exhilarating.

Roger Protz
St Albans

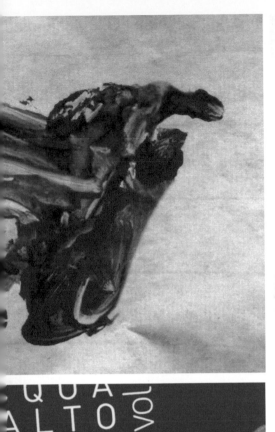

IPA

6.5% A.B.V.

birrificio RuRAle ®

BIRRA · Alc.4,4% vol

QUA
ALTO
EVITO
PPOLO

SESSION IPA ESTIV
VARIETÀ DI LUPPO
HOPART E' IL LATO
8°C. DA CONS

SUMMER SESSION IP
SELECTED IN ORD
SIDE OF THE HOPS.

0.33L

WARNING:(1) ACCORDING TO THE SURGEO
CY BECAUSE OF THE RISK OF BIRTH DEFE
DRIVE A CAR OR OPERATE MACHI

FLAGSHIP

ALC 5.3% VOL (3.2 UNITS PER PINT)

STRONG, ZESTY & FULL

HANDCRAFTED IN THE COTSWOLD HILLS SINCE 1849

HOOK NORTON
BREWERY

Restored to glory

India Pale Ale was the great beer style that transformed brewing in Victorian England and refreshed the world, but by the turn of the 20th century was under attack by new golden lager beer and all but disappeared during World War One when the government drastically reduced the strength of all beers. The first steps in restoring the style were taken in the summer of 1990, in an upstairs room of the White Horse pub at Parsons Green, in south-west London. Mark Dorber worked for a law firm in the City of London during the day, but such was his passion for the pale ales brewed in Burton-on-Trent in the English Midlands that he devoted evenings and weekends to the White Horse, where he learned the cellar skills necessary to serve impeccable pints of Draught Bass. He later became the full-time manager of the pub and created an international reputation for the quality of its beer. Visitors to the annual Great British Beer Festival at nearby Olympia, including many Americans, would beat a path to the White Horse to sample the pale ales on tap.

The meeting in 1990 was attended by head brewers from several Burton breweries, along with barley and hop farmers, and selected beer writers, including Michael Jackson and myself. They all agreed that the tradition and legacy of Burton-brewed pale ales and IPAs were under-appreciated by modern beer drinkers. Dorber was inspired to organize a festival of Burton beers at the White Horse. In 1993 he approached Bass, the leading brewer in Burton and owner of the White Horse, with the suggestion it should recreate a Victorian IPA for the event. Bass was enthusiastic and called in a retired brewer, Tom Dawson, for advice. He recalled brewing a beer called Bass Continental for the Belgian market from the 1950s to the 1970s. It was based on recipes for Bass pale ale produced in the 1850s and represented an unbroken line of descent from the original IPAs.

On Saturday 19 June a team of young brewers under Tom Dawson's guidance assembled at Burton-on-Trent, along with Mark Dorber and cellar staff from the White Horse. The atmosphere, Dorber said, was electric as they set out to brew a taste of history. They used a small, five-barrel pilot brewery where Bass tried out new recipes. Two brews were necessary to meet the White Horse order for 324 gallons of beer. Brewing lasted for close to thirty hours before the exhausted but exhilarated participants announced themselves satisfied. Tom Dawson's recipe consisted of 90 per cent Halcyon pale malt and 10 per cent brewing sugar. East Kent Goldings and Progress hops were used at the rate of 22 ounces per barrel and were added in two stages during the copper boil. The hopped wort circulated over a bed of Progress in the collecting vessel following the copper boil for additional aroma. When the fermented beer was racked into casks, it was dry hopped with East Kent Goldings for aroma at the rate of six ounces per barrel. The yeast strain was a traditional Bass two-strain culture.

The beer reached 7.2 per cent alcohol with a stunning 83 units of bitterness, twice the rate of even the most heavily hopped beer at the time. The bitterness was far more than Dawson had expected – but modern varieties of hops such as Progress are some 40 per cent higher in the alpha acids that create bitterness than 19th-century varieties.

The finished beer was aged in casks for five weeks before it was served at the White Horse on 31 July 1993. I described it as follows:

The beer is burnished gold in colour. The colour rating is eighteen units. Placed next to a glass of modern Draught Bass and the classic Pilsner Urquell lager beer, the White Horse IPA was midway between the two. The aroma was pungent and resinous. Hops dominated the palate and the long, intense, bitter finish. 'It's like putting your head inside a hop pocket [sack] from the Kent fields,' Mark Dorber said. Malt and yeast also had their say in the aroma and palate of the beer. Ripe banana, pear drop and apple esters began to make themselves felt as the beer warmed up. Mark Dorber said the beer would remain in drinkable condition for some three months. Tom Dawson, with his long experience of Bass yeast, thinks it will survive for even longer. Both think the beer will become softer over time but will not lose the enormous hop character.

The interest created by the White Horse IPA led to Dorber and myself, with the support of the British Guild of Beer Writers, organizing a further seminar on the subject in the summer of 1994. This time the event was not in a small pub room but in the imposing surroundings of Whitbread's Porter Tun Room in the former Chiswell Street Brewery in London's Barbican. In the cavernous cellars where Whitbread had once aged porter for months, brewers from Britain and the United States presented their interpretations of IPA along with historians, journalists and wine writers, including Oz Clarke and Andrew Jefford. Two Burton brewers, Ind Coope and Marston's, brewed special versions of IPA for the occasion, along with Whitbread's Castle Eden Brewery in north-east England. There were also samples of the White Horse version, by then eleven months old. Mark Dorber said that in order to counter the pronounced banana ester on the beer he had dry hopped the casks a second time in the pub. The beer had become much softer over time. The fruitiness was almost Madeira-like, with a pungent apricot fruit note on the nose, with fruit, hops and nuts in the mouth and a long bittersweet finish.

From the United States, Thom Tomlinson brought a beer called Renegade Red from Boulder, Colorado, which had a massive 90 units of bitterness: it was a beer which paved the way for the heavily hopped American IPAs that have inspired brewers in many other countries. Garrett Oliver from the Manhattan Brewing Company in New York City contributed his interpretation of the style, a beer that developed into the East India Pale Ale at Brooklyn Brewery, where Oliver established a reputation as one of the finest craft brewers of his generation. Teri Fahrendorf brewed Bombay Bomber at the Steelhead Brewery in Eugene, Oregon; she has gone on to work as a brewery consultant throughout the US. Brewing historian Dr John Harrison provided a beer that was as close as he could get to the India Pale Ale brewed by George Hodgson's Brewery at Bow Bridge in East London early in the 19th century, the first known beer produced for export to the subcontinent. He used Thames Valley well water and 100 per cent pale malt, with no brewing sugar. The hops were East Kent Goldings and the yeast strain came from the former Truman Brewery in East London. The beer was fermented with a starting gravity of 1072 degrees and it was six weeks old when it was served. It had a powerful peppery and resinous aroma from the hops and was packed with tart fruit in the mouth, while the finish was exceptionally dry and bitter with a fine balance of hops and fruit.

The seminar ended with an agreement that brewers on both sides of the Atlantic should make every effort to raise the profile of IPA and encourage others to produce examples of the style. Of the English breweries that contributed beer to the event, only Marston's has survived. As a result of government intervention in the brewing industry in the 1990s, with a demand that the national brewers should sell off many of their pubs and turn others into 'free houses', offering rival brewers' beers, Bass, Ind Coope and Whitbread sold their breweries, pubs and brands. Marston's abiding contribution to the seminar was Old Empire, a nationally available IPA sold on draught and in bottle.

In Boston, Massachusetts, Dan Kenary, one of the founding members of the Harpoon Brewery, was unaware of the events in Britain when he launched his IPA in 1993, though by coincidence 'it pays homage to the British style – but with an American twist,' he says. 'We had thought of using English Fuggles hops but in the end opted for American varieties.' With his beer-drinking friends Rich Doyle and George Ligetti, he had toured Britain and Europe in the 1980s and discovered that beer could have taste, unlike the bland lagers available in the United States.

Back home, they opened Harpoon in 1986, the first new brewery in Boston for a quarter of a century. Their first beer was Harpoon Ale, which was well received, and was followed by several other beers before the decision was made to launch an IPA. Dan Kenary says there were older drinkers who could remember a famous IPA called Ballantine's from years earlier, but there were no modern versions on the East Coast and the term IPA meant nothing to younger people. 'At first, the consumer response wasn't good,' Kenary recalls. 'The beer was dry, floral and hoppy and people said it would never sell – it was too bitter and women in particular would never drink it, they said. Look at it now: just 42 units of bitterness – compare that to some of the West Coast IPAs today!' IPA is now Harpoon's leading brand. Its success in the 1990s encouraged other pioneers: Bert Grant in the remote, hop-growing Yakima Valley in Washington State, Pike in Seattle, Samuel Adams in Boston, and Shipyard in Portland, Maine, created IPAs which opened the floodgates that engulfed American craft brewing.

By the second decade of the 21st century, IPA accounts for more than a quarter of the American craft beer sector, with sales increasing by 36 per cent a year. In 2012, it accounted for 9.9 per cent of craft beer sales; by 2016 the percentage had grown to 26.2. In the take-home sector, IPA sold 5,625,645 cases in 2012 and 20,208,600 cases in 2016. It is now the leading category at the annual Great American Beer Festival held in Denver, Colorado: 312 versions entered the judging competitions in 2016.

With their renowned ability to 'push the envelope', American brewers have developed interpretations of IPA that are a long way removed from the original beers brewed in 19th-century England. Today there are double IPAs, imperial IPAs and, controversially, black IPAs.

The West Coast versions have become the benchmark for 'hop forward' beers with high levels of bitterness. Anchor Brewing in San Francisco and Sierra Nevada in Chico have invented special containers where their beers circulate over beds of hops to increase aroma and bitterness. Russian River's Pliny the Elder, brewed in Santa Rosa, is regarded as one of the finest modern interpretations of the style. Stone Brewing of Escondido has taken the message abroad: in 2016 it opened a large brewery in Berlin, where it brews its full range of IPAs that are delivered fresh to European countries.

In Britain there are now more than 300 IPAs. Burton-on-Trent has not forgotten its heritage, with Worthington's White Shield, which dates from the 19th century, still in production. It's been joined by such flag-waving beers as Old Empire from Marston's, Empire Pale Ale from Burton Bridge and Imperial IPA from Tower. In London, notable IPAs are brewed by Five Points, Fuller's (Bengal Lancer), Kernel, and the splendidly named Howling Hops. Charles Wells, the large family-owned Bedford brewery, bought the rights to McEwan's and Younger's beers and has breathed life back into the most famous of all Scottish IPAs, McEwan's Export. Deuchars IPA, brewed by Caledonian Brewery in Edinburgh, is one of the most popular beers in Scotland and smaller brewers, including Fyne Ales and Stewart Brewing, have added to the range. Versions of the style exist in such remote areas as the Lake District, while the Welsh, who have long enjoyed Worthington's beers since Bass owned a brewery in Cardiff, now produce their own interpretations of IPA.

The impact of the revival has been international. IPA is made in English-speaking countries such as Canada, Ireland, Australia and New Zealand and the style has spread to Belgium, France, Italy, Japan and Scandinavia. The Canadian beer writer Stephen Beaumont remarks, with dry humour, that 'all beers are IPAs today.' Not quite, but a style that was originally designed for travel lives up to its reputation.

Reviving the revival

The White Horse IPA was a one-off brew, but given its critical role in kick-starting the revival, and in discussion with Mark Dorber, I decided to attempt to brew the beer again. I had been invited by UBREW in Bermondsey, south London, to make a beer with them and so I sent them the recipe for the White Horse beer. UBREW is a community enterprise founded by two keen home-brewers, Matt Denham and Wilf Horsfall, which enables fellow home-brewers and wannabe commercial brewers to design beers using UBREW's equipment. I made two changes to the original recipe. In place of Halcyon malt, I used Maris Otter, considered the finest modern English malting variety, and I replaced Progress hops with Fuggles. East Kent Goldings and Fuggles were widely used by brewers in Victorian England. Maris Otter was not grown in the 19th century, but it's a direct descendant of barley varieties grown then.

On 24 May 2016 I met Stuart Sewell in the brewhouse and we started the process of making what we called Catalyst IPA. Stuart – Stu for short – had learned beer-making skills at Brewlab in Sunderland before joining UBREW. The main vessels traditionally used to make ale are a mash tun, boiling kettle and fermenter. In the mash tun, barley malt is blended with hot water – called 'liquor' by brewers – and during the mashing period natural enzymes in the grain convert starch into a type of sugar known as maltose which can be fermented by brewers' yeast. The liquid, called wort, produced by the mash is then boiled with hops: the hops add aroma and bitterness, and their oils and tannins keep the wort free from infection. The hopped wort is clarified in a vessel known as the hop back or whirlpool, cooled and transferred to the fermenters where it's thoroughly mixed with yeast.

To produce 30 litres of beer, we used 7.65kg of Maris Otter pale malt and 0.85kg of invert sugar. 100 grams each of East Kent Goldings and Fuggles were used at the start of the boil, with 40 grams of each hop added 20 minutes before the end of the boil. A further 40 grams of Fuggles were placed in the whirlpool for additional aroma. The yeast culture used was a traditional ale yeast labelled WLP002 and described by its supplier as 'a classic yeast from a large independent brewer', believed to be Fuller's.

In the mash tun, Stu added 15.85mg of gypsum (calcium sulphate) to harden the brewing liquor: along with magnesium, gypsum is one of the mineral salts found in Trent Valley water, which enabled 19th-century brewers in Burton-on-Trent to produce sparkling pale ales rich in malt and hop character. The mash lasted for 45 minutes. The starting gravity of the mash was 1063 degrees. The water started with a temperature of 82°C, which came down to 67°C as the malt was blended with the liquor. Stu aimed for a final temperature of 76°C prior to the boil in the kettle.

Forty litres of wort were transferred to the kettle. It took 15–20 minutes to bring the wort to the boil and Stu waited a few more minutes to get a good, rolling boil.

He added the brewing sugar first, followed by the first batch of whole flower hops. The boil was left for 40 minutes before Stu added the second batch of hops. He then hooked up the kettle to a chiller to lower the temperature in preparation for fermentation. At UBREW, the kettle doubles as the hop whirlpool, where the final addition of Fuggles was added.

When the hopped wort reached a temperature of 20°C it was transferred to the fermenting vessel. This is the magical moment in brewing, when nature takes over. Liquid yeast is 'pitched' or thoroughly mixed into the wort and then brewers stand aside as the yeast nibbles away at the sugars and begins the transformation into beer and carbon dioxide gas. After a few days, a thick blanket of yellow, brown and black – the yeast head – will cover the wort. The head will eddy and heave until, after a week, the yeast will have no further sugars to gorge on and will start slowly to sink to the bottom of the vessel.

We left the beer to age in an oak cask for three months to replicate the length of a sea voyage to India in the 19th century. We toyed with the idea of putting the cask on board a boat on the River Thames, but we abandoned the plan on the grounds that we might never see the beer again. I returned to UBREW on 22 September 2016 and tasted the beer straight from the wood. It had been dry hopped in cask with East Kent Goldings and it had received a further dosage of brewing sugar to encourage a strong second fermentation. The beer was 7.6 per cent alcohol and had a massive 81.4 units of bitterness. As a result of losses from boiling and evaporation, we had 30 litres to bottle. Stu was keen the beer should condition for a further month and I took two bottles home and stored them in my cellar until 21 October.

It was the moment of truth. I opened a bottle with considerable nervousness. Would all this effort go to waste? Would the beer be poor, even undrinkable? I poured it slowly into a glass. A thick collar of foam developed: it was clearly in good condition. It was pale gold in colour and had an oak and smoke aroma, with lemon fruit and spicy hops and a funky note from a wild yeast strain, *Brettanomyces*, which is a feature of beers aged in wood. It was intensely bitter and acidic in the mouth with biscuit malt and tart lemon fruit. The finish was bitter, with further funky notes from the wild yeast, biscuit malt, spicy hops and lemon fruit. It was magnificent. I sensed the hair standing up on the nape of my neck, the feeling I get when passing Stonehenge or buildings of great antiquity. We had brewed something special: Catalyst IPA is as close as we will get to the true aroma, taste and character of a Victorian India Pale Ale.

UBREW, Old Jamaica Business Estate, 24 Old Jamaica Road, London SE16 4AW; 020 3172 6089; www.ubrew.cc

Facing page above: Stu Sewell (right) with the author discussing the brewing system to be used for the Catalyst IPA. Below left: Stu stirs the mash. Below right: the fermentation vessel with an airlock in place.

The beer of the Raj

In 1894, Lord Curzon, the Viceroy of India, crossed into Afghanistan on horseback; in his memoirs he recalled his urgent need for a refreshing drink.

I turned back towards India, crossed the shallow trough of the Baroghil Pass, and came down on the upper waters of the Yarkhun River...I was expecting to join my friend Younghusband, and march with him to Chitral. But I felt sure that as soon as I crossed the frontier and entered the territory of British India, he would send out someone to meet me and guide me to his camp. Sure enough, as I rode down the grassy slopes, I saw coming towards me in the distance the figure of a solitary horseman. It was Younghusband's native servant. At that moment I would have given a kingdom, not for champagne or hock and soda, or hot coffee, but for a glass of beer! He approached and salaamed. I uttered but one word, 'Beer'. Without a moment's hesitation, he put his hand in the fold of his tunic and drew therefrom a bottle of Bass. Happy forethought! O Prince of hosts! Most glorious moment! Even now, at this distance of time, it shines like a ruddy beacon in the retrospect of thirty years gone by.

The episode shows how deeply ingrained the thirst for beer had become in the upper echelons of the Raj. Raj means 'rule' in Hindustani and it referred to the nobility, senior civil servants and army officers who governed British India as representatives of Queen Victoria. Pale ale from England was their chosen beer – but it was never the main type of beer consumed by the British in India; ordinary civil servants and soldiers continued to drink cheaper mild, porter and stout. The ruling classes saw pale ale as their preserve. Lord Curzon was a controversial and arrogant man: when he was studying as Balliol College in Oxford, his fellow students immortalized him in a piece of doggerel:

My name is George Nathaniel Curzon
I am a most superior person
My cheeks are pink, my hair is sleek
I dine at Blenheim twice a week.

Blenheim Palace near Oxford is the ancestral home of the dukes of Marlborough, and Curzon was related to them. He would not have contemplated mixing with Rudyard Kipling's Tommies in India and drinking their inferior beers.

The beer that became known as India Pale Ale had upper-crust origins in England. Nobody invented it; there was no big bang in brewing. It developed from a style known as October beer which had been designed to suit the tastes of the gentry living in the country. During the interminable wars with France in the 18th and early 19th centuries, patriotic English gentlemen and women refused to drink imported French wine and preferred instead strong ales that matched Bordeaux or Burgundy wines in strength. October beer was made using the first and freshest grains and hops of the harvest, and then aged in oak casks for a year or more to round out and mellow the flavours. It was described as a pale beer, because the malt was kilned or gently roasted

22 The beer of the Raj

George Hodgson's brewery at Bow Bridge, East London, in the late 19th century. It was one of the first breweries to send pale ale to India.

over coke fires rather than the wood ones used for dark beers – it was the first beer that was paler than dark brown or black. It was heavily hopped, the plants giving not only aroma and bitterness to the beer but also helping to keep bacterial infection at bay during its long rest in oak casks. The result was an expensive beer, way beyond the means of ordinary people, who quaffed dark mild, porters and stouts.

As London turned into a major metropolis in the 18th century, the gentry moved into elegant town houses and London brewers were quick to grasp the opportunity to provide them with October beer. Among them was George Hodgson, a brewer at Bow Bridge in East London. His was a small brewery, opened in 1752, but he had the good fortune to be in the right place at the right time. His production plant was alongside the River Lea and this enabled him to bring the finest Hertfordshire malting barley from Ware by river and send finished beer down the Lea to the East India Docks at Blackwall.

Hodgson was a convivial fellow. He drank with sailors and dockers, notably at a pub called the Bombay Grab, named after a two-masted sailing vessel known in Arabic as a *gurab*. (The building that was the Bombay Grab is still standing and is now, by a neat twist of history, a mosque.) Hodgson learned that the costs of transporting goods to India were low. Ships left London half empty; they returned heavily laden with silks, spices, tea and other goods in great demand in England, and shipping costs were far higher for the return journey. Hodgson was also told that the army officers and senior employees of the East India Company were desperate to receive a more refreshing beer than the dark London brews being shipped to the colony. It was a potentially profitable business. By 1750, some 1,500 barrels of beer were being exported to India and that figure rose to 9,000 barrels by 1800. Hodgson sent beers from his regular list to India, including porter, small or weak beer and strong ale, and his brewery continued to do so well into the 19th century. But he found that his October beer met with particular success and praise.

Hodgson was not the only London brewer engaged in the India trade. Abbott's Brewery and WA Brown's Imperial Brewery, both based at Bromley-by-Bow, were also active: Abbott was later to merge with Hodgson. But contemporary records show that it was Hodgson's pale beer which enjoyed the greatest acclaim in India. In 1801, the *Calcutta Gazette* carried an advertisement for the arrival of 'beer from Hodgson…just landed and now exposed for sale for ready money only.' In 1809 the same newspaper described Hodgson's 'select Pale Ale, warranted of superior excellence'.

A number of sources make the link between October beer and the beer sent to India. In January 1822, the *Calcutta Gazette* mentioned a recently landed shipment that included 'Hodgson's warranted prime picked pale ale of the genuine October brewing, warranted fully equal, if not superior, to any ever before received in the settlement.' In England in October 1856, the *Leeds Intelligencer* carried an announcement from Tetley's Brewery: 'East India Pale Ale – this season's brewings are now being delivered', a clear indication that the beer was an annual harvest-time brew. As late as 1898, Waltham Brothers' Brewery in Stockwell, south London, said of its India Pale Ale: 'This Ale is heavily hopped with the very best Kent hops, and nearly resembles the fine Farmhouse Stock-Beer of olden times.' Stock ale was another term for October beer or a beer that had been aged for some considerable time.

A brewer in the 1760s named George Watkins recorded the large amounts of barley malt used to make October beer as between 16 and 20 bushels per hogshead (54 gallons). The result would have been beers of around 11.5 per cent alcohol in modern terms. Watkins said October beer would be ready for bottling after one year in cask but should then be kept in bottle for a further year, making it two years old before it was ready to drink.

The fact that the same or similar beer was ready for consumption four or five months after leaving England for India is explained by the nature of the voyage. It was a rough trip: an East Indiaman ship could make only four or five round voyages before being broken up. The tumultuous nature of the voyage was tracked by the American brewer and scientist Thom Tomlinson in 1994. He worked with the Climate Diagnostics Center in Boulder, Colorado, to trace the temperatures that a shipload of ale would encounter on a voyage from Liverpool or London to India in the mid to late 1800s. The ships left between late November and early February, arriving in India between March and May. The winter departures were timed to ensure the ships reached the Indian Ocean before the start of the monsoon season.

Heading south from England, the ships cruised along the coast of Africa, rounded the Cape of Good Hope and then crossed the Indian Ocean to Bombay, Madras or Calcutta. 'Even though the hogsheads of ale were stored in the lowest level of the ship's hull – the coolest place in the ship – the temperature fluctuations were tremendous,' Tomlinson wrote in the March/April 1994 issue of *Brewing Techniques*, published in Eugene, Oregon. His research found that for the first few weeks of the voyage, water temperatures were approximately 52°F/11°C. As the ships entered equatorial regions, temperatures climbed to 81°F/25°C. As they rounded the Cape, temperatures dropped to 65–69°F/17–19°C. In the southern Indian Ocean they rose to 73°F/21°C and on the final leg of the voyage, nearing the coast of India, temperatures soared to 83–86°F/26–28°C. Tomlinson observed: 'Combine the temperature fluctuations and the rough waters off southern Africa and you have one hellish trip for ale.'

Historian Martyn Cornell, in *Beer: The Story of the Pint*, agrees with Thom Tomlinson that the voyages were rough:

...but the slow, regular temperature changes and the rocking the beer received in its oak casks as the East Indiamen ploughed the waves had a magical maturing effect. By the time

Overleaf: The East Indiaman ship, Bridgeman, was one of the fleet that carried IPA from England to India.

the beer arrived in Bombay, Madras or Calcutta…it was as ripe as a brew six times its age that had slumbered unmoving in an English cellar. The expatriate British running the East India Company's 'factories' [trading posts] and commanding its three private armies loved it, and by the beginning of the 19th century, Hodgson's was 'the beer in almost universal use' in India.

Hodgson's success was in large part due to his location, with easy access to both pale malts from Hertfordshire and to the India-bound ships. Like other pale October ales being made at the time, his beer would have been high in alcohol and heavily hopped to prevent spoilage. Thom Tomlinson suggests that Hodgson may have made his own interpretation of the style:

Hodgson also added dry hops to the casks at the time of priming, which provided a further measure against infection. During priming he conditioned the beer with more sugar than was typical for pale ales. The high priming rate probably helped keep the yeast alive during the long voyage. Although high priming rates might suggest excessive carbonation, leakage from the wooden casks may have offset this effect. In any case a 'high state of condition' would have been important to offset large amount of carbon dioxide lost during the primitive bottling process used when the beer arrived in India.

But fermentation during the long voyages created obvious problems: bottles or casks could break under pressure, creating havoc and mess in the holds of ships. Casks used for export were made with staves twice the thickness of those used for domestic trade. A tableau in the National Brewery Centre in Burton-on-Trent shows casks in the hold of a ship with battens criss-crossing the ends of casks to prevent them exploding. Porous venting pegs made of red oak were hammered into the 'shive holes' on top of each cask to allow carbon dioxide to vent as a slow fermentation continued during the long voyage to the Indian sub-continent.

Peter Mathias, in *The Brewing Industry in England, 1700–1830*, says:

Beer in the bottle probably did better than beer in casks, aided by being airtight and under pressure through corking. Benjamin Wilson and Samuel Allsopp [Burton brewers] advised customers to bottle the ale which they wanted to survive into the summer, leaving the bottle uncorked for a time to allow the ale to go flat. This was the procedure adopted by a London wine merchant, Kenton, who is said to have been the first to have shipped porter successfully to the East Indies. Once 'flat', it was corked and sealed so that secondary and tertiary fermentation on the voyage brought it up to the necessary state of 'briskness' by the time it reached India.

Hodgson's beer may have left London as a muddy-looking brew, but it must have improved during the lengthy voyage to India, where it was described as 'clear, brilliant and straw-coloured'. Despite Hodgson's success, what is beyond dispute is that London in the early 19th century was not best suited to brewing pale beer. The city's water was rich in calcium carbonate, which was ideal for making dark beers such as porter. While brewing water with high levels of sulphates, as in Burton-on-Trent, extracts less colour from malt and emphasizes hop flavours, water rich in carbonate makes pale beer production more difficult and there is also a lower conversion rate of starch to fermentable sugar, leading to a finished beer with a rich malt character.

But it was not the quality of Hodgson's beer that led to its downfall: it was the brewery's ability to annoy the mighty East India Company and its ships' commanders. The company had been created by royal charter in 1600 by Elizabeth I to develop trade with India. It grew to exercise almost monopoly control over imports and exports with the subcontinent and it had its own shipping fleet, docks at Blackwall, and private armies to protect its factories, warehouses and employees in India. It depended on the loyalty of its ships' commanders as the bedrock of its business and it allowed the commanders to engage in some private business as well as acting for the company. Selling English goods to the British stationed in India became highly profitable: it was estimated that some ships' commanders made as much as £12,000 a year. The entrepreneurial sailors naturally turned to local brewers in East London to supply them with beer.

In 1811, George Hodgson was succeeded by his son Mark, who energetically expanded the export side of the business. By 1813 he was shipping some 4,000 barrels a year to India, four times the amount sent in 1801. By 1821, the brewery was in the hands of Frederick Hodgson and Thomas Drane, who rebuilt and expanded the site and then took the catastrophic decision to cut out both the East India Company and the ships' commanders. Hodgson and Drane registered as shippers in the City of London and transported beer to India themselves, where they appointed their own agents. They refused all credit and would accept only cash payments: Hodgson's had previously given employees of the East India Company twelve or eighteen months' credit. To add insult to injury, they raised the price of their beer by 20 per cent. The brewery's behaviour caused outrage and led to a meeting of historic importance in London in 1822, not in the smoke and grime of the East End but in the more elegant surroundings of Upper Wimpole Street near Regent's Park.

Campbell Marjoribanks (pronounced 'Marchbanks') was a director of the East India Company and served as chairman of the company three times. He was a wealthy man who had made three voyages to India between 1795 and 1807. In 1822 he invited Samuel Allsopp, a brewer in Burton-on-Trent, to dinner in his mansion. Marjoribanks had a problem he wished to discuss with Allsopp, namely the behaviour of Hodgson's Brewery. He was also aware that Allsopp, in common with all the Burton brewers, had an equally pressing problem: the loss of his lucrative trade with Russia and the Baltic States. As a result of the wars with France, Napoleon had blockaded the Russian and Baltic ports. For many years, the Burton brewers had done profitable business with the region, sending large quantities of a strong, nut brown beer called Burton Ale.

Campbell Marjoribanks of the East India Company who encouraged the Burton brewers to send pale ale to India.

Now that business had gone and Burton was in crisis, with a number of breweries closing down. Marjoribanks told Allsopp to forget the Baltic and attack the India trade instead. 'India,' he said, offered 'a trade that can never be lost: for the climate is too hot for brewing. We are now dependant on Hodgson who has given offence to most of the merchants in India. But your Burton ale, so strong and sweet, will not suit our market.'

It's possible to report the conversation because Samuel Allsopp later recounted it to a Burton journalist and it was recorded in a book, *Burton and its Bitter Beer*, by John Stevenson Bushnan in 1853. Marjoribanks added that as a result of England's dominion over India, brewers who sold beer there would not face tariffs of any kind. This was music to Allsopp's ears for, before the French blockade, Russia had imposed punitive tariffs on Burton beer. But if Burton ale was not suitable for the India trade, what type of beer would suffice?

On cue, Marjoribank's butler appeared with a bottle of Hodgson's India ale, which he poured for the two diners. Allsopp was intrigued by the flavour and he said he would take a bottle back to Burton and ask his brewers for their advice. He also took with him the message from the powerful director of the East India Company: Burton needed to produce a paler and more bitter beer if its business were to recover.

Burton-on-Trent had been an important brewing town for centuries: monks had first brewed at the Benedictine abbey in the town in the 11th century. In *Ivanhoe*, Sir Walter Scott recorded that during the reign of Richard I (1189–99) Burton had acquired a 'lofty reputation' for its ale. By the 18th century, the improvements in roads and the opening up of canals meant that Burton-brewed beers reached London, where they were met with acclaim. The celebrated diarist Samuel Pepys noted his appreciation of what he called 'Hull ale': this was almost certainly Burton ale transported by canal to Hull and then shipped to London. In 1712, 638 barrels of Burton beer came to London via Hull and Joseph Addison noted in the *Spectator* that year: 'We concluded our walk with a glass of Burton ale.' Burton prospered and large breweries developed in the town. The Wilson family were major brewers and in 1807 sold their company to their relative Samuel Allsopp. He faced keen competition from, among others, Bass, Thomas Salt and William Worthington.

It wasn't until the Burton brewers were faced with the opportunity to brew pale ale for India that they realized the special qualities of the spring and well waters in the Trent Valley. Unlike London water, which was rich in calcium carbonate, the Trent water had heavy deposits of calcium sulphate (gypsum) and magnesium sulphate (Epsom salt). Burton's brewing 'liquor' – brewers' term for water – plays a crucial role in the flavour and keeping qualities of pale ale. Calcium sulphate, in particular, enhances hop bitterness and keeps the yeast active, reduces haze and decreases beer colour leading to a much paler end product.

It was the remarkable quality of the Trent Valley water that gave IPA its springboard. When Samuel Allsopp returned to Burton, he handed the bottle of Hodgson's pale ale to his head brewer, Job Goodhead. He tasted it and spat it out in disgust, affronted by

*Beer casks being unloaded in the Calcutta docks following
the long voyage from England. The fact that this image
is a photograph and that there is a steam ship on the left
suggests that this would have been mid to late 19th century.*

its extreme bitterness. But he said he could kiln his malt to a lighter colour to produce a similar beer. According to a local legend, Goodhead made a trial brew in a teapot. This seems unlikely as he had a brewery at his fingertips, with small vessels where new beers could be tested, but the tale has become Burton folklore.

In a small town such as Burton, news of the pale beer spread fast as brewery workers met in pubs for a drink and a chat. Bass and Thomas Salt were soon experimenting with their own ales for India. They faced considerable costs. As well as making oak casks with thick staves to withstand the journey, they had to supply bottles and corks when the beer arrived in India and was decanted from the casks. And when the beer finally arrived at its destination, it had to pass muster with tasters who could either accept or reject a whole consignment.

Samuel Allsopp heard to his distress that his first consignment, while accepted by the tasters, earned only twenty rupees a hogshead while Hodgson's rated twenty-five. But the second and third consignments brought forty rupees per hogshead each and Allsopp never looked back.

A letter from a J C Bailton in Calcutta in 1825 gave Allsopp great heart:

With reference to the loss you have sustained in your first shipments, you must have been prepared for that, had you known the market as well as I do: Here almost everything is name, and Hodgson's has so long stood without rival that it was a matter of astonishment how your ale could have stood the competition; but that it did is a fact, and I myself was present when a butt of yours reached 136 rupees, and a butt of Hodgson's only eighty rupees at a public sale.

The helpful Bailton also described how Allsopp's beer improved when it reached its destination: 'One month after bottling: dark, turbid, and decomposed. Three months: starting to clear, sparkling, Champagne-like appearance. Eight months: bright, amber, crystal clear; very peculiar fine flavour.' The use of 'peculiar' may be a quirk of 19th-century English or it could be a reference to the particular character given to oak-aged

34 The beer of the Raj

Burton-on-Trent in 1840, with breweries and water towers seen on the far side of the river. It was the mineral-rich waters of the Trent Valley that gave IPAs their special character.

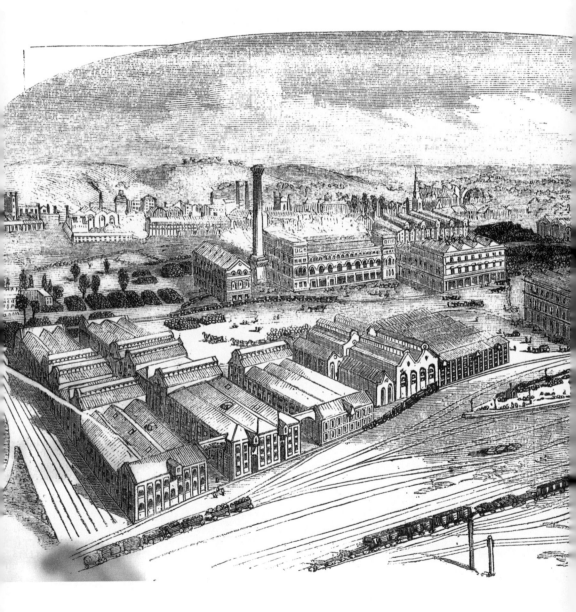

Allsopps' brewery in the second half of the 19th century. Burton-on-Trent was a town devoted to beer and the arrival of the railway in 1839 meant its pale ales could be transported swiftly around the country.

beers by the wild yeast strain *Brettanomyces*. It gives an aroma and palate variously described as funky, tart and 'horse blanket'.

Of course, there were conflicting views on how the English beers were appreciated once they arrived in India. Hodgson's ale continued to receive praise, but it would seem that Allsopp and Job Goodhead had improved on Hodgson's beer in every sense: it was paler, hoppier and arrived in India in better condition. As the other brewers

in the town rushed to follow Allsopp's route to India, Burton was about to be transformed. Historian Peter Mathias says: 'Burton-on-Trent remained the only true example of a "brewing town" in the same economically significant sense that Dundee was a jute town or Merthyr Tydfil was an iron town.'

Burton's rise was made possible by the new technologies of the Industrial Revolution: by the middle of the 19th century, beer-making in Burton was no longer a slow, laborious, artisanal craft that took place only between the months of October and April. Brewing in the summer had been impossible before cooling was introduced, because fermentation couldn't be controlled during hot weather. But brewing was now an industry based on year-round mass production, using all the skills, scientific knowledge and machinery unleashed by the Industrial Revolution. Within a few decades, not only brewing but the town itself had changed out of all recognition. By 1861, the population was three times as high as in 1801 and then it doubled by 1878. The figure doubled again to 50,000 by 1901. In 1851, the breweries employed around a third of the male population, rising to half by the late 1880s.

Driven by the quest for new markets to replace the lost Baltic trade, and aided by new technology, the Burton brewers, with Allsopp and Bass to the fore, set out to dominate the export of pale ale to India. To Allsopp's annoyance, Bass became both the major brewer and exporter. In the years 1832 and 1833, of 12,000 barrels of beer reaching Bengal, Bass accounted for 5,200, Allsopp 1,400 and Hodgson 3,600. Within a decade, Allsopp and Bass accounted for more than half the beer shipped to Calcutta. Hodgson's dropped their prices in a desperate attempt to win back market share, but the superiority of the Burton beers led to the Bow brewery's demise. It was put up for sale in 1855 and was bought by Smith, Garrett & Co. The brewery survived until 1927 when it was taken over by one of the leading London brewers, Taylor Walker. The former Hodgson site closed in 1933 and was replaced by London County Council social housing.

But Hodgson was not forgotten. Lord Curzon's memoirs, *A Viceroy's India: Leaves from Lord Curzon's Notebook*, were written many years after his sojourn in India and published posthumously in 1926. But his memory of the acute pleasure of a bottle of Bass made him recall the comic poem by Charles Stuart Calverley written in 1861:

O Beer, O Hodgson, Guinness, Allsopp, Bass!
Names that should be on every infant's tongue,
Shall days and months and years and centuries pass,
And still your merits be unrecked, unsung?

When the poem was written, the Hodgsons had had no involvement in their old brewery for at least a dozen years, but the name and its reputation lived on.

But IPA was now synonymous with Burton. The Victorians, never slow to use hyperbole, dubbed the town 'Beeropolis'. Brewers rushed to Burton in the hope they could make their fortunes with the aid of the magical waters of the Trent Valley. During the 1840s, the output of Burton's breweries increased from 70,000 barrels a year to 300,000. Allsopp and Bass were jointly responsible for 70 per cent of the increase. Between 1850 and 1880, the Burton brewing industry trebled in size every ten years. As London brewers saw their sales of porter go into steep decline, they were desperate for a slice of the pale ale market. They attempted to brew the style in London but met with mixed success. Several of them decided the only course of action was to open plants in Burton to take advantage of the water there. Ind Coope of Romford arrived in 1856 and built a brewery adjacent to Allsopp's. Charrington, Mann Crossman & Paulin, and Truman followed. Provincial brewers arrived, including Boddingtons of Manchester, Peter Walker from Warrington, and Everards of Leicester. In 1834 there were nine breweries in the town. The number rose to fifteen by 1851 and by 1888 there were no fewer than thirty-one breweries in Burton producing three million barrels of beer a year. Burton was now wholly a 'beer town' and had achieved the seemingly impossible of producing twice as much beer as London by the late 19th century.

Casks, including giant tuns and hogsheads, stored in Bass's yard in Burton and waiting to be despatched by train. The triangle on the bottle label was the first registered trademark, in 1876.

7
BURTON-ON-TRENT

Ale and Beer.

POPULATION, 48,260.

BURTON BREWERIES.

MR. BASS, M.P.

Michael Thomas Bass spearheaded the company's dramatic growth in the 19th century. As well as chairing the brewery, he was the Liberal MP for Derby and helped develop a railway network in the area to transport his beer around the country.

   The incomers did not enjoy universal success. Allsopp and Bass were too dominant and enjoyed a fine reputation in both Britain and abroad for the quality of their beer. By 1867, Bass was brewing close to one million barrels a year and had opened two new breweries in the town to cope with demand. Allsopp built a second brewery in 1860 opposite the railway station and had a combined workforce of 1,600, including its own maltings. At the peak of Burton's power there were thirty-two maltings in the town, all soaking, germinating and kilning vast amounts of pale malt. Thomas Salt's brewery continued to play a major role in the town and had four maltings, while William Worthington carved out a niche for himself by concentrating on bottled beers: his White Shield IPA is still brewed today and remains a potent link with the original beers of the 19th century.

Stock Ale

Great interest was aroused in 2016 by a beer called Brewery Yard Stock Ale, produced by Goose Island in the United States but launched in London. The formula was drawn up by British beer writer and historian Ron Pattinson. Stock Ale, in common with October Beer, was one of the styles from which IPA developed. The beer was based on a recipe from Truman's brewery in 1877: Truman was one of the London brewers that went to Burton-on-Trent in the 19th century to avail themselves of Trent Valley water.

The revised recipe used by Goose Island used Maris Otter pale malt, brewing sugar, East Kent Goldings and American Cluster hops. The beer was 7.29 per cent ABV and had 95.5 units of bitterness.

The beer was aged in oak casks for a year as Pattinson's research revealed that the Burton brewers stored casks of IPA in their brewery yards for a year before they were despatched to India. During that long period, the wild yeast strain *Brettanomyces*, which buried itself deep in the wood of the casks, attacked remaining sugars in the beer and gave it what brewers call a 'horse blanket' character. Goose Island's brewers deliberately added some 'Brett', as it's known for short, to the Stock Ale they brewed. The result was that after a year the beer had reached 8.4 per cent ABV while bitterness fell to 62 IBUs and the Brett added a distinctive funky and musty note. In common with the Catalyst IPA brewed for this book at UBREW, this is another fascinating glimpse of what IPA and its parent beers tasted like in the 19th century.

By the middle of the century the nature of the export trade was changing. Business rose to a peak of 217,000 barrels by 1870. Allsopp said the production of pale ale was its 'first consideration' as new markets opened up. The Australian gold rush in the 1850s sent 400,000 British emigrants Down Under in search of wealth – and pale ale followed them. Clipper ships could make the journey in sixty-eight days. The Burton brewers were also busy in the American market. Bass Ale was listed on the dining cars of the Union Pacific transcontinental railroad, while Allsopp's pale ale won prizes in the Centennial Brewers' Exhibition in Philadelphia in 1876.

Bass became a colossus. India remained an important market until the end of the century, but by the 1840s the company was selling as much beer to Australia as it was to the subcontinent. Sydney was the main city, but the brewery had agents in Tasmania, Adelaide, Melbourne and the Swan River region. New Zealand was also served and Bass built sales in Java, the Cape of Good Hope, China, Hong Kong, Ceylon and Singapore. Its beer reached Boston, New York and San Francisco, the Caribbean and as far south as British Guiana, Peru and Chile. Bass pale ale was sold in 58 countries.

Bass's Red Triangle was the first registered trademark when new laws to protect companies came into effect in 1876. Bass sent a clerical worker to sit on the steps of the registrar's office in London to wait there all night in order to be the first in the queue when the office opened on 1 January.

IPA was also changing. Strong October beers had gone out of favour. There were growing complaints from India that the beers sent there took too long to settle, had too much alcohol, and were even 'narcotic'. The last named complaint was probably due to the high level of hops: the hop is a member of the same plant family as cannabis. In 1858, an agent in Calcutta complained to William Younger, an Edinburgh brewer: 'Your beer is well known for its body. This is an obstacle to its becoming a favourite brand; it takes so long to ripen. The few casks of your last lot were fully 18 months before sufficiently ripe to drink.' One colonial critic of Burton beers said they had 'too much alcohol, too much sediment, too much hops and too little gas.'

After a long sea voyage in hogsheads (large casks) it took some time for the beer to 'drop bright' – the point at which yeast cells settle at the bottom of the vessel. As industrial glass production developed and bottles became stronger, brewers were able to send increasing amounts of beer in bottle to India. These small containers had less yeast sediment than a cask and would clear within a few hours. It was also possible to chill bottled beers: in 1828 a correspondent in India wrote to Samuel Allsopp telling him that in the hot season his beer 'was always cooled with saltpetre before it is drank [sic]: we can make it by this article as cold as ice'. Saltpetre, or potassium nitrate, was widely used in India in the manufacture of ice cream.

Complaints about the high alcohol level of IPAs were met by the simple process of reducing their strength – it also significantly reduced the brewers' tax bill. By the second half of the 19th century Burton pale ales were brewed between 6 and 7 per cent alcohol, a considerable reduction on the October and stock beers from which they had evolved.

With the exception of Ind Coope, the other incomers to Burton gradually retreated back to their towns and cities of origin, armed with a wealth of experience based on new scientific knowledge. Thanks to the work of Louis Pasteur and the scientists and chemists employed by the Burton breweries, they now understood the importance of keeping their brewing equipment scrupulously clean to avoid yeast infections and spoilt beer. Another important development was a better understanding of the chemical qualities of Burton's water. A chemist called C W Vincent taught brewers in London and elsewhere how to add such minerals as gypsum and magnesium sulphate to their brewing liquor to replicate Burton water. The terms 'Burtonizing' and 'Burtonization' entered the brewers' lexicon and today brewers throughout the world talk of Burtonizing their liquor to make the best possible IPAs and pale ales.

The Burton brewers now faced competition at home from pale beers brewed throughout the country. And their trade with India was also coming under attack. The peak figure of exports from Burton in 1870 is significant: India Pale Ale went into decline after that. The success of the beer contained the seeds of its downfall, a downfall that came from an unexpected source: central Europe. In the 1820s and '30s, Anton Dreher and Gabriel Sedlmayr the Younger made extensive tours of major brewing countries to help them perfect their own products. Dreher owned a brewery in Vienna while Sedlmayr ran the Spaten Brewery in Munich. Both made lager beer.

Navvies digging the cellars under St Pancras Station in London in 1867. The cellars, known as the Undercroft, were designed to store casks of ale from Burton: three train loads arrived every day. Today the Undercroft is the departure lounge for Eurostar services.

Lager means 'storage' in German and – until the invention of refrigeration – the beers were stored or aged in cellars packed with ice cut from lakes and rivers. Lager beers were dark, the result of malt cured over wood fires. Dreher and Sedlmayr were aware of developments in England and were anxious to see pale ale being produced at first hand. They were generously treated in Burton and Bass presented them with saccharometers that enabled them to measure the fermentable sugars in wort. The visitors responded with acts of industrial sabotage. They used thermometers to secretly measure temperatures and they had hollowed-out walking sticks with hidden valves in which they kept samples of beer and wort for later analysis. Dreher and Sedlmayr wrote home to say that while they had been warmly welcomed in one brewery 'we stole as much as we could.' 'It always surprises me that we can get away with these thefts without being beaten up,' Sedlmayr added to his colleagues in Munich.

The young brewers were impressed in particular by the new methods of kilning grain to produce pale malt. They returned home to fashion pale lagers but they were beaten to the punch by a new brewery that opened in Pilsen in Bohemia in 1842. The Burghers' Brewery produced the first golden lager, dubbed Pilsner, with the aid of a malt kiln imported from England. The new beer was exported throughout the Austro-Hungarian Empire and to the rest of Europe and Scandinavia, while the skills to make pale lager were taken to the United States with the 'second wave' of immigrants from Europe. Brewers rushed to follow Pilsner's success. As well as supplying domestic markets, the new breed of lager brewers started to supply countries crying out for cold, refreshing beer such as Africa, India and Australia. Lager had a clear advantage over IPA: lager had its second fermentation in the lager cellar in the brewery and was then filtered. When it arrived at its destination, it was ready to drink. It didn't take weeks or months to settle and clear. And to rub salt in the English brewers' wounds, when American brewers joined lager's gold rush to African and Indian colonies, they sent ice as well as beer.

However, as sales of IPA tumbled, there was no panic in Burton and no need for the help of the East India Company. The most potent symbol of the Industrial Revolution – the steam engine – came to their aid.

The railway had arrived in Burton in 1839, linking the town with Birmingham and Derby. The brewers now had easy access to England's 'second city', where hordes of thirsty industrial workers clamoured for beer. The railway spread at dizzying speed and industrialists saw the enormous advantages of moving goods quickly across the country: freight, not passengers, was the first consideration of the early railway companies. Allsopp, Bass and their competitors found they could convey beer at a pace that would have seemed unimaginable when canals and coaches offered the only means of transport. Soon, most parts of Britain could be reached within a day. When St Pancras Station opened in London in 1868, the Midland Railway brought Burton beer to the capital via Derby in a few hours. Bass rented a large warehouse close by with a capacity of 120,000 barrels and a workforce of 150, where hogsheads were broken down into smaller casks and bottles for onward travel to London's pubs. A year later, Bass moved this operation to the cellars of the station itself. The large space, known as the Undercroft, was designed by consulting engineer W H Barlow, who used iron columns and girders to maximize space. He said that 'the length of a beer barrel became the unit of measure, upon which all the arrangements of this floor were based.' The Undercroft is now the Eurostar departure lounge.

The cost advantages offered by the railway were enormous. Before the arrival of the train, it cost £3 to transport one ton of ale – approximately five barrels – to London on a journey that lasted more than a week. The same amount of ale went to London by train at a cost of 15 shillings. The impact of fast transport, lower costs and higher profits led to production of beer in Burton increasing from around 70,000 barrels a year in 1849 to 300,000 ten years later. By 1867, Bass was the biggest brewer in the world. Several directors became millionaires and Michael Thomas Bass was elevated to the peerage – dubbed the 'Beerage' by critics of their enormous wealth and pomp – as Baron Burton.

Tastes and society were changing, though. The Burton brewers, witnessing declining sales overseas as the lager revolution took hold, concentrated on the domestic market. But strong beers such as IPA were no longer in vogue. The rising middle class wanted beer of a more moderate strength they could drink at home or in the comfort of the pub saloon, distinct from the more basic public bar frequented by hoi polloi quaffing mild ale. The result was pale ale with a strength of between 4 and 5 per cent. It was not cheap and its price was pitched above those for mild and porter at around seven to eight pence a quart (four pints) against four or five pence for darker beers. Richard Wilson, co-author, with T R Gourvish, of *The British Brewing Industry 1830–1980*, says 'Quality and cost...made it [Burton pale ale] a status drink for the expanding lower middle class of clerks and shopkeepers, the armies of rail travellers and "aristocrats of labour" [highly skilled workers] whose standards of living rose appreciably after 1850.'

A powerful temperance movement, supported by the Liberal Party, railed against the 'demon drink' and its influence drove down the strength of beer further still. The Burton brewers also faced pressure from their shareholders. Allsopp and Bass became limited companies and their shareholders expected a return on their investment. The days when a hogshead of IPA could quietly mature for six months were long gone. The brewers started to build 'tied estates' – pubs they directly owned and supplied – and developed 'running beers' that needed just a day or two to drop bright in the cellar before they were pumped to the bar.

IPA's death knell was sounded by World War One. David Lloyd George, leader of the Liberal Party, became Minister of Munitions and now had the power to tackle his old enemies, the brewers. In an infamous speech in Bangor in 1915 he ranted that 'Drink is doing us more damage in the war than all the German submarines put together. We are fighting Germany, Austria and Drink; and as far as I can see the greatest of these three deadly foes is Drink.' Supplies of grain were rationed in order to direct the bulk of it to the bread industry, while excise duty on beer was massively increased. Production of beer was cut to 25.3 million barrels a year and this was further reduced to 10 million when Lloyd George replaced Herbert Asquith as wartime prime minister. There was no respite when the war ended, as post-war reconstruction had to be paid for and beer remained a convenient milch cow. Gourvish and Wilson say that in real terms, allowing for wartime inflation, the increase in duty between 1914 and 1920 was a staggering 430 per cent.

The beers that emerged from these punitive restrictions were poor things of around 3 and 3.5 per cent alcohol. Strengths did increase as the country's economy revived, but they never regained their 19th-century levels. IPA was a shadow of its former self, indistinguishable from its junior partner, pale ale. Draught 'running beers' – mild and bitter – were now the preferred style and it would take the best part of a century for IPA to be restored to its former glory.

THE ILLUSTRATED LONDON NEWS

REGISTERED AS A NEWSPAPER FOR TRANSMISSION IN THE UNITED KINGDOM, AND TO CANADA AND NEWFOUNDLAND BY MAGAZINE POST.

No. 3976.—VOL. CXLVII.   SATURDAY, JULY 3, 1915.   SIXPENCE.

The Copyright of all the Editorial Matter, both Engravings and Letterpress, is Strictly Reserved in Great Britain, the Colonies, Europe, and the United-States of America.

"I DO NOT KNOW WHETHER I AM IN ORDER, MR. SPEAKER, IN SHOWING THIS ARTICLE": MR. LLOYD GEORGE, THE MINISTER OF MUNITIONS, EXHIBITS IN THE HOUSE OF COMMONS A HIGH - EXPLOSIVE FUSE.

There was a dramatic moment during Mr. Lloyd George's speech in Parliament introducing the Munitions Bill. He was explaining the difficulties of suddenly and enormously increasing the output of complicated mechanism. To point his words he held up an object. "I do not know whether I am in order, Mr. Speaker," he said, "in showing this article. It is the fuse of the high-explosive, and is one of the greatest difficulties of all in the turning out of shells. This fuse is not nearly so complicated as the fuse of the shrapnel—which is one of the most intricate and beautiful pieces of machinery—before it explodes. (Laughter.) This, indeed, is supposed to be simple. Yet it takes a hundred different gauges to turn it out." Mr. Lloyd George mentioned that in France much delicate fuse-making is done by women.

DRAWING BY S. BEGG. (COPYRIGHT IN THE UNITED STATES AND CANADA.)

A storm in a beer mug

Burton folklore says the reason why IPA found a ready market in England was due to a ship carrying casks of beer being wrecked in a storm in the 1820s off the Liverpool coast. When the beer was salvaged, it was sold in Liverpool pubs, where drinkers enjoyed this hoppy new style. Both Allsopp and Bass claimed the beer was theirs. A Bass guidebook published in 1902 said: 'A quantity saved was sold in Liverpool on behalf of the Underwriters. The quality was so much appreciated that the fame of the new "India Beer" spread in a remarkably rapid manner throughout Great Britain.'

The problem with the story is that there is no record of any violent storm in the Irish Sea in the 1820s. It was originally given credence by a writer named Walter Molyneux who said in a book *Burton-on-Trent: Its History, its Waters and its Breweries* in 1869 that a ship carrying some 300 hogsheads of beer was wrecked in the Irish Channel in 1827.

Research by Martyn Cornell proves that Molyneux was 12 years out with his claim. Writing in the *Journal of the Brewery History Society* in autumn 2015, Cornell said he had discovered a different story that appeared in 1870 in an obscure publication called *English Mechanic and World of Science*. This said that in 1839 an English ship called the *Crusader* foundered and contained a large quantity of 'export bitter ale'. Armed with the name of the ship, Cornell was able to track down its fate. It was due to leave Liverpool for Bombay in January 1839 with a cargo that included beer from both Allsopp and Bass: the entire cargo was worth around £8 million in modern value. The ship was struck by what Irish victims called 'the night of the big wind' – a storm that caused terrible damage in Ireland and the west coast of England. The *Crusader* struck a sandbank, still today called the Crusader Bank. The crew was rescued by lifeboats, but the ship broke up and much of the cargo floated ashore, including 79 casks of beer.

It may well be true that the beer was sold to pubs by the underwriters but, as Cornell points out, it seems unlikely it would have suddenly led to a clamour for 'India beer'. Hodgson in London had appointed an agent in Liverpool as early as 1825 and a Liverpool newspaper used the term East India Pale Ale in 1835, four years before the *Crusader* was wrecked.

David Lloyd George, seen here in 1915 as Minister of Munitions, was the bête noire of the brewers. He was responsible for driving down the strength of beer during the war and as a result IPA became a pale shadow of its old self.

The Edinburgh brewers

The success of England's pale ales prompted Scottish brewers to attempt to make the style. Robert Disher brewed the first pale ale in Edinburgh in 1821. He owned the Edinburgh & Leith Brewery in Edinburgh's Canongate and found that the city's water was ideally suited to brewing a sparkling pale beer. As was the case in Burton-on-Trent, Edinburgh's water was high in calcium and sulphate and bubbled to the surface through the sandstone layers of the 'charmed circle', an underground trough of water-bearing strata that rings the centre of the city through Canongate, Cowgate and the Grassmarket to Fountainbridge.

Scottish brewers had exported beer for many years. As a result of the Auld Alliance, beers from Scotland were popular in France and they also reached the Low Countries and the Baltic States. Scottish beer was also supplied to Scots who had settled in the Caribbean and New Zealand. As the 19th century progressed, other Edinburgh brewers followed Disher into pale ale production; they included Campbell, Drybrough, McEwan and Younger. The town of Alloa, on the north bank of the Firth of Forth, about 35 miles north-west of Edinburgh, was equally blessed with hard, pure water and became another major brewing centre. It had eight breweries in the second half of the 19th century and was dubbed 'the Burton of the North'. George Younger's brewery in Alloa became the third biggest in Scotland. Glasgow, with soft water, concentrated on darker beers and later moved into lager production.

As a result of the colder climate, the production of pale beer in Scotland was different to that in England. Mashing took place at a far higher temperature than in England while fermentation was a long, slow process at a low temperature, similar to primary fermentation in a lager brewery. Hops did not grow in Scotland's cold climate; as they had to be imported from England, costs were high and they were often used sparingly. T Thomson, in *Brewing & Distilling* (1842), quoted a pound of hops per bushel of malt for Edinburgh 'keeping ales', two-thirds the rate of Burton ales. When hops were added to the copper, the boiling time was long by English standards. This led to some caramelization of the brewing sugars. As brewers also used some amber malts, the finished beers tended to be darker, maltier and less hoppy than English IPAs. And many Scottish brewers continued their practice of adding some roasted barley to their IPAs, which gave the beers a distinctively different colour and flavour from the ones in the south.

Production methods changed with the arrival of new technology. The biggest breweries, notably McEwan and Younger, introduced steam, gas and electric power, installed laboratories, and employed trained brewers and chemists. Refrigeration cut down on cooling and conditioning times, allowing faster turnover. The brewers promoted and advertised their beers with vigour and by 1890 a third of exported British beer came from Scotland. Edinburgh, which by then had some forty breweries, enjoyed the lion's share of the trade.

When Alfred Barnard, the noted historian of British brewing, visited Younger's sites in Edinburgh in the late 1880s, he found that the entire production was given over to pale ale: 'Their principal manufacture is India Pale Ale, which is well known and appreciated in all parts of Britain as well as in foreign countries.' By 1900 Scotland was exporting 123,000 barrels of beer annually and Edinburgh accounted for 80 per cent of the country's beer production. Barnard said the Scottish capital was Burton and London rolled into one.

Scotland's export trade was so crucial that its versions of IPA were better known by the name of Export, with McEwan's Export the best-known example. But reliance on exports proved to be the brewers' undoing. The retreat from Empire in the 20th century and the dismantling of British garrisons overseas, which had always had a high proportion of Scots, saw sales of beer fall alarmingly. At home, the severe economic depression and unemployment of the 1930s adversely affected consumption and production. Breweries closed and merged. McEwan and Younger joined forces in 1931 as Scottish Brewers and in 1960 merged with Newcastle Breweries to form Scottish & Newcastle. For decades, Scottish brewing was dominated by S&N and another giant, Tennent Caledonian of Glasgow. Both concentrated on lager, though S&N did continue to brew McEwan's Export in keg and canned versions. It would take the success of Deuchars IPA towards the end of the 20th century to start to revive Scotland's great contribution to the style.

The first American IPAs

IPA was brewed in the United States in the 19th and early 20th centuries but it was never a dominant style there. The founding fathers brewed ale and advertised for brewers to follow them to the American colonies to build commercial plants, and for a period porter was widely produced. But while IPA was booming in Britain in the 19th century, the 'second wave' of immigrants to the US led to the rapid development of lager brewing.

In the early 19th century, brewers in the north-east of the United States were still influenced by brewing practice in Britain; English ales, including IPA, were also imported. The common practice was to brew strong stock ales that were aged in wood for up to a year and heavily hopped. Barley was grown in the region but was of poor quality – better varieties were imported from Canada – while hops grew in abundance in New York State. The water in the Hudson Valley was virtually identical to that in Burton-on-Trent. In his book *IPA: Brewing Techniques, Recipes and the Evolution of India Pale Ale*, Mitch Steele, former brewmaster with Stone Brewing in California, says that when attempting to produce their own versions of IPA the brewers used pale malt, high hop rates and long aging in wood. Because the malted barley was of poor quality, the brewers blended in wheat, rye, honey, molasses, corn, sugar and rice to provide additional fermentable sugar.

Peter Ballantine became arguably the best-known of IPA brewers in the US. His was the only IPA brewery to survive Prohibition and the beer has now been revived. He came from Scotland and opened a brewery in Albany, New York, in 1833. In 1840 he moved to Newark, New Jersey, and the brewery remained there until 1971. He brewed Burton Ale and IPA, beers aged in wood for a year or more: it's claimed one version of Burton was aged for 20 years.

The Vassar Brewery was founded in 1797 by an Englishman, James Vassar: a descendant founded Vassar College. James started on his farm, where he grew barley and used wild hops from the fields. In 1801 the family went into partnership with Oliver Holden and opened a brewery in Poughkeepsie. At its peak Vassar produced 20,000 barrels a year and its beers were sold in bottle and cask as far away as New York City; it closed in 1899.

Other notable IPA brewers included C H Evans in Hudson, New York, which at its peak produced 70,000 barrels a year. Its IPA had 7 per cent alcohol. Frank Jones Brewery in Portsmouth, New Hampshire, was founded in 1859. By the 1880s, it was producing 150,000 barrels of beer a year, making it the biggest ale brewery in the United States.

The Christian Feigenspan Brewery was founded in Newark, New Jersey, around 1870. It was famous for its 'Monks' Cellar', which held 100-barrel oak vats where its IPA was aged for two years; the brewery claimed this was the longest aging time in the US and advised that the beer was 'for sipping'. It had the misfortune to have 4,000 barrels in the cellar at the start of Prohibition and the beer had to be dumped. It never recovered and was taken over by Ballantine's during World War Two.

Economic recession in the late 19th century saw many breweries close or merge, with beer styles disappearing. But it was Prohibition, the ban on the manufacture and sale of alcohol from 1920 until 1933, which led to the virtual disappearance of IPA from the US. Only a handful of breweries survived the ban and they concentrated on a thin, bland version of lager. On the day Prohibition was repealed, President Franklin D Roosevelt said: 'Today would be a good time for a beer.' But he would have been hard-pressed to find an American version of IPA with which to celebrate.

Peter Ballantine from Scotland became the major brewer of IPA in the US in the 19th century. His beer has been revived by the national Pabst brewing group.

How IPA is brewed

India Pale Ale, in common with all styles of beer, is the result of blending malted grain and hops, and then fermenting the liquid to create alcohol and natural carbon dioxide. It sounds easy, but beer is arguably the most complex form of alcohol and requires enormous skill, training and dedication. At their simplest, wine and cider can be made by crushing fruit and allowing natural yeasts on the skins to create alcohol, though of course wine production can be far more sophisticated than that. But beer is the result of blending two radically different raw ingredients: malted grain and hops. The correct balance between the two is critical to the final character of the beer.

Malt

Grain delivers the natural sugars needed for fermentation, but it takes a complex set of procedures to turn the grain's starch into a fermentable sugar called maltose. Barley is the preferred grain for brewing: brewers call it 'the soul of beer'. It produces a sweet, clean, biscuit and honey character and delivers the most 'extract' of fermentable sugars. It differs from other grains in having a tough husk that acts as a natural filter during the mashing stage. Other grains, such as wheat, can become soggy and clog up pipes and valves. Even Bavaria's famous 'wheat beers' are a 50:50 blend of barley malt and wheat.

Brewers choose their barley with care. Only a small proportion of the grain is suitable for beer-making. Most is used as cattle feed or as an ingredient in breakfast cereals, bedtime malted drinks, candy bars and in some forms of instant coffee. Barley for malting must be low in protein and nitrogen: if they are too high the finished beer may be hazy. The preferred type of barley for brewing is considered to be 'two row' (the grains are arranged in two rows, on opposite sides of the stalk). The finest varieties of two-row are maritime barleys grown close to the sea. The early brewers of IPA would have chosen the pick of the crop from East Anglia, known as the 'grain basket of England', where much of the land has been reclaimed from the sea and fens, and as a result has rich, dark alluvial soil ideal for cereal growing. In warmer climates, six-row barley is the norm. It gives a more grainy texture to the finished beer and a number of American producers of IPA import English malt for their IPAs for a more refined character. Anchor Brewing in San Francisco, one of the early pioneers of craft brewing, uses two-row barley.

The Burton brewers had their own maltings, where enormous amounts of barley were transformed into grain suitable for brewing. Today brewers prefer to use the

Overleaf: The start of the journey – harvest time where barley is threshed and the best quality grain is sent to maltings to start the transformation of starch into fermentable sugar.

services of specialist malting companies. The skill of the maltster is to control the germination and kilning of the grain. First, the grain is thoroughly cleaned and then 'steeped', or soaked in water for several days. The grain is then placed on large, warm open floors or in rotating drums and left to germinate. The embryo of the grain starts to grow while tiny roots break through the husk. As the embryo grows, it triggers complex chemical changes that turn proteins into enzymes, natural organic catalysts. At the same time, starches are converted into soluble sugars.

Grain can be turned by hand on open floors (below) or mechanically in rotating drums (overleaf). This is Thomas Fawcett maltsters who have been malting barley for over 200 years in Yorkshire.

When the maltster is satisfied with the 'modification' – the embryo is fully grown, the roots forming a beard outside the husk and the hard grain now soft and chewable – the grain, called green malt, is loaded into a kiln, and the malt spread on a mesh floor to be heated from below, or – more usually today – into drums that rotate and are heated externally. A low heat at first gently dries the grain, stops germination and preserves the vital enzymes. Then the heat is increased to cure the malt to the brewer's own specification.

Pale malt is not only the essential backbone of IPA but also the base of all beers, including the blackest stout, as it contains the highest level of enzymes. The temperature is raised to 80°C/180°F and held for 24 hours. Higher temperatures will be used for darker malts, but pale malt is now ready for the brewer.

Hops

Even the most casual drinker knows hops add bitterness to beer. But this remarkable plant contributes far more than bitterness. In the 1990s, when Sean Franklin at Rooster's Brewery in Yorkshire, who had studied both wine-making and brewing in depth, coined the phrase 'hops are the grapes of brewing', he opened a window onto the complex contribution the plant makes to beer.

The hop delivers aromas and flavours that are spicy, herbal, grassy, perfumy, fruity (citrus in particular), peppery, woody/piny and resinous. It gives added dimension and depth to beer. It balances the biscuit sweetness of the malt's juices. An English Fuggle or Golding, a Czech Žatec (Saaz in German), a German Hersbrucker or Perle, a Slovenian Golding, an American Cascade or Citra, or a New Zealand Nelson Sauvin will give aromas and flavours to beer as distinctive as the world's great grape varieties.

The cultivated hop plant is called *Humulus lupulus*, the 'wolf plant', so called because of its voracious growing and climbing habits. The hop is dioecious, meaning the male and female plants grow separately. With the exception of English and some American and Belgian varieties, hops are not fertilized. Only the female hop is used in brewing and most brewers want seedless hops because they feel the more pungent character of fertilized hops does not marry well with the delicate flavours of lager beer. Ale brewers, on the other hand, consider that seeded hops better balance the more robust and fruity nature of their beers.

The hop thrives in well-drained loamy or sandy soil. In some regions, such as the American Pacific North-west, the soil has to be irrigated. The plants need warmth as well as moisture and long hours of sunlight. They are trained to climb tall trellises in order to attract the sun and they grow at spectacular speed, as much as 30 centimetres (12 inches) in a single day. By early July in the northern hemisphere, the hops will reach the tops of their trellises – 4.8 metres (16 feet) in height – and will then start to flower, allowing the cone to form and mature. The cones will be ready for picking in late August and September.

Humulus Lupulus.

The wolf plant: left to its own devices, it would rampage across the ground but hop growers encourage it to climb trellises for easy picking. Overleaf: the cones are the key part of the plant and any leaves and stalks are removed.

The hops are picked by a machine that removes stalks, leaves and earth. They must be dried quickly, or they will rot within a few hours. The plants are laid out on perforated floors in buildings known in England as oasthouses. Heat from kilns beneath the floors dries the hops, with the temperature held at 60°C/140°F for around 10 hours.

The hop cones contain a fine yellow powder called lupulin, which has the essential oils and bitter compounds needed by the brewer. The compounds break down into humulone and lupulone: the former creates the alpha acids that give bitterness to beer, while lupulone helps stabilize the wort during brewing. The oils in the cone give distinctive flavours to beer. Tannins also play a part, adding flavour and helping to prevent infection during the brewing process: it was vital to prevent bacteria infecting IPAs on their long journey to India. Hops divide into two main groups: bittering and aroma. Bittering hops are high in alpha acids while aroma hops have low rates of acid and are used mainly for the delightful bouquet they give to beer.

A traditional hop farm in Kent with trellises leading to the oasthouses where hops are dried. The rotating cowls on top of the houses direct warm air on to the drying hops below.

At the brewery, hops are added in stages during the boil in the copper. A proportion is added to the wort at the start of the boil in order to extract the oils and bittering compounds. But most of the aroma evaporates during the boil and there are further additions midway through the boil and a few minutes before it ends. Ale brewers often add a handful of hops to casks before they leave the brewery to intensify aroma and minimize the risk of infection – a process known as dry hopping.

Brewers with traditional coppers, which have slotted bases to separate hopped wort from spent hops, use the plant in its whole flower form. Modern plants that use two vessels for the boiling stage, a brew kettle followed by a whirlpool or separator, use pelletized hops. Pellets are made by crushing the hops into small tablets. Hop oil, a green juice extracted from the plant, is used by many large breweries but is frowned on by producers of handcrafted beer, who feel the oil gives a harsh back taste.

Starting in England, a new type of hop called a hedgerow variety has been developed. Hedgerow hops climb to only half the height of conventional varieties and are easier to pick. They are also less prone to the pests and diseases that plague hop farms and which can, in extremis, wipe out an entire harvest. The First Gold variety in England has been especially popular.

The unstoppable demand for new and exciting hop aromas and flavours, in the US in particular, has led to the development of new varieties such as Amarillo and Citra that give even more pronounced citrus/grapefruit character to beer. New Zealand hops are prized for their fine floral and fruity character. One hop is called Nelson Sauvin because it grows in the Nelson region where Sauvignon grapes are also harvested: the hop has a floral, citrus character similar to the grape.

In England new hop varieties, such as Endeavour and Jester, have been developed in an attempt to deliver the citrus notes demanded by modern craft brewers. The American Cascade is being trialled in England: time will tell whether this is a success, as terroir – a combination of climate, soil, environment and agricultural practices – is as important to hop growing as it is to vines. England's damp, often chilly environment is radically different to the hot summers of the Pacific North-west in the United States where hop fields have to be irrigated.

Units of Bitterness

Many of the beers listed in this book include their IBUs, short for International Bitterness Units. This is a scale that resulted from an international agreement in the 1960s. The level of bitterness of a beer is measured in a laboratory by chromatography. Until the revival of IPA, 40 units of bitterness was considered high, but many IPAs today have IBUs of 90 or more. The perceived bitterness of beer is a subjective assessment and no two people have identical taste buds. And extreme bitterness is often offset by the malts used in a particular beer.

Water

The importance of water in brewing is often overlooked. Brewers even have a special name for the water they use in mashing and boiling: liquor. Water differs from region to region and country to country and helps determine the types of beer that are brewed. You cannot make a genuine IPA with soft water – neither can you produce a true Pilsner lager with hard water. The total salts present in the water of Burton-on-Trent amount to 1,226 parts per million. In Pilsen, in the Czech Republic, where golden lager was first brewed, the figure is just 30.8.

As rain percolates through the earth it absorbs mineral salts. The type and quantity of salts depend upon rock formations in a given area. Soft water is the result of rain falling on insoluble rock such as slate or granite. It cannot pick up salts and is almost mineral free. When rain falls on soluble rock such as sandstone, water will pick up such sulphates as calcium and magnesium, which are present in the waters of the Trent Valley. Calcium sulphate is highly beneficial to the brewing of pale ale. It helps create the correct level of acidity in the mash, known as the pH (short for 'power of hydrogen'). It also encourages enzymes in barley malt to convert starch into maltose during the mashing stage.

Paul Bayley, the retired head brewer at Marston's, says Burton brewing liquor plays a crucial role in the flavour and keeping qualities of pale ale. According to Bayley, 'Calcium reduces sugar and helps produce

more alcohol. It keeps the yeast active, reduces haze, decreases beer colour and improves hop utilization. The result is a more bitter beer. Magnesium acts in a similar fashion and sulphates give a drier flavour and enhance bitterness.' Yeast, he adds, thrives on magnesium, making it 'greedy' as it converts malt sugars into alcohol.

Before scientists were able to 'Burtonize' water by adding calcium and magnesium sulphates, brewers in other parts of England were forced to move to Burton to produce IPA and pale ale. London brewers found that while they could make excellent dark beers such as mild, porter and stout in the capital, the level of sodium chloride present in London water made pale ale production difficult.

The Trent Valley in Staffordshire: the mineral-rich waters from springs in the valley were vital to the character of Burton IPA.

Today IPA brewers not only 'Burtonize' their liquor but strenuously filter it to remove impurities and modern 'agrichemicals'. As water accounts for around 90 per cent of even the strongest beer, it has to be good.

Yeast

Beer is as old as civilization, yet it wasn't until the 18th and 19th centuries that scientists were able to analyse yeast's role in the brewing process. Until then, fermentation was viewed as some kind of witchcraft and the foam produced by this strange alchemy was known in England as 'God-is-Good'.

The renowned French scientist Louis Pasteur showed brewers that yeast is a type of fungus, a single-cell plant that feeds on sugary liquids, converting them into equal proportions of alcohol and carbon dioxide – the process known as fermentation. All brewers bought copies of Pasteur's seminal work *Études sur la Bière*, published in 1876; among other things he convinced brewers of the need for absolute cleanliness.

As a result of the Industrial Revolution, factories were built in towns and cities and a large army of workers demanded beer to refresh them after long hours of backbreaking labour. Brewers responded by attempting to brew all year round, rather than only in the cooler months, when fermentation was easier to control. But when they brewed in the summer their yeast cultures were susceptible to many different competing strains of wild yeasts, some of which created sour, undrinkable beer. The major breweries in Burton-on-Trent built laboratories and employed scientists and chemists to perfect their products. Bass appointed John Matthews as its 'chemist and principal brewer' and in 1865 he was joined by Cornelius O'Sullivan, whose outstanding work on the theory and practice of brewing led to him being appointed a Fellow of the Royal Society. It was his pioneering work that enabled brewers to move from seasonal brewing to year-round production. Dr Horace Tabberer Brown at Worthington carried out groundbreaking research into barley germination, yeast nutrition and microbiology.

In the Carlsberg laboratory in Copenhagen, the scientist Emil Christian Hansen worked tirelessly to perfect a pure strain of brewer's yeast that eradicated infected strains and he was eventually successful in 1883. His strain was made available to other brewers and was called *Saccharomyces carlsbergensis*. The Carlsberg culture was designed to make lager, but Hansen's work had a knock-on effect among ale brewers, who cleaned up their cultures to avoid infection. The scientific term for ale yeast is *Saccharomyces cerevisiae*, but not all ale brewers reduced their yeasts to a single culture. Some preferred to use a two-strain yeast culture that they felt works best during fermentation, converting malt sugars at different times and speeds, which is essential when secondary fermentation is needed in cask or bottle. The Bass yeast culture, used to produce IPA in Burton in the 19th century, is famously a two-strain one still used to brew Draught Bass.

Women brewery workers at Burton during World War One: they replaced men who were away fighting. The funnel in the foreground removed surplus yeast from an open fermenter.

While lager yeast works slowly at a low temperature, ale yeast ferments at a warmer one and creates a dense head on top of the fermenting liquid. Ale fermentation usually lasts for a week: brewers say they like to give their beer 'two sabbaths'. Yeast cultures are carefully stored and refrigerated, as they are vital to beer-making. Yeast picks up, retains and imparts flavour characteristics from one brew to the next.

In Britain, brewers deposit a sample of their culture with the National Collection of Yeast Cultures in Norwich. They know that if they should suffer the nightmare of a yeast infection they can get a fresh supply: there are similar facilities in the United States, Germany and Denmark. When the London brewery Truman was revived in 2013, the owners were able to get the original yeast cultures from Norwich to give their ales the authentic East London character. Truman was one of the London brewers who went to Burton in the 19th century to produce pale ale and became the second biggest brewery in England after Bass.

Adjuncts

Adjuncts are ingredients added to malt, sometimes to reduce the cost – some global brewers use substantial amounts of rice – but they can also add distinctive flavours: the head brewer at Harvey's in Lewes, Sussex, says adjuncts allow him to 'play tunes with his beer'. The main adjuncts used in ale brewing are wheat, which helps create a lively head of foam, flaked (gelatinized) grains or torrefied (scorched) grains – the latter is similar to popcorn.

The first IPAs, we know from their recipes, used brewing sugar. This comes either in the form of candy sugar (sucrose) or invert sugar (glucose and fructose). Sugar encourages fermentation and reduces haze in the beer. As people are concerned about levels of sugar in modern diets, it should be stressed that brewing sugar, added during the copper or kettle boil, creates a dry beer rather than a sweet one because the yeast converts sugar to alcohol. In general, the level of adjuncts used in modern IPAs is low and many craft brewers avoid them completely.

Esters

As well as aromas and flavours derived from malt and hops, there are other flavour compounds known as esters. These are created naturally during fermentation and they are similar to banana, butterscotch, pear drop, apple, rose, honey, sultana, raisin and fresh tobacco. Brewers will use yeast strains either to avoid powerful esters or to encourage them. Lager brewers want clean aromas and flavours and will use yeast cultures that create low levels of esters. They are especially keen to avoid a compound called diacetyl which gives a buttery or butterscotch character to beer. Some ale brewers, on the other hand, positively welcome diacetyl.

Developments in brewing

Benjamin Wilson, the first major commercial brewer in Burton-on-Trent, was frustrated by the way in which beer was brewed in the late 18th century. In a letter in 1791 to a customer in Germany, he explained at length the outdated technology available to make beer at that time:

> *From the unusual impatience of the shipowners and masters to depart so early in the spring, I ought to begin to brew before the winter sets in; but let me tell them and all whom it may concern that it would be very dangerous to the preservation of the ale, which is a material object both for me and my friends to consider. I commonly begin to brew in the beginning of November, and am not willing, notwithstanding the importunity of the shipowners, to open my winter business sooner.*

The Industrial Revolution would dramatically change brewing technology. The largescale development of coke was of huge importance to the Burton brewers.

Wilson, whose family later sold the business to their relative Samuel Allsopp, was equally frustrated by his failure to meet domestic demand. A cotton mill had opened in Burton and thirsty workers wanted beer. But brewing remained a seasonal occupation and Wilson complained that even a mild winter could force him to suspend brewing because he couldn't control mashing and fermenting temperatures. Brewing methods were archaic. In a letter to Joseph Brooks in London, Wilson wrote: 'Every part of the business is done by hand-pail, from drawing of the mash to filling casks for exportation. It occurs to me that this quantity of business could be done with the aid of machinery to some great expense, and with equal certainty of purpose.' Country brewing lagged far behind the big porter brewers in London, where Samuel Whitbread had installed a steam engine, built by James Watt, in 1785 to provide power for the brewing processes. And the Burton brewers were still comparatively small. As late as 1830, most of the brewers in the town were producing around 3,000 barrels a year each.

The Industrial Revolution came to their rescue. Within a few decades, science and technology transformed brewing: without them it wouldn't have been possible to brew pale ale on a vast scale. Brewers started to use attemperators to control the temperatures of mashing and fermenting. Attemperators, known colloquially as 'worms', were lengths of coiled copper piping through which cool water circulated. The worm was placed in mash tuns to control the heat of malt and 'liquor' – brewing water – and the device was also put into fermenting vessels to maintain an even temperature. The worm could be used in reverse, with warm water used in winter if temperatures fell so low that fermentation couldn't get under way. It was now possible for brewers to extend the brewing season and their problems were further eased later in the 19th century with the arrival of ice-making machines and refrigerators.

Wilson and Allsopp learned not only from the East India Company but also from domestic customers in London and the south-east, that their beers needed to be paler in colour. The availability of pale malt was vital to Burton's future and its production was made possible by the rapid development of the coke industry. Pale malt is more gently heated or kilned than brown malt and retains a higher level of the enzymes that turn starch into brewing sugar. This means less malt is needed to produce beer, an important cost consideration. Brown malt was traditionally kilned using wood fires. Wood is hard to control and can flare, producing a scorched or charred end product. Coal had been used to make pale malt in country areas but it wasn't a satisfactory fuel as a result of the gases created when it was burnt, which infected the malt with off flavours. Early in the 19th century, Abraham Darby started to turn coal from the Staffordshire mines into coke. Coke had been available since the late 17th century but it became more widely available for brewers when it was made on a much bigger commercial scale in the 19th. Benjamin Wilson's record books refer to buying 'coaks' from Derby. Coke was much easier to control than wood and gave off consistent heat. As the Industrial Revolution gathered pace and coke was made on a large scale, the Burton brewers had the ideal fuel for their maltings.

Brewing equipment was changing, too. Cast-iron mash tuns held heat better than wood and were far larger, holding up to 200,000 gallons of the sugary extract called wort. They had a far longer lifespan, too. A large funnel placed above the mash tun, known as a Steel's Masher after its inventor, contained an Archimedes screw that mixed grain and brewing liquor at the correct temperature before it entered the tun. Previously, horses had plodded, hour after hour, round the tun and mixed the mash with rakes attached to their harness.

For centuries, one batch of grain was used to produce two or three brews, a system developed by monastic brewers at the dawn of Christianity. The first brew produced a strong beer, the second a weaker one and, if a third beer was made, it was a watery drink deemed suitable for impoverished pilgrims and nursing mothers. In the middle of the 19th century, Scottish brewers developed a method calling 'sparging' – from old French *esparger*, meaning to sprinkle – that sprayed the grain in the tun at the end of the mash with hot brewing liquor from rotating arms in the roof of the vessel: it's similar to the revolving rinsing arm in a modern dishwasher. Sparging effectively washed out any remaining malt sugars and meant mash tuns could be used more effectively by pushing through new, full-strength brews every few hours.

Coppers, where the wort is boiled with hops, were turned from open pans into enclosed domed vessels that avoided heat loss and evaporation, and captured the essential aromas of the hops. Open pans, where the 'hopped wort' cooled prior to fermentation, were inefficient and were also prey to wild yeasts in the atmosphere. They were phased out in favour of heat exchange units in which the wort is pumped through plates that alternate with plates containing running cold water.

Improvements in agriculture led to better-quality grains and hops being grown, while the work of Louis Pasteur and Burton's own brewing scientists created purer yeast strains that gave cleaner and more effective fermentations, free from contamination by infected strains. Water could be scientifically analyzed and treated: the role of sulphates in producing a bright, pale and sparkling beer had repercussions throughout the brewing industry.

The Burton Unions

Without doubt the greatest advance in brewing IPA was the invention of the 'Burton Union' system of fermentation. The unions were a stroke of genius by Peter Walker, a brewer from Liverpool who was one of the 'incomers' who came to Burton to use the Trent Valley spring waters. In 1838 he devised a method of fermentation that turned an ancient system known as the 'carriage cask' on its head. The carriage cask, dating back to monastic times, was a messy and unhygienic method, in which fermenting beer rose from the bung holes of casks, ran down the sides and was collected in troughs below. The beer was returned to the casks in jugs while most of the yeast was held back for future brews.

The 'Cathedrals of Brewing' – the unions at Marston's brewery.
Fermenting beer and yeast in the giant oak casks are driven
by carbon dioxide up pipes into troughs above. Most of the
yeast is retained in the troughs while the beer runs back into
the casks.

Peter Walker's innovation was brilliant in its simplicity. He placed the troughs above the casks and linked them by pipes. In the old system, once fermentation was finished, the casks were sealed and sent to inns and taverns, but Walker installed large oak casks, each one holding 150 gallons of beer, that remained in the brewery in what became known as Union Rooms. The term 'union' stems from the fact that the casks, troughs and pipes are linked together, or 'held in union' as the Victorians said.

Strictly speaking, the union casks are not fermenting vessels but finishing vessels. At Marston's, the only Burton brewery that still uses the system, fermentation begins in shallow open vessels. As soon as a vigorous fermentation is under way, the liquid is pumped to the unions. As fermentation continues, the carbon dioxide created drives the liquid from the casks up swan-neck pipes into the troughs above: as the name suggests, the pipes curve at the top in order that the liquid can drip into the troughs, known as 'barm trays' in the local Staffordshire dialect. The troughs are held at a slight incline: the liquid runs down them and flows back to the unions, leaving most of the yeast behind.

Not all the yeast is cleared as a result of the unions. Richard Westwood, managing director of brewing at Marston's, told me that sufficient yeast is left to ensure a powerful secondary fermentation in the cask when it leaves the brewery: between 0.5 million to 1 million yeast cells per millilitre are left in the beer. The ability of the Burton brewers to produce a clear, sparkling beer was vital to the success of IPA and pale ale. As commercial glass-making developed, drinkers moved from pewter tankards to glass and appreciated a beer that was temptingly clear and free from dregs.

When the American brewer and scientist Thom Tomlinson studied the sea journey of the India-bound ales in the early 19th century, he concluded that the 'hardy yeasts produced in Burton unions combined with high rates of priming sugar protected the beer on its stormy voyage and helped give it a long shelf life.' Priming sugar is added to casks as they leave the brewery and help encourage a strong second fermentation. Paul Bayley, the former head brewer at Marston's, who is a passionate devotee of Burton pale ale, says yeast as much as alcohol and hops kept beer destined for India in good condition.

The union system fell out of favour as a result of the high costs of oak and the labour required to build and repair them. Brewers turned instead to mechanical skimming devices to remove yeast from fermenting beer. But the Burton brewers remained faithful to them well into the 20th century. The former Bass unions now stand forlornly in the car park alongside the Molson Coors brewery, the successor to Bass, but Marston's still proudly uses them and says they are critical to the flavour and character of their beers. Its union rooms are vast; the only sound is the quiet drip of wort into the barm trays and the hiss of carbon dioxide. I once described them as 'the cathedrals of brewing' and visitors are sometimes surprised to find a member of staff dressed in a bishop's robes and mitre saying benediction over the oak vessels.

An article in the *Daily News* in 1880, which was reprinted as a pamphlet, paints a vivid picture of Bass as a vast Victorian enterprise and also gives a graphic description of the brewing process of the day. William Bass had started his company little more than a century before on an acre of land. By 1880 the Bass empire occupied 140 acres. It used 267,000 quarters of malt a year, 36,000 hundredweight of hops, and paid £300,000 to the government in excise duty.

The writer's description of the brewing process illustrates the way in which all the new technologies had been assimilated. When the wort has been run off through the slotted base of the mash tun, 'the malt left is "sparged" by a shower bath of hot water to extract from it the last remains of saccharine-matter.' After the wort has been boiled with hops it has to be cooled in preparation for fermentation. The writer notes that before the arrival of refrigeration the temperature was often too high to allow brewing to take place. But now the hopped wort is pumped to heat exchangers: 'It is difficult to make these out to be anything else than huge boxes; but by climbing up and peeping over the edge, we can see a shallow lake, laced by successive long straight coils of copper piping...the boiled wort is flowing slowly from the coolers through this mighty submerged snake, while the cold water that covers it has given to it a slow, steady motion at right angles to the flow of wort, so as to intensify the refrigerating power.' Once fermentation has started, the fermenting wort is transferred from vessels called squares to the great union room, where it continues to work inside large wooden casks linked by one long pipe. 'What a ball-room would this Union-room make if its floor was clear...but instead of dancers it holds 2,500 casks, each one containing 160 gallons.'

Page 79 Ale brewing, including IPA, starts on a farm where barley is harvested and sent to a maltings where it's washed, allowed to germinate and then heated to turn into malt. In the brewery, the malt is stored in a grist case, then crushed in a mill and fed to the mash tun where it's thoroughly mixed with pure hot water. The sweet wort produced flows to a copper for boiling with hops. The 'hopped wort' is clarified in a whirlpool, then cooled before being pumped to fermenting vessels and mixed with yeast, which converts the malt sugars into alcohol. After conditioning for a short period, the beer is ready to be packaged in casks, kegs, cans and bottles.

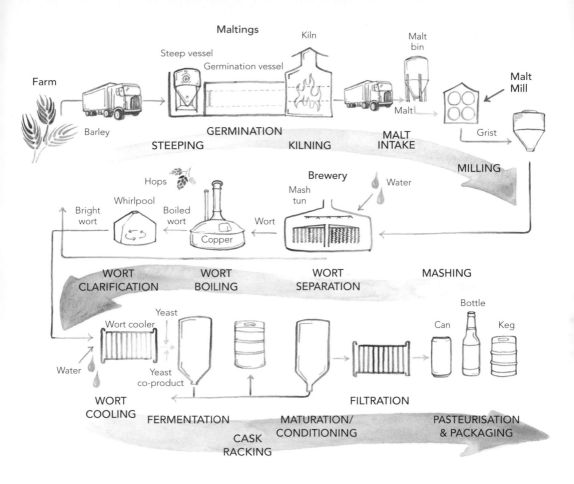

Maltings

Farm
Barley

STEEPING

Steep vessel
Germination vessel

GERMINATION

Kiln

KILNING

Malt
bin

Malt

MALT
INTAKE

Malt
Mill

Grist

MILLING

Hops

Brewery

Water

Bright
wort

Whirlpool

Boiled
wort

Copper

Wort

Mash
tun

WORT
CLARIFICATION

WORT
BOILING

WORT
SEPARATION

MASHING

Yeast

Wort cooler

Bottle

Can

Keg

Water

Yeast
co-product

WORT
COOLING

FERMENTATION

CASK
RACKING

MATURATION/
CONDITIONING

FILTRATION

PASTEURISATION
& PACKAGING

Overleaf, clockwise from top left: In sharp distinction to Marston's traditional brewing system, these cylindro-conical vessels are used to ferment beer in modern breweries; hops prepared for the copper boil with the sweet wort producing mash; 'spent grain' spilling out of the mashing vessel when the wort has been run off; preparing hops for dry hopping; digging out the mash, a slow and laborious task. The spent grain is used as cattle feed; preparing hops for 'dry hopping' the finished beer.

How IPA is brewed   79

Classic IPAs

New interpretations of India Pale Ale beguile us from all parts of the globe. But what were the early beers like? It's possible to taste three versions of the style with their roots in the 19th century, which give a fascinating glimpse of IPA with all its Victorian pomp and swagger.

Ballantine India Pale Ale

United States

Ballantine India Pale Ale. Jesus, this beer is a holy sacrament! Dangerous, high-test, 44 magnum ale, its bitter, woody suds, reeking of spruce sap, overwhelm the nose and palate – God, this is fabulous ale...Ballantine India Pale Ale, last bright jewel in the tarnished crown of American brewing, you haunt me still.

Alan D Eames, *Ale Dreams* (1986)

Alan D Eames was often called 'the Indiana Jones of beer', so we can take his word that this was a very special beer. And yet, passed from pillar to post from the 1970s, the beer finally disappeared in 1996 when its latest owner, the giant Pabst Brewing Company, sidelined the brand and then killed it off. But eighteen years later, in 2014, Pabst brought it back from the grave as it saw the craft brewing movement's IPA bandwagon gathering pace.

Ballantine's was founded in 1840 by Peter Ballantine, a Scot who had emigrated to the US. At first he rented an old brewery, but his early success enabled him to build a new brewery in Newark, New Jersey, in 1850 where he was joined by his three sons. They launched their India Pale Ale in 1878 and by 1879 P Ballantine & Sons had become the sixth largest brewery in the US and it had achieved fame for beers that were rooted firmly in the British tradition, such as its flagship XXX Ale.

Ballantine's survived Prohibition by making malt syrup, but in 1933, the year Prohibition ended, the brewery was bought by two energetic brothers, Carl and Otto Badenhausen, who grew sales of Ballantine Beer, a lager, through aggressive advertising, including sponsoring the famous baseball club, the New York Yankees. Through the 1940s and '50s, Ballantine's became the third biggest-selling beer brand in the country.

The brewery went into steep decline in the 1960s as light lagers became more popular. In 1972 Ballantine's was sold to the Falstaff Brewery, based in St Louis, Missouri. But these were difficult times for middle-ranking brewers: giants such as Budweiser, Coors and Miller dominated more and more of the market. From a high point of seven million barrels in 1965, Falstaff lost 70 per cent of its sales over the next decade and was sold to the giant Pabst brewing group in 1985. Pabst moved Ballantine IPA from plant to plant, reducing its strength and changing its recipe until it was a shadow of its former self. Finally, in 1996 it was put out of its misery.

When Pabst decided to revive IPA, it understood it had to be restored to its former glory if it were to compete successfully in the modern beer world. Master brewer Greg Deuhs was asked to make a study of the beer and he found to his astonishment that the original recipe for the beer no longer existed. He told Jeff Alworth of *All About Beer* magazine in October 2014: 'With all the acquisitions related to Ballantine, none of the records made it to me. All the records you'd expect just aren't there; no one handed me a couple of boxes and said, here are the recipes.'

But Deuhs wasn't working completely in the dark. He knew from anecdotal evidence that Ballantine's IPA in its heyday had been aged for a year in 800-barrel pitch-lined oak tanks and it had been both dry hopped and dosed with hop oil. Dry hopping refers to hops added after fermentation for additional aroma and bitterness. The fact that the oak tanks were lined with pitch is of particular interest, as it's a departure from English practice in the 19th century. Lining oak casks with pitch or resin prevents wood flavours from penetrating the beer: the first brewer of golden lager, Pilsner Urquell in Bohemia, lined its oak casks with pitch, a practice followed by other lager breweries in Bavaria. This prevented any wild yeasts such as *Brettanomyces* attacking the beer. English brewers didn't use pitch lining, although they vigorously steam-cleaned their casks. We can therefore assume that Ballantine's IPA lacked the funky note of a Victorian IPA brewed in Burton, though some contemporary writers referred to the beer's 'woody' character.

In the 19th century and for most of the 20th, brewers were not required to declare the strength of beer, so again Deuhs was using guesswork in recreating Ballantine's: he had seen references ranging from 6.9 per cent to 8 per cent. Units of bitterness were also not given and were claimed to range from 65 to 80. The beer's colour was less of a problem, as Deuhs found many descriptions citing a deep golden to amber colour. He discussed the colour with maltsters and came to the conclusion that the beer had been made with pale malt, caramel malt and Munich malt 'with maybe some black malt for colour adjustment'. This is also a departure from English practice because we know the Burton brewers used only pale malt and brewing sugar and no darker malts. In fact, 'stewed malts' such as caramel malt – known as crystal malt in Britain – and Munich malt were not used in brewing until late in the 19th century.

As well as IPA, Ballantine's also brewed a pale ale called XXX. It was hugely popular, not least among such literary giants as Ernest Hemingway, John Steinbeck and Hunter S. Thompson.

Hops were critical to the revival of Ballantine's IPA. Deuhs opted for a combination of old and newer hops, arguing that all breweries change and update the varieties they use. He used Magnum as the main bittering hop and added Cascade, Columbus, Brewer's Gold and English Fuggles. He was intrigued to discover that Ballantine had also used hop oil, which is made by grinding hops into a fine powder, adding water and cooking them in a process that effectively distils the oils from the plant. The oil is used solely for aroma and is added following fermentation. It's said the beer had a hop aroma unlike any other beer brewed in the United States at the time. Deuhs was so anxious to recreate this characteristic that he had to track down a manufacturer of hop oil in Britain. To add to the hop character, he also dry hopped trial batches of the beer with Cascade and Columbus.

Deuhs gave great thought to the wood character of the beer. As contemporary reports referred to a little or even a lot of wood flavour and Alan Eames spoke of the beer's 'woody' and 'spruce sap' appeal, Deuhs wondered if some exposed, unlined staves had been used in the oak tanks. He estimated that perhaps five per cent of the staves were untreated and he created an 'oak torpedo' that goes into the modern bright beer tank, where the beer rests following fermentation, for 'a bit of oak nuance'.

The beer is brewed for Pabst by the Cold Spring Brewery in Minnesota. It's not a small brewery. It was founded in 1874 and produces around 80,000 barrels of beer a year, but unlike Pabst it can handle short-run brews in 75-barrel batches. The beer

Promotions for Ballantine's IPA and other beers made much of their purity and popularity with sportsmen.

is fermented with a yeast culture called Chico, considered to be close to the type of culture that was used in the 19th century. The IPA designed by Greg Deuhs has 7.2 per cent alcohol and 70 units of bitterness. I think Alan Eames, who died in 2007, would have approved.

The verdict

The beer has a bright gold/amber colour with a superb and complex aroma of spicy, cinnamon hops, caramel, sappy malt and a light oak note. Juicy malt, caramel/butterscotch and spicy hops dominate the palate, with a wood note developing as the beer warms up. The finish is bittersweet, with luscious malt, caramel, resinous hops, and a continuing cinnamon spice note. It's finally dry and quenching. This American/English hybrid IPA is magnificent.

ABV	7.2%
First brewed	1878; revived 2014
Brewery	Pabst
Website	www.pabstbrewing.com

Worthington's White Shield

England

I shy away from the over-used term 'iconic', but it's surely true of White Shield. It's a beer beloved of connoisseurs and is a potent link with the India Pale Ales brewed in Burton-on-Trent in the 19th century. But in the modern world of brewing giants, whose main interest is producing large volumes of unremarkable and undemanding beers, White Shield lives a precarious existence. Its current owner, Molson Coors, a Canadian-American group that bought the former Bass breweries in Burton, is at the time of writing offering to sell White Shield to a smaller brewery that can be bothered with a beer which contains live yeast in the bottle and requires patience and even passion to bring to fruition.

William Worthington was one of the great Burton brewers. He was a cooper by trade and moved from Leicestershire to Burton, where he worked for a brewery that he bought out in 1760. He and his family achieved success and fortune, becoming bankers as well as brewers. The banking side developed from trading in oak imported from Europe. So much English oak had been used to make warships to fight the threat from Napoleon's France that brewers were in desperate need of imported wood to make their casks.

As well as banking, the Worthingtons carved out their own special niche in brewing. They seized on the advantages of glass as commercial glass production developed in the 18th century and produced a sizeable proportion of their beers in bottled form, winning great acclaim for the quality of their products. The quality was in no small measure due to Worthington's brewing chemist Horace Tabberer Brown, who pioneered the science of separating and cultivating pure strains of brewer's yeast. The brewery opened the industry's first laboratory in 1872 to enable Brown to carry out his research.

White Shield, with its logo of a dagger on a shield, was launched in 1829 and has been in continuous production ever since. Bass and Worthington merged in 1926, but the Worthington beers continued to be brewed under their own names. As more and more brewers in the 20th century started to filter and pasteurize their bottled beers, White Shield became an aficionados' drink, treated with the reverence given to vintage wine as a result of its bottle-aging with live yeast. In the turbulent times of the 1960s and '70s, with a spate of brewery mergers, Bass closed the Worthington brewery in 1965, but the draught and bottled beers continued to be produced. White Shield took on an extra lustre during the dog days of poor but heavily promoted keg draught beers that created a consumer backlash and the formation of CAMRA, the Campaign for Real Ale. White Shield, dubbed 'real ale in a bottle' by CAMRA, kept drinkers happy in areas of the country where real draught beer was hard to find. It became a cult beer and encouraged the production of more bottle-conditioned ales.

Above: Worthington's IPA is generally known as White Shield.
Overleaf: the arrival of the railway in the mid-19th century
helped transport Worthington's beers all around the country.

A river idyll, enjoying a cool White Shield after a row on the river. The clothing suggests this is either late Victorian or Edwardian England.

The message of the popularity of White Shield didn't get through to Bass, which concentrated on Carling lager and other major brands. It said volumes were too small to brew in Burton and switched production of White Shield to its breweries in Birmingham and Sheffield and finally to the family brewery of King & Barnes in Horsham, Sussex.

But after Bass left brewing in 2002, Molson Coors brought the beer back to Burton, where its return was marked by members of the Staffordshire Regiment marching through the town. Steve Wellington, a veteran Bass brewer with a great love of White Shield, was put in charge of brewing the beer in the small plant within the Bass Museum, which Molson Coors renamed the National Brewery Centre.

As sales took off, Molson Coors had to move production to its main brewery and all seemed set fair for the future of White Shield. I was delighted to join a select party in Burton in 2005 which celebrated the production of the millionth bottle.

But global brewers are fickle beasts. Molson Coors bought a small brewery in Cornwall, Sharp's, which had achieved considerable success with a draught and bottled bitter called Doom Bar. Molson Coors invested heavily in Sharp's, turned Doom Bar into Britain's biggest-selling draught cask ale and moved production of the bottled version to Burton. As a result, White Shield has been sidelined and in 2016 Molson Coors put the beer out to tender. At the time of writing, there are two contenders, one outside Burton, the other Steve Wellington's Heritage Brewery at the National Brewery Centre. I hope – fervently – that it stays in its native town.

Worthington's White Shield is 5.6 per cent alcohol, has 26 units of colour and 40 units of bitterness: its amber/gold is almost identical to Ballantine's IPA. It is now brewed with pale and crystal malts and hopped with Challenger, Fuggles and Northdown varieties. It is unlikely crystal malt was used in the original beer and Fuggles hops were the only variety of the three that were available in the 19th century. Challenger and Fuggles are used for bitterness, Northdown for aroma.

The brewing regime is complex. Two strains of yeast are used for primary fermentation. The beer is conditioned in tanks for three weeks, filtered and re-seeded with a different yeast culture described as 'sticky' by the brewers because it clings like a limpet to the bottom of the bottle. In common with Champagne, a 'dosage' of brewing sugar is added to encourage fermentation in bottle. Finally, the beer is held in the brewery for a month before it's released. Consumers are advised to drink bottles that are not more than two years old, but I have tasted versions dating back to the 1980s. Some have oxidized, but those that have survived well are not only drinkable but are also fascinating to compare to a young version: aging makes the beer darker, less bitter and extremely fruity.

The verdict

An enticing and complex beer with spices, peppery hops, light apple fruit and sulphur on the aroma, followed by juicy malt, tart and tangy hop resins and spices in the mouth. The long and lingering finish has a bitter hop character but is balanced by nutty malt and apple fruit: apple is a defining note in Burton pale ales. The beer has been named CAMRA's Champion Bottled Beer of Britain in 1991, 2000 and 2006. A brewing icon.

ABV	5.6%
First brewed	1829
Brewery	Heritage Brewery
Website	www.worthingtonswhiteshield.com

1759. AULD REEKIE.

Edinburgh in 1910. Its nickname of 'Auld Reekie' stems either from the high number of breweries in the city or the smell from the tenements ... or both.

McEwan's Export

Scotland

There are unconfirmed stories that William McEwan was teetotal, which would make
him a rare member of the brewing community. If true, it's as tragic as Beethoven being
unable to hear his symphonies as a result of acute deafness: McEwan developed a
historic Scottish variant of IPA but may never have tasted it.

He built one of the biggest and most influential breweries in Britain, and he may
have exported more beer to more countries than even the Burton brewers. He was
born in Alloa, an important brewing town, in 1827. His father, John McEwan, was
a shipowner, and the family business proved vital to his success. William McEwan
was taught the brewing skills by his uncles John and David Jeffrey, who ran the
Heriot Brewery in Edinburgh. He decided to branch out on his own and with
the help of a £2,000 loan from his family opened a brewery in 1856 in the city's
Fountainbridge district, which takes its name from the spring waters in the area that
bubble up from the 'charmed circle', the rock strata beneath the city. He was clearly
a canny businessman. He paid a geologist to find a site with a plentiful supply of
the finest well water with a high content of calcium and sulphate making it ideal for
producing pale ale. He was not above engaging in industrial espionage. In common
with brewers from Austria and Bavaria, who stole samples of beer and yeast when
they visited the Burton breweries, McEwan also went to Allsopp and Bass to make
copious notes about ingredients, temperatures and brewing techniques. He knew that
success lay in producing a beer similar to the Burton IPAs, and moving away from
traditional Scottish beers that were strong, dark and sweet: they were dubbed 'Scottish
Burgundies' by French aristocrats who settled in Edinburgh to escape the guillotine.

McEwan wasn't the first Edinburgh brewer to make a paler ale than the traditional
dark Scottish beers. Robert Disher's Edinburgh & Leith Brewery was brewing pale
ale in the 1820s; others followed, including Younger and Campbell. But McEwan had
the advantage of his proximity to the railway, which enabled him to sell beer to the
Newcastle and Sunderland regions of north-east England, with a large army of thirsty
coal miners and shipbuilders, and to export courtesy of his father's ships.

His export success was aided by the large number of Scots who had moved abroad
as a result of the hardships caused by the Highland Clearances in the 18th and 19th
centuries. A high proportion of soldiers in the British army in India were Scots and
they also found their way to Australia and the United States to dig for gold. Both
Canada and New Zealand also had strong links with the old country. By the 1890s,
one third of all British beer sent abroad came from Scotland and expatriate Scots
not only welcomed pale ales from their homeland but dubbed them 'export'. A new
member of the IPA family had arrived and travelled the world.

McEwan and his rivals were keen to emulate Burton IPAs, but Scottish brewing
practice and the climate made their beers distinctively different. Mashing temperatures

The Laughing Cavalier became one of the most recognizable images in Britain for decades and gave a global impetus to McEwan's beer.

were higher than in England and the result was a sweeter beer. As hops don't grow in Scotland, they were used more sparingly, around one-third less than in Burton. As a result of low ambient temperatures, fermentation was cooler and slower than in England. Younger is known to have used Burton Unions but records don't show if McEwan did: however, as he had seen them in action at Allsopp and Bass, it's likely he had union sets installed.

Most Scottish brewers used open wooden vats and when fermentation was complete the beer was allowed to settle for a few days in a receiving vessel before being racked into casks. The casks were then stored for a year before being shipped abroad. While McEwan and his rivals used the finest malting barley from Scotland and England, both brewing sugar and amber malts were also used, giving the finished beers a darker colour than English IPAs.

McEwan, like Worthington in Burton, was quick to grasp the opportunities offered by industrial glass production and his Export, with the prominent image of the Laughing Cavalier on the label, made it stand out from the crowd. By 1880 his brewery covered twelve acres and when McEwan became a registered company in 1889 it was worth half a million pounds with capital of £1 million. At its peak, McEwan brewed around two million barrels a year and was one of the biggest breweries in Britain. As well as dominating Scotland with Younger, McEwan enjoyed a 90 per cent share of the Tyneside beer market.

In 1930, McEwan and Younger put aside their long rivalry and merged to form Scottish Brewers, which enabled them to further their domination of the beer market north and south of the border. Following World War Two, the group saw its export sales decline as Britain pulled down the curtain on the age of empire. Nevertheless, sales of Export remained strong, especially in North America. In 1960, Scottish Brewers merged with Newcastle Breweries to form Scottish & Newcastle (S&N); McEwan's Export remained a key brand in cask, keg, bottle and can. By 1973, the Fountain Brewery was still producing some two million barrels a year, but as a result of rationalization early in the 21st century, S&N closed both its Edinburgh and Newcastle plants, with production centred at John Smith's in Yorkshire and the Royal Brewery in Manchester. CAMRA scornfully dubbed the group 'Neither Scottish nor Newcastle Breweries', but McEwan's Export lived on, brewed under licence by the Caledonian Brewery in Edinburgh.

In 2008 S&N was bought by Heineken, the world's third biggest brewery and now the biggest UK brewery. In 2011 it agreed to sell the McEwan's brands to Charles Wells, a large, independent, family-owned brewery in Bedford. Wells has invested heavily in the beers and has seen a substantial revival in Scotland. The company is also a vigorous exporter and runs a dozen pubs in France, bringing McEwan's Export – still brewed by Caledonian for the Bedford company – to new audiences.

The beer is brewed with pale and crystal malts, with, in the Scottish tradition, a touch of roasted barley. The hop varieties are East Kent Goldings, Hersbrucker from Bavaria and Styrian Goldings from Slovenia.

The verdict

The deep, burnished, copper-red beer will come as a profound shock to drinkers used to the bold hop character of modern IPAs. It must be judged on its merits, as a Scottish traditional beer. The aroma has a rich malt and butterscotch character, but there is a subtle yet firm spicy and floral hop note. The palate is dominated by juicy and gently toasted malt, but again the hop notes provide balance. The finish is far from sweet, ending dry and refreshing and with continuing notes of rich malt, butterscotch and spicy hops.

ABV	4.5%
First brewed	c.1860
Brewery	Charles Wells, Bedford
Website	www.mcewans.co.uk

The great revival

IPA, originally a beer style from just one country, Great Britain, is now produced throughout the world and often in the most surprising places. Who would expect to encounter IPAs in Italy? It's a country with no beer culture, and so new craft brewers look to Britain and the United States for inspiration. Belgium on the other hand has a profound and ancient beer culture, but brewers there are widening their horizons and looking beyond the borders of the country for new styles, including IPAs – made with a definable Belgian twist.

In France, haughty and proud of its viniculture, brewing has largely been confined to areas close to Belgium or in the Strasbourg region with its Germanic influences. But beer-making is spreading south and IPAs are appearing in regions where until now the grape has reigned supreme. Scandinavia, dominated for decades by the might of Carlsberg and its subsidiaries, has brought back the ancient style of *øl*, or ale, and is invigorating the style with the use of New World hops and pale malts.

Australia and New Zealand, as a result of their strong and even emotional links to the 'Old Country', are brewing exhilarating interpretations of pale ale and IPA and are proving there is more to beer than the bland offerings of Foster's, XXXX and Steinlager. Far more surprising is the discovery of IPAs in China and Japan, proving that the style is emerging in the most unusual places and pleasing a new generation of drinkers who have never encountered the beer style before.

But undoubtedly the United States is the powerhouse, the driving force of the IPA revival. A type of ale that was little known there in the 19th century, made by just a small number of brewers, has been taken up by the modern craft movement and become the sector's major style. In a sense, it was a revival that was waiting to happen. Since the 1960s, there has been a symbiotic relationship between craft brewers in the US and Britain. A small number of American home-brewers, some on military service, discovered pale ale in Britain and went home to create the style there on a commercial basis. Fritz Maytag, who rescued an ailing brewery in San Francisco and turned Steam Beer into an American classic, made an extensive tour of Britain to see how the likes of Timothy Taylor in Yorkshire and Young's in London brewed their pale ales and was inspired to launch his Liberty Ale and, later, IPA.

Scroll forward to the 1980s and Dan Kenary and friends were sufficiently inspired by the ales they discovered in Britain and Europe to open the Harpoon Brewery in Boston, Massachusetts, and – with some trepidation – to launch an IPA they thought might be too hoppy and bitter for modern tastes. It rapidly became popular and is still the brewery's main brand. On the far side of the country in Seattle, close to the hop fields of the Pacific North-west, Charles Finkel, who ran a wine and beer import business called Merchant Du Vin, added the small Pike Place Brewery and launched an IPA with a reverential bow in the direction of the English model. In Portland, Maine, a British ex-pat Alan Pugsley added a distinctively English note to his Shipyard IPA, importing both Fuggles hops and a yeast culture from his homeland. In New York City, Garrett Oliver, who was to become the best-known and most revered craft brewer in the country, weighed in with East India Pale Ale at Brooklyn Brewery.

And then the country went hop crazy. Craft brewers realized that a beer based on pale malt provided the perfect platform for building a powerful hop character using home-grown varieties. The special climate of Oregon and Washington States, with bountiful sunshine rarely found in England, produced hops brimming with the aromas and flavours of passion fruit, grapefruit, mango and pine. These helped create IPAs that led to an insatiable demand for the style – a style which has now taken the world of beer by storm.

United States

Sales of IPA are growing by more than 30 per cent a year and it's the top category in the awards at the annual Great American Beer Festival, attracting some 250 entries. Brewers, restlessly seeking even more distinctive versions of the style, have added double and imperial IPAs (strong beers, generally with 7 to 10 per cent alcohol – sometimes more) and – controversially – black IPAs. And growth goes roaring on, with no sign of the bubble bursting. Imperial, double, black, spiced and fruited: new interpretations of IPA tumble from American craft breweries with a restless desire to seize on once-forgotten beers, restore them to life and give them a modern twist.

The IPA boom is doubly remarkable, for when the pioneers of American craft brewing, such as Fritz Maytag at Anchor in San Francisco, toured Britain to study local brewing they found precious few IPAs. The English and Scottish versions had slipped below the radar and in England the favoured beer was bitter. Fortunately pale ale, the domesticated version of IPA, was still to be found and Americans, entranced by its character, returned home determined to fashion their own versions of the style. Others were encouraged to follow them when Michael Jackson's seminal *World Guide to Beer* appeared in 1977 and included a lengthy section on English pale ale. He praised in particular Bass Ale and Worthington's White Shield. While he did not call them IPAs, it took only a small amount of research by American brewers to discover the true export origins of these formidable Burton beers.

IPAs began to flow from American breweries and, in the hop-crazy world of the 21st century, took on their own identity as a result of rapid innovations in hop farming. While English varieties give both a deep bitterness and a characteristic peppery and spicy note, with restrained fruitiness, new American varieties, thanks to the terroir and blazing summers of the Pacific North-west, developed scintillating, nose-tingling aromas and flavours of gooseberry, grapefruit, lime, lychee, mango and tropical fruits.

American hops gave IPAs an unmistakable swagger that other countries couldn't hope to match. The rush to brew the style created a divide, with West Coast pale ales outdoing the rest of the country with the sheer zing of their hop delivery. But commonsense has intervened: while beers with 100 units of bitterness may be impressive, they do not make for comfortable drinking and more approachable 'session IPAs' are now making an appearance.

But, over-hopped or more restrained, the IPA juggernaut roars on. At the end of 2016, there were more than 5,000 craft breweries in the US, 90 per cent of which are independent producers. A quarter of their sales are now accounted for by IPA and demand for the beer shows no sign of slowing.

Samuel Adams, Rebel IPA

The brand celebrates Samuel Adams, who led the opposition to British rule and played a key role in the Boston Tea Party in 1773. He helped draft the Declaration of Independence and became a senator and governor of Massachusetts. He was also a maltster in Boston and was involved in the brewing industry in the city.

Jim Koch, owner of the Boston Beer Company which makes the Samuel Adams brand, is descended from a family of German immigrants who ran several breweries: his father's closed during Prohibition. In 1985 Koch gave up a successful business career to brew Samuel Adams Boston Lager and he has seen the company grow spectacularly to become one of the biggest craft breweries in the US. As well as the best-selling Boston Ale, Koch has added Rebel IPA, which has become so popular that there is now a series of Rebel IPAs.

Rebel IPA, though brewed on the East Coast, makes a deep bow in the direction of West Coast IPAs with a big input of American hops: Cascade, Centennial, Chinook, Mosaic and Simcoe, which create 45 units of bitterness. The grains are two-row pale malt and cara malt. As the bitterness units are relatively modest by West Coast standards, it's a well-balanced beer with good malt character.

The verdict

Bronze beer with sherbet lemons, peaches and grassy and perfumy hops dominating the aroma along with fresh biscuit malt. Juicy malt and bitter hops combine on the palate with a strong undercurrent of bittersweet fruit. The finish is dry, with biscuit malt, hop resins and lemon and peach fruit notes.

ABV	6.5%
First brewed	2014
Brewery	Boston Beer Company, Boston, Massachusetts
Website	www.samueladams.com

Anchor Brewing, Go West! IPA

Fritz Maytag, founder of Anchor, was a student at Stanford University in California in the 1960s; while there, he enjoyed a local speciality known as steam beer. It dated from the days of the gold rush in the 1850s when brewers in San Francisco, lacking refrigeration, met the prospectors' demand for refreshment by making a beer with lager yeast but fermented at ale temperature. The result was a beer with such a high level of carbonation that when casks were tapped in bars they gave off an audible hiss of gas that sounded like steam escaping. Maytag used his stake in the family's washing machine empire to buy the last remaining steam beer brewery. He modernized it and fashioned a legend with Anchor Steam Beer.

Go West! hints at the brewery's roots in the 19th century, when prospectors coined the expression 'Going to see the elephant' to underscore their spirit of adventure.

Brewmaster Scott Ungermann uses two-row pale barley malt backed with a massive attack of hops: Apollo and Bravo in the kettle followed by Citra, Calypso, Equinox and Eureka! for dry hopping. He uses a special piece of equipment, nicknamed the Odeprot, where the beer is filtered through whole flower hops to extract maximum aroma and flavour. The odd name is a wink in the direction of the Sierra Nevada Brewing Company (see page 141) and its torpedo used for dry hopping. Anchor launched its dry-hopped Odeprot IPA, with 8.2 per cent alcohol, in 2016.

The verdict

A pale bronze beer with pine needles, a 'malt loaf' grain note, spicy hops and orange and lemon fruit on the nose. Bitter hops vie for attention in the mouth with tart fruit, pine and juicy malt. The finish is dry, with biscuit malt, spicy hops and a continuing powerful fruit note, with an intensely bitter end.

ABV	6.7%
First brewed	2015
Brewery	Anchor Brewing Company, San Francisco, California
Website	www.anchorbrewing.com

Brooklyn, East IPA

Brooklyn's renowned brewmaster Garrett Oliver has a sharp eye for tradition and his IPA – originally named East India – is inspired by the role played by London brewers and the East India Docks before the style was taken up by brewers in Burton-on-Trent, England. Brooklyn Brewery is best known for reviving a style of lager – Vienna red – that was lost during Prohibition, and Oliver has added a raft of new beers to the portfolio.

Brooklyn has grown to become one of the leading craft breweries in the US, while Garrett Oliver has achieved worldwide acclaim not only as a brewer but also as a writer. He is the author of *The Brewmaster's Table* that details beer-and-food pairings and he edited *The Oxford Companion to Beer* that has helped give beer the same recognition as wine around the world.

For his IPA he uses two-row malting barley imported from Crisp's in East Anglia, England. The beer has a complex blend of hops: East Kent Goldings from England, Celeia from Slovenia and American Amarillo, Cascade, Centennial and Summit. The beer is also dry hopped. But Oliver stresses he is not brewing a 'hop bomb' to 'peel the enamel from your teeth' but is concerned with a good balance between malt and hops.

The verdict

A deep bronze colour and an aroma of lemongrass, citrus fruit, piny hops and cracker-like malt. Bitter hop resins accompanied by tart citrus fruit build in the mouth, with a rich juicy malt backbone. The finish has a superb balance of tangy fruit, biscuit malt and lingering piny hop bitterness.

ABV	6.9%
First brewed	1996
Brewery	Brooklyn Brewery, New York City
Website	www.brooklynbrewery.com

Deschutes, Inversion IPA

Deschutes is a rags-to-riches brewery. It was founded in 1988 by Gary Fish and produced just 300 barrels in its first year; it now brews some 400,000 barrels a year and is the fifth biggest craft brewery in the country. It stands in beautiful countryside alongside the Deschutes River.

In spite of being at the heart of the hop-growing region of the Pacific North-west, the brewery's key IPA is a subtle blend of both malt and hop character, allowing the grain to balance the large range of hops used. Pale, Munich and cara malts are blended with Bravo, Cascade, Centennial, Delta, Millennium and Northern Brewer hop varieties that create 80 bitterness units. Deschutes brews several other IPAs: see their website.

The verdict

A copper-coloured beer with a massive aroma of toasted malt, bittersweet fruit – grapefruit, mango, orange and peach – with piny and floral hops. Intense hop bitterness builds in the mouth but is balanced by nutty and toasted grain and ripe fruit. The finish is long and complex, with a quinine-like hop bitterness mellowed by nutty malt and bittersweet fruit notes.

ABV	6.8%
First brewed	2013
Brewery	Deschutes Brewery, Bend, Oregon
Website	www.deschutesbrewery.com

Dogfish Head, 90 Minute Imperial IPA

Brewery founder Sam Calagione is a legendary figure in the craft beer movement. He not only produces several versions of IPA but he has also developed a system of 'continuous hopping' to give them intense aroma and flavour. 90 Minute was his first beer in a series that now includes 60- and 120-minute versions. His innovation was to add hops throughout the boil in the kettle, not just at the start and finish, which is the conventional method. At first the hops were piled onto an old table football board and were shaken by hand into the kettle, but this has been replaced by a more sophisticated 'Me So Hoppy' device that fires the hops into the boiling wort.

The method means that every last vestige of hop oils and tannins are extracted, adding enormous depth of flavour to the beer. 90 Minute IPA takes a full month to brew and condition, and delivers 90 bitterness units from hops from the Pacific Northwest region.

The verdict
Gold-coloured beer with pale malt creating a luscious biscuit note on the nose, balancing a great blast of citrus fruits and piny hop notes. Hop bitterness, grapefruit, mango, tropical fruits and juicy malt combine on the palate, followed by a finish in which the hops take full control and lead to an intensely bitter end.

ABV	9%
First brewed	2003
Brewery	Dogfish Head Craft Brewery, Milton, Delaware
Website	www.dogfish.com

Flying Dog, The Truth Imperial IPA

In common with IPA, Flying Dog has been on a journey. It started life as a brewpub in Aspen, Colorado, run by George Stranahan, entrepreneur, philanthropist and rebel. He teamed up with his neighbour Hunter S Thompson, founder of 'gonzo' journalism and author of *Fear and Loathing in Las Vegas*. Thompson introduced Stranahan to British artist and cartoonist Ralph Steadman, who from the 1990s has designed the brewery's distinctive, eye-catching labels. The success of the brewpub led to a move to a bigger plant in Denver and then way over to the east to Maryland, where 100,000 barrels a year are now brewed.

Imperial IPA has changed over the years. At first it was 10 per cent alcohol and a single hop beer using just the Simcoe variety. But it has been scaled back to 8.7 per cent and now has a potpourri of hops – Amarillo, Citra, CTZ, Summit and Warrior – that deliver 80 bitterness units. The grains are pale, Munich and malted wheat. Flying Dog also brews Easy, a session IPA; Snake Dog IPA at 7.1 per cent; a Belgian-style IPA called Raging Bitch; Double Dog, a double IPA at 11.5 per cent; and has also made a number of small-batch single hop imperial IPAs.

The verdict

The beer has a burnished bronze colour and a big grassy hop, citrus fruit and cracker wheat aroma. Bitter hops and ripe fruits – grapefruit, lemon and mango – fill the mouth while the finish is long and complex with succulent bittersweet fruit, bitter hops and lightly toasted malt.

ABV	8.7%
First brewed	2013
Brewery	Flying Dog Brewery, Frederick, Maryland
Website	www.flyingdogales.com

Founders, All Day IPA

Brewmaster Jeremy Kosmicki says he fashioned his session IPA so he could enjoy an everyday beer that didn't blow him away with too much hop attack: he was seeking a good balance of grain and hop. While Founders, launched in 1996 by Dave Engbers and Mike Stevens, has other IPAs in its portfolio, All Day marks a change in the beer scene in the US, where drinkers now want to enjoy a few glasses rather than just one 'hop bomb'. Its drinkability has proved popular and All Day accounts for half Founders' sales of its beer range.

The brewery has grown from humble beginnings and now produces some 900,000 barrels a year. It has won a number of awards at both the World Beer Cup in Chicago and the Great American Beer Festival in Denver. All Day IPA is brewed with two-row pale malt and cara malt. The hops are not revealed but are understood to be Amarillo and Centennial, which create 42 units of bitterness. It may be a session beer but it's not shy on hops.

The verdict

A pale copper colour with lightly toasted malt and floral hops on the nose, with hints of apricot and peach. Bitter hops, toasted malt, pine notes and bittersweet fruit challenge for attention on the palate. The finish has a dryness from the darker malt, with continuing notes of floral and piny hops and rich, tart fruit.

ABV	4.7%
First brewed	2012
Brewery	Founders Brewing Company, Grand Rapids, Michigan
Website	www.foundersbrewing.com

Great Lakes, Commodore Perry IPA

Brothers Patrick and Daniel Conway, who opened Great Lakes in 1986, admit it's a trifle odd to name a quintessentially British beer style after a man who sank the Royal Navy's ship in the Battle of Lake Erie in 1812. But several of their beers honour American heroes: during the great battle, Commodore Oliver Hazard Perry flew a flag that declared 'Don't give up the ship!'

Great Lakes started life as a brewpub, which still operates in Cleveland, but the brothers now also have a state-of-the-art plant, which is one of the major American craft breweries. The IPA is brewed with two-row pale malt and cara malt; Cascade, Simcoe and Willamette hop varieties create 70 units of bitterness. As Willamette is a descendant of the English Fuggle, there is a faint touch of 'Britishness' about the beer.

The verdict

Bronze beer with a pine and vanilla note on the aroma from the cara malt, with a balancing act of citrus fruit from the hops. Grapefruit and mango build in the mouth, but the cara malt continues to make a big impression with vanilla and toffee notes. The finish starts bittersweet and fruit-led but segues into a dry, hoppy and bitter finale.

ABV	7.7%
First brewed	c.1991
Brewery	Great Lakes Brewing Company, Cleveland, Ohio
Website	www.greatlakesbrewing.com

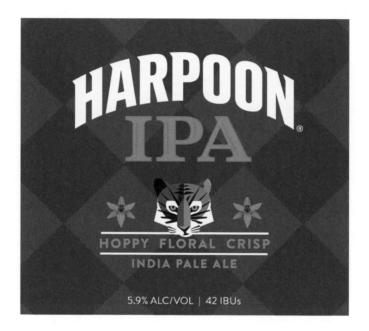

Harpoon, IPA

This is the beer that helped spark the IPA revival in the US. The brewery was founded in 1986 by Dan Kenary, Rich Doyle and George Ligetti, following a tour of Britain and Europe where they discovered beers, unlike American bland lagers, with taste and hop character. They launched their IPA in 1993 when it was almost a forgotten style and they were uncertain whether drinkers would accept a beer with 42 units of bitterness. It is Harpoon's main brand, its bitterness modest compared to West Coast versions. The company, now owned by its employees, has a second brewery in Windsor, Vermont.

The signature flavour of Harpoon IPA is the result of around 5 per cent of the pale malt being lightly toasted. The hops are Apollo and Cascade, with Cascade also used to dry hop the beer following fermentation.

The verdict

A beer with a deep bronze colour and an enticing aroma of fresh cracker biscuits, earthy hop resins, orange and lemon fruit and a hint of basil. Hop bitterness builds in the mouth, but there's a fine balance from biscuit malt, bittersweet fruit and spice notes. The finish starts bittersweet, with a good balance of toasted malt and spicy hops, but finally ends dry with continuing fruit notes, earthy hop resins and lingering spice.

ABV	5.9%
First brewed	1993
Brewery	Harpoon Brewery, Boston, Massachusetts
Website	www.harpoonbrewery.com

Lagunitas, IPA

Lagunitas is one of the fastest-growing craft breweries in the US, with IPA its main brand. It was founded in Lagunitas in 1993 by Tony Magee and moved to Petaluma to build a bigger plant and keep up with demand. Investment in further equipment enabled the brewery to produce 600,000 barrels a year by 2012 and that figure has been matched by a second plant built in Chicago.

Heineken has taken a 50 per cent share in the company and distributes IPA in Europe as well as the US. The arrival of global brewers in the craft sector is controversial, but there's been no perceived drop in the quality of Lagunitas' beers, which are given lengthy periods of conditioning following fermentation.

IPA is brewed with pale malt and a touch of darker cara malt and is hopped with Cascade and Centennial: other hops may be added during conditioning but they are not revealed. The beer has 51.5 units of bitterness, modest by West Coast standards, but it still has a resounding hop impact.

The verdict
The beer has a bright gold colour and a grassy and herbal aroma with powerful hints of camomile and fennel balancing toasted malt. Bitter hops dominate the palate, with a solid underpinning of rich malt and tart fruit notes of peach and lychee. Hop bitterness subsides in the finish to give fruit and malt the last word.

ABV	6.2%
First brewed	1995
Brewery	Lagunitas Brewing Company, Petaluma, California
Website	www.lagunitas.com

Laughing Dog, Alpha Dog Imperial IPA

Michelle and Fred Colby, founders of Laughing Dog, say they make 'fetchingly good beer': their yellow Labrador Ben gives the paws-up or down to each new brew they produce. Apparently it's one bark for 'yes' or two barks for 'no'. He might find it hard to bark at all after sampling a beer that has a redoubtable 126.8 units of bitterness, the result of adding some 6 pounds of hops to each barrel brewed. Ben is now well past middle age but he has a son called Ruger, who will take over tasting duties in due course.

Laughing Dog is surrounded by the Selkirk Mountains, which supply pure water for the brewery. The Colbys use the finest malts and hops money can buy and avoid cheaper ingredients. Their Alpha Dog is brewed with pale and Munich malts with a touch of honey that counters the extreme bitterness of the hops: the varieties are Columbus and Mount Hood.

The verdict

A copper-coloured beer with a massive hit of citrus fruit on the aroma, with blood orange to the fore and further notes of lemon and grapefruit. The hops are balanced by a teasing hint of honey sweetness alongside nutty malt. Powerful piny hops and fruit notes dominate the palate, but toasted malt and a gentle hint of honey are also present. Honey and malt make a big impression in the long finish, but the beer ends dry with a powerful bitterness and continuing citrus and pine notes.

ABV	8%
First brewed	2009
Brewery	Laughing Dog Brewing, Ponderay, Idaho
Website	www.laughingdogbrewing.com

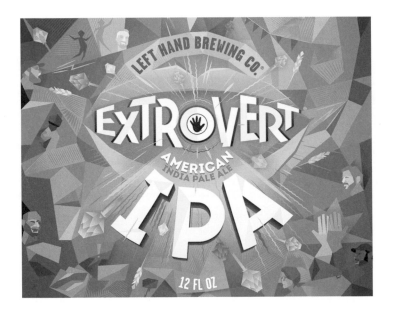

Left Hand, Extrovert American IPA

With 75 units of bitterness, the beer is well named: in your face and a bit mouthy. It's an outstanding example of the big flavoured West Coast style of modern IPAs. It was created as a complement to Introvert Session IPA, with 4.8 per cent alcohol and 55 bitterness units.

The brewery dates from 1993 and was founded by Dick Doore who, in common with many American craft brewers, had started out as a home-brewer before turning professional. The brewery is named after Chief Niwot (meaning left-handed) of the Arapahoe tribe, which wintered in the area. Doore has achieved a fistful of awards for his beers, including 27 medals at the Great American Beer Festival. Left Hand produces more than 50,000 barrels a year and is one of the top 50 American craft breweries.

Extrovert IPA is brewed with two-row pale malt and CaraMunich darker grain and also rye and wheat. The hops are Cascade, Comet and Equinox.

The verdict

A bronze beer with a delightful, nose-tingling aroma of fresh pine, floral and earthy hop resins, orange fruit and a 'fresh bread' malt note. Orange fruit bounces across the tongue, with bitter hops building in the mouth, balanced by chewy malt. The finish starts bittersweet and fruity, but the hops take over, leading to a bitter and dry end.

ABV	7.1%
First brewed	2016
Brewery	Left Hand Brewing Company, Longmont, Colorado
Website	www.lefthandbrewing.com

Odell, Myrcenary Double IPA

Doug Odell is a legendary figure in the American craft brewing movement and he's now a roving ambassador, lecturing about the joys of beer in his home country and abroad. With other family members, he launched his brewery in 1989 after spending years as a dedicated home-brewer, researching old recipes and beer styles. At first he sold beer door-to-door in Seattle from an old pick-up truck, but his success enabled him to open his plant in a former grain store in Fort Collins, where he can produce 45,000 barrels a year. The current 125-barrel brewhouse was custom-built in Germany and will provide approximately 300,000 barrels of future brewing capacity.

Doug's double IPA pays tribute to myrcene, one of the essential oils of the hop plant delivering both aroma and bitterness. The varieties used in the beer are Cascade, Centennial and Chinook which create 80 units of bitterness. Grains are a complex blend of pale, Pilsner, cara and Vienna.

The verdict

A hazy bronze colour and a massive aroma of passion fruit, lemons, pine, cobnuts and freshly baked bread. Bittersweet citrus fruits coat the tongue, but there is a strong malt backbone and a big build-up of hop bitterness in the mouth. The finish has a warming hit of alcohol, rich citrus fruit, biscuit malt and bitter hops full of resins and pine.

ABV	9.3%
First brewed	2011
Brewery	Odell Brewing Company, Fort Collins, Colorado
Website	www.odellbrewing.com

Pike, IPA

Pike IPA is one of the pioneering versions of the style, first brewed in 1990 in a small plant in the Pike Place area of Seattle, famous for its food market and fish restaurants. It has since moved to a bigger plant but remains in the hands of founder Charles Finkel and his family. In common with Harpoon on the East Coast, sceptics doubted when it was launched that drinkers would accept a beer with a high level of bitterness, but 60 units seems modest today.

Apart from imported English Goldings, Finkel is dedicated to using local ingredients. His other hops come from the Pacific North-west and he works with farmers in the Skagit Valley region to obtain the finest malting barleys.

Pike IPA has a complex grain bill of pale, crystal, Munich and cara pils along with some malted wheat. The hop recipe is lengthy: Amarillo, Cascade, Chinook, Columbus, Goldings and Willamette.

The verdict

Pike IPA has an appealing burnished pale copper colour with a massive burst of floral hops and grapefruit on the nose. Underlying the hops is a nutty and cracker biscuit malt note. Quenching malt, citrus fruit and bitter hops combine in the mouth, followed by a finish that has a creamy note from the wheat along with earthy, resinous hops and bittersweet fruit.

ABV	6.3%
First brewed	1990
Brewery	Pike Brewing Company, Seattle, Washington State
Website	www.pikebrewing.com

Rogue, Brutal IPA

The founders of Rogue, Jack Joyce, Rob Strasser and Bob Woodell, have a mission to brew beers made – as far as possible – from locally grown ingredients free from fertilizers and without additives or preservatives. Their own farms now provide their two-row malts from barley grown on volcanic land in the Pacific North-west, where there are strict regulations about the use of fertilizers. Some grain is also imported from Europe and has a similar ecological background.

The founders soon outgrew their first small plant in Ashland and now have a substantial site in Newport, where brewing is conducted by John Maier, who was recruited in 1989.

For his Brutal IPA, Maier uses cara wheat along with pale malt and, unusually, just one hop, Rogue Farms' own Alluvial™ hops.

Since 2008, Rogue has had its own hop farm in Oregon and its range of beers makes increasing use of homegrown hops. These are showcased in its 'hop family' IPAs: 4 Hop, 6 Hop, 7 Hop and 8 Hop.

The verdict

Brutal IPA has a bronze colour and a pungent aroma of citrus fruit, with lemon and grapefruit to the fore, and cracker wheat malt and spicy hop resins. Bittersweet fruit builds in the mouth against a solid backbone of biscuit malt and bitter hops. The finish is long and complex, finishing dry and bitter, but with continuing notes of rich fruit and malt.

ABV	6.2%
First brewed	circa 1996
Brewery	Rogue Brewing Company, Newport, Oregon
Website	www.roguc.com

Russian River, Pliny the Elder

This is the most talked-about IPA in the United States. It has won a shed-load of awards, including top medals in the World Beer Cup and the Great American Beer Festival. It's brewed in small batches and, in a similar fashion to beers brewed by Trappist monks in Belgium, aficionados hot-wire the bush telegraph to announce a new batch's arrival and hurry to pick up stock. The bottling date of each batch is printed on the label.

The brewery and bar, in beautiful countryside surrounded by vineyards alongside the Russian River, opened in 1997 and were sold in 2003 to brewmaster Vinnie Cilurzo and his wife Natalie. They moved to a new site in Santa Rosa but have maintained the original brewpub where they stage many charity events. They have also planted their own hop fields.

Their double IPA honours Pliny the Elder (AD23–79), who died during the eruption of Mount Vesuvius but who had analyzed and possibly grown what was called *lupus salictarius* – now known as hops. His work was continued by his nephew: Russian River also brews a Pliny the Younger IPA.

Pliny the Elder is brewed with Amarillo, Centennial, CTZ and Simcoe hops. Pale malt is the base; the brewery does not reveal any additional grains.

The verdict

Bright gold beer with a delightful aroma of freshly planed pine wood, earthy, spicy hops, fresh tobacco, biscuit malt and a hint of butterscotch. The palate is bittersweet with tropical fruits vying for attention with the attack of bitter hops and juicy malt. The finish lingers, with hops dominating but balanced by juicy malt and a returning hint of butterscotch, but ending dry and bitter.

ABV	8%
First brewed	1999
Brewery	Russian River Brewing Company, Santa Rosa, California
Website	www.russianriverbrewing.com

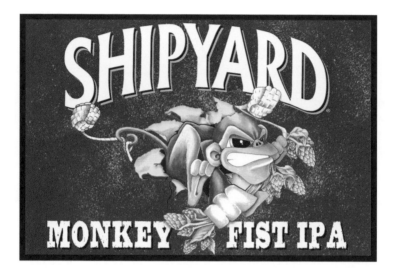

Shipyard, Monkey Fist IPA

Alan Pugsley trained at the Ringwood Brewery in Hampshire, England, and when he moved to the US in 1992 he brewed Ringwood's award-winning Old Thumper strong ale under licence, using the brewery's yeast culture. It was also used to ferment Shipyard's first IPA, made with Fuggles hops, in 1994.

Pugsley also uses the English yeast culture for Monkey Fist, which he calls an aggressive IPA, for which he imports British two-row pale malt, which is blended with malted wheat, Munich, crystal and cara malts. The hops, on the other hand, are all-American – Cascade and Chinook – which create 67.5 units of bitterness.

The verdict

The copper-coloured beer has a big hit of citrus fruit on the nose, with grapefruit to the fore, and biscuit malt, pine and spice notes from the hops. Nutty, chewy malt, tart fruit and spices combine in the mouth, followed by a long finish that has a powerful malt backbone overlain with tangy fruit and a spicy and woody bitterness.

ABV	6.9%
First brewed	2012
Brewery	Shipyard Brewing Company, Portland, Maine
Website	www.shipyard.com

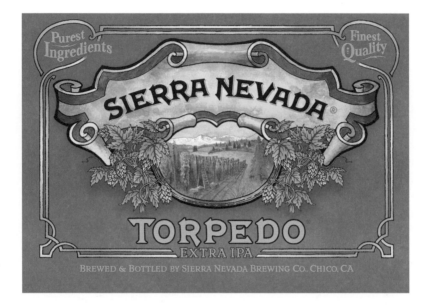

Sierra Nevada, Torpedo Extra IPA

'Brewing legend' may be an overused term but it surely applies to Sierra Nevada. Founded in 1981 by two passionate home-brewers, Paul Camusi and Ken Grossman, in the university town of Chico, students spread the word about the wonders of the early beers, Pale Ale and Big Foot barley wine. The insatiable clamour for the beers enabled Camusi and Grossman to install a modern, German-built brewhouse and today Sierra Nevada produces around 800,000 barrels a year.

For years, the brewers had been determined to extract maximum aroma and flavour from their hops, and this led to the invention of the torpedo. Fermenting beer is pumped into the stainless steel vessel known as a torpedo, which is packed with whole flower hops, and then returns to the fermenter. The result is 65 units of bitterness and a profound attack of hop character in the finished beer. The varieties used are Magnum for bitterness, with a further addition of Magnum along with Crystal at the end of the kettle boil. The two hops are joined by Citra in the torpedo. The grains are two-row pale and cara malt.

The verdict

The beer has a burnished bronze colour with a big waft of grapefruit and lemon jelly on the nose, with spicy hop resins and a 'fresh bread' malt character. The palate is shatteringly bitter with touches of iodine and quinine, but the hop character is softened by bittersweet fruit and juicy malt. Grapefruit, lemon, passion fruit and lime marmalade pack the finish with spicy hop resins and toasted malt.

ABV	7.2%
First brewed	2009
Brewery	Sierra Nevada Brewing Company, Chico, California
Website	www.sierranevada.com

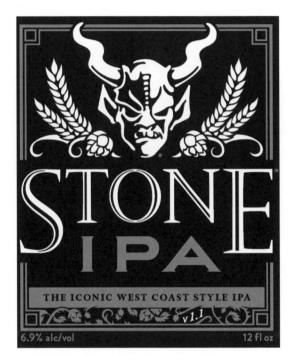

Stone, IPA

In spite of the terrifying-looking gargoyle image on labels and glasses, the brewery has a gentle disposition – they say the gargoyle wards off evil spirits – and has won awards for its contribution to the environment. It gets around 40 per cent of its electricity from solar power and it has added a waste water treatment plant.

The brewery was founded in 1996 by Greg Koch and Steve Wagner; they released their IPA to mark their first anniversary in business. They have since added Go To, a session IPA Delicious, with 7.7 per cent alcohol and Ruination, with 8.5 per cent; and many seasonals, reserves, collaborations and small-batch IPAs.

The flagship IPA has a vast range of hops in its makeup – Azacca, Calypso, Centennial, Chinook, Ella, Magnum, Motueka and Vic Secret – which combine to produce 71 bitterness units.

The Stone beers can be enjoyed in the sylvan surroundings of the brewery's World Bistro with its large garden. In 2016 Greg Koch unveiled a similar brewery, beer garden and bistro complex in Berlin (see page 266).

The verdict

A pale gold beer with pine and citrus notes dominating the aroma, but with balancing biscuit malt, and floral and peppery hops. The palate has a fine juicy malt backbone overlain by bittersweet fruit and intensely bitter hops. The finish is long, with sappy malt combining with deep and luscious citrus fruit, but finally ending hoppy and bitter.

ABV	6.9%
First brewed	1997
Brewery	Stone Brewing, Escondido, California
Website	www.stonebrewing.com

Uinta, Hop Nosh IPA

Will Hamill launched his brewery in an old garage in 1993; success led to a move in 2001 to a large, modern plant that can produce some 77,000 barrels a year. The brewery slogan is 'Earth, Wind and Beer' and the company is environmentally friendly, using wind power to drive the brewery. While the water from the Salt Lake might be ideal for brewing pale ale, Hamill and his colleagues prefer to use the pure waters from the surrounding Uinta Mountains and add salts as required.

Hop Nosh is brewed with pale malt and small amounts of Munich and cara malts. The complex hop regime includes Apollo, Cascade, Chinook, Bravo and Zythus, which produce 82 units of bitterness.

The verdict

The beer has a pale gold colour and a big aroma of peaches and mangoes, with creamy malt and spicy hop resins. Bitter hops and ripe fruit dominate the palate with a strong backbone of juicy malt. The finish has a pleasing malty sweetness but is balanced by earthy hop resins and a mellow fruitiness.

ABV	7.3%
First brewed	circa 2010
Brewery	Uinta Brewing Company, Salt Lake City, Utah
Website	www.uintabrewing.com

Alchemist, Heady Topper

This double IPA is in such demand that each batch sells out within hours. The recipe is kept a closely guarded secret but is thought to be pale, Pilsner, cara malt and wheat malts with Amarillo, Apollo, Cascade, Centennial, Chinook, Columbus and Simcoe hops: the hops create no fewer than 120 bitterness units. The unfiltered beer has grapefruit, lemons, mango and spice on the aroma with sweet malt balancing the extreme bitterness on the palate.

ABV	8%
First brewed	2003
Brewery	The Alchemist Brewery, Stowe, Vermont
Website	www.alchemistbeer.com

Anderson Valley, Hop Ottin' IPA

This is one of America's pioneering craft breweries, founded in 1987. It has grown, moved site and now has a 100-barrel capacity plant. The owners are committed to helping the environment and use solar panels for energy, recycle and clean brewing water, and send used malts and hops to local farms. The name Hop Ottin' is local slang and means 'hard-working hops'. There's certainly a powerful hop punch to the beer thanks to large amounts of Cascade and Columbus in the kettle, which deliver 78 bitterness units. The malts are pale, crystal and Munich.

The beer has a burning bronze colour with a powerful aroma of earthy and peppery hops, orange fruit and freshly baked biscuits. Bitter hops build in the mouth with chewy malt and ripe fruit, and there is a lingering finish of peppery hops, bittersweet fruit and juicy malt.

ABV	7%
First brewed	mid-1990s
Brewery	Anderson Valley Brewing Company, Boonville, California
Website	www.avbc.com

Ballast Point, Sculpin India Pale Ale

A sculpin is a spiked fish found off the coast of California and the beer named after it has a big spiky attack of hops from Amarillo, Centennial and Warrior varieties that create 70 bitterness units. The malts are pale, crystal and cara pils. There's a big hit of fruit – apricot, peach, lemon and mango – on the nose and palate with toasted malt and bitter hops in the finish.

ABV	7%
First brewed	circa 2006
Brewery	Ballast Point Brewing Company, San Diego, California
Website	www.ballastpoint.com

Bell's, Two Hearted Ale American IPA

When Larry Bell opened his plant in 1985 it was the first new brewery in Kalamazoo since Prohibition. Larry started with a converted soup pot and open fermenters and produced small batches of beer. He has been so successful that his current plant makes half a million barrels a year.

Two Hearted is named after the river that runs through Michigan. It's unusual in two ways: only one hop, Centennial, is used and it's added to the fermenting vessels as well as during the boil in the kettle. The aim is to extract the maximum amount of aroma and flavour: bitterness units are around 50. The malts used are pale with a touch of crystal and Vienna.

The beer has a hazy orange colour with a big hit of orange fruit on the nose, toasted grain and floral hops. Centennial hops add a delicate hint of rose petals to the palate with continuing notes of biscuit malt, orange fruit and hop resins. The long finish is bittersweet to start, but as fruit and malt fade there's a bitter, hoppy finale.

ABV	7%
First brewed	1992
Brewery	Bell's Brewery, Kalamazoo, Michigan
Website	www.bellsbeer.com

Boulevard, Single-Wide IPA

From humble beginnings in 1988, Boulevard has grown to become one of the major craft breweries in the US. In 2011 it was bought by the major Belgian brewer Duvel Moortgat, which has invested around $20 million and enabled additional equipment to be installed. A Bavarian-built brewhouse can now produce around 600,000 barrels a year. The takeover has not affected beer quality. Boulevard specializes in bottle-conditioned beers and the owners of the famous Duvel golden ale in Belgium could scarcely quarrel with that.

This IPA has a complex recipe of pale, amber, wheat and Munich malts, with Cascade, Centennial, Citra, Magnum and Summit hops. Bitterness units are 57.

The deep bronze beer has a delightful aroma of floral hops, grapefruit and gooseberry fruit and creamy malt. Malt provides a solid backbone in the mouth and allows floral hops and bittersweet fruit to build their presence. The finish has creamy malt, ripe fruit and lingering floral and bitter hops.

ABV	5.7%
First brewed	circa 2006
Brewery	Boulevard Brewing Company, Kansas City, Missouri
Website	www.boulevard.com

Breakside, IPA

Bronze/gold beer brewed with pale, cara and Munich malts and hopped with Chinook, Citra, Columbus, and Falconer's Flight: it has 74 bitterness units. There's a fine balance of apricot and orange fruit with sweet caramel notes on the palate and finish, but floral and pine dominate the bitter finale.

ABV	6.3%
First brewed	circa 2013
Brewery	Breakside Brewery, Portland, Oregon
Website	www.breakside.com

Captain Lawrence, Palate Shifter Imperial IPA

From an early age, Scott Vaccaro knew that his ambition was to brew beer. He made beer at home, then studied the art and science of brewing in the US before working as an intern at Adnams' brewery in Suffolk, England. In 2006 he realized his ambition by opening a small commercial brewery and has since upgraded to a 40-barrel plant.

Scott's brewery is named after the road where he grew up in South Salem. The road took its name from a captain who served in the Westchester Militia during the American War of Independence.

The imperial IPA is a hefty beer with a big hop character from the use of Cascade, Chinook, Columbus and Simcoe varieties. To give the finished beer an extra kick, it's dry hopped with Chinook and Simcoe and chalks up an impressive 90 units of bitterness. The only grain is pale two-row barley malt.

A deceptively pale colour doesn't prepare you for the explosion of fruit on the nose: apricots, peaches, mangoes and orange, backed by floral and spicy hops and sappy malt. Fruit bombards the palate but bitter hops build in the mouth along with a biscuit malt note. The finish has warming alcohol with intensely bitter hops, ripe fruit and juicy malt.

ABV	9%
First brewed	circa 2010
Brewery	Captain Lawrence Brewing Company, Elmsford, New York
Website	www.captainlawrencebrewing.com

Cigar City, Jai Alai IPA

Cigar City is the nickname for Tampa, which was once a centre of cigar manufacturing, with large numbers of Cubans employed to hand-roll the cigars. It was thirsty work and breweries supplied them with both ale and lager. Brewing ceased in the 20th century but was restored in 2008 when Wayne Wambles and Joey Redner opened their brewery and began with a brown ale that had been popular with the cigar workers. They have busily expanded the range and produce 60,000 barrels a year, of which Jay Alai accounts for more than half of the production.

The beer takes its name from a once-popular ball game played by Tampa's cigar workers, based on a sport from the Basque region of Spain. Jai Alai is brewed with pale and cara malts and generously hopped with Amarillo, Cascade, Centennial, Columbus, Motueka and Simcoe hops that create 70 bitterness units.

A bronze beer with a superb aroma of pine needles, melon, orange and tangerine fruit and biscuit malt. The palate is packed with floral hops, bittersweet fruit and chewy malt, followed by a long finish that ends hoppy and bitter but is balanced by biscuit malt and rich fruit.

ABV	7.5%
First brewed	2009
Brewery	Cigar City Brewing, Tampa, Florida
Website	www.cigarcitybrewing.com

Crow Peak, 11th Hour IPA

Brewed in Dakota's famous Black Hills, Crow Peak's IPA chalks up 70 bitterness units from a generous dose of Amarillo, Centennial, Columbus and Simcoe hops, balanced by pale malt. Aroma and palate offer apple and peach fruit, grass and pine backed by honeyed malt with a big fruity, hoppy and sweet malt finish.

ABV	6.5%
First brewed	circa 2010
Brewery	Crow Peak Brewing, Spearfish, South Dakota
Website	www.crowpeakbrewing.com

Firestone Walker, Union Jack IPA

An American beer named in honour of the British flag – that's a rarity in the United States. But brothers-in-law Adam Firestone – related to the tyre maker – and David Walker were so enthused by the Burton-on-Trent 'union system' of fermentation that they use oak barrels to make their IPA and pale ales. In this case the casks come from the Bourbon whiskey industry.

Head brewer Matt Brynildson has even made a trip from California to Burton to study traditional pale ale brewing at Marston's. Back home, he ferments Union Jack in conventional steel vessels but transfers each batch to the oak casks where it stays for seven days. Following the kettle boil, further hops are added in the whirlpool and then again three days later. The hops are Amarillo, Cascade, Centennial and Simcoe and bitterness units are 70. The grains are two-row pale malt, Munich and cara pils.

A bronze beer with a nose-tingling aroma of fresh pine, pineapple and grapefruit with cracker-like malt and floral hops. Hop bitterness builds in the mouth but is balanced by toasted malt and bittersweet fruit. The finish is long and deep, the bitter, floral hops interweaving with toasted malt and bittersweet fruit.

Firestone Walker became part of the Belgian Duvel Moortgat group in 2015.

ABV	7%
First brewed	circa 1996
Brewery	Firestone Walker Brewing Company, Paso Robles, California
Website	www.firestonebeer.com

Florida Beer, Swamp Ape IPA

A swamp ape is a mythical beast said to roam the swamps and Everglades and is described as having 'a potent aroma and bite'. This imperial IPA exemplifies the description, with a powerful strength and a massive dose of five hops.

The brewery opened in 1997 and moved to its present location as a result of a merger with several other craft breweries in the region. It has an impressive portfolio of beers, but Swamp Ape is the standout brew. The beer has five hop varieties – Amarillo, Cascade, Centennial, Chinook and German Tettnanger – and the malt bill is equally complex, with pale, Europ and cherrywood smoked malt.

A gold/bronze beer with a massive aroma of ripe pears, strawberries, spicy, floral and grassy hops and a smoky note from the malt. Fruit dominates the palate, but smoky malt and bitter hop resins break through. The finish starts fruity but ends with a blast of pungent hops and toasted malt.

ABV	10%
First brewed	2010
Brewery	Florida Beer Company, Cape Canaveral, Florida
Website	www.floridabeer.com

Good People, Snake Handler Double IPA

This is a hazy pale bronze imperial IPA with a mighty 100 bitterness units from Cascade, Chinook, Columbus, Simcoe and Warrior hops. Two-row pale malt provides the backbone, with colour and flavour from speciality malts. There are big aromas and flavours of pine, grass, spice and pineapple on a base of rich, toasted grain.

ABV	10%
First brewed	circa 2009
Brewery	Good People Brewing Company, Birmingham, Alabama
Website	www.goodpeoplebrewing.com

Goose Island, Goose IPA

This is a very good IPA but it's no longer the standout modern American interpretation of the style. What began as a Chicago brewpub run by father and son John and Greg Hall in 1988 is now the leading craft brewery in world giant AB InBev's 'high end' division. Goose IPA is brewed in various sites: a large plant in Fort Collins, Colorado, a new plant in New York State, and at two Labatt's breweries in Canada (also owned by AB InBev).

The beer is now an all-American brew. Czech Saaz hops have been phased out as a result of the long-running dispute between AB, owner of Budweiser, and the Czech Budweiser Budvar. The hops – including Amarillo, Cascade, Centennial, Pilgrim and American Saaz – are grown on AB's Elk Mountain farms in Idaho. Pale malt is the only grain and bitterness units are 55.

A pale gold beer with a spicy and orange fruit aroma. Cracker-like malt builds in the mouth with bitter hops and fruit and has a bitter, fruity and spicy hop finish.

ABV	5.9%
First brewed	1993
Brewery	Goose Island Beer Company, Chicago, Illinois
Website	www.gooseisland.com

Great Basin, Ichthyosaur IPA

Known as 'Icky' for short, this is a comparatively mild version of IPA with 47 bitterness units from Cascade hops and pale malt. It has a pale gold colour and a spicy, citrus aroma balanced by honeyed malt. Malt, bitter floral hops and bittersweet fruit dominate the palate with a lingering fruity and hoppy finish.

ABV	6.4%
First brewed	2010
Brewery	Great Basin Brewing Company, Sparks, Nevada
Website	www.greatbasinbrewingco.com

Kane, Head High IPA

Generous hopping with Chinook and Columbus followed by dry hopping with Cascade, Citra and Columbus create 80 bitterness units. The grain recipe of Pilsner, light crystal, cara pils and wheat balances aromas and flavours of pine, grapefruit and tropical fruit with a lightly toasted note.

ABV	6.5%
First brewed	2011
Brewery	Kane Brewing Company, Ocean Township, New Jersey
Website	www.kanebrewing.com

Kern River, Citra Double IPA

The name says it all: a strong version of the style with a flavour profile dictated by Citra hops that create 75 bitterness units. The grains are pale malt with a touch of cara malt and Munich. The aroma has grapefruit and gooseberry with gently toasted malt followed by a palate and finish with a good balance of hop bitterness, toasted malt and bittersweet fruit.

ABV	8%
First brewed	2014
Brewery	Kern River Brewing Company, Kernville, California
Website	www.kernriverbrewing.com

Melvin, 2x4 DIPA

Groomed by the Great Plains and the Rockie Montains, this double IPA is a loud hosanna to American hops: Centennial, Citra, Columbus and Simcoe contribute a tongue-curling 101 units of bitterness. The grain base is light malt to allow the hops to shine. There are floral hops and citrus fruit on nose and palate with a biscuit malt underpinning. The finish is long with bittersweet fruit, juicy malt and spicy hops.

ABV	10%
First brewed	2010
Brewery	Melvin Brewing Company, Alpine, Wyoming
Website	www.melvinbrewing.com

Nebraska, IPA

A pale bronze beer with a massive hop hit from Centennial, Chinook, Citra and Warrior: 72 bitterness units. The grains are two-row pale, Munich and wheat. There's citrus fruit on the nose with honeyed malt and spicy hops, followed by a palate and finish rich in bittersweet fruit, creamy malt and spicy, bitter hops.

ABV	6.9%
First brewed	2007
Brewery	Nebraska Brewing Company, Papillion, Kalamazoo, Nebraska
Website	www.nebraskabrewingco.com

Redhook, Long Hammer IPA

Redhook, founded in 1981, is one of America's pioneering breweries; it brewed in a former trolley car depot in Seattle and in 1994 opened a large plant at Woodinville which produces 250,000 barrels a year. It also has a brewery in Portsmouth, New Hampshire, and is a member of the Craft Brew Alliance, in which global brewing group AB InBev has a 32 per cent stake; AB helps with distribution. Time will tell if the mega brewery's involvement will affect beer quality.

Long Hammer was introduced in 1997 and quickly established itself as one of the leading West Coast IPAs. It has a straightforward recipe more in keeping with the English style: pale and crystal malts and just one hop, Cascade, which creates 44 bitterness units.

It is a pale bronze beer with an aroma of pine wood, grapefruit and tangerine, floral hops and honeyed malt. There's a fine balance of sweet malt, ripe fruit and bitter hops in the mouth, leading to a finish in which bitter hops have the final say but with continuing notes of bittersweet citrus fruits and biscuit malt.

ABV	6.2%
First brewed	1997
Brewery	Redhook Ale Brewery, Seattle, Washington State
Website	www.redhook.com

Reuben's Brews, Crikey IPA

The brewery acknowledges the London origins of IPA: Crikey is a Cockney exclamation; another beer in the range is called Blimey That's Bitter, a triple (imperial) IPA. Crikey uses a fistful of American hops, though the choice is not revealed. The beer has pine, tangerine and tropical fruit on the nose, with biscuit malt providing a solid backbone on the palate and a finish packed with fruit, juicy malt and bitter, spicy hops.

ABV	6.8%
First brewed	2012
Brewery	Reuben's Brews, Seattle, Washington State
Website	www.reubensbrews.com

Sebago, Frye's Leap IPA

The beer is named after the cliffs that overhang Sebago Lake on Frye Island. The brewery has an acclaimed restaurant where beer and food are matched: IPA was introduced in 1998 and visitors to the restaurant spread the word about the beer, making it one of the most popular on the East Coast. The Sebago chef recommends drinking the beer with lobster and shrimp risotto.

It's brewed with two-row pale malt, crystal malt and, unusually, a touch of dark chocolate malt to create a deep bronze colour. The hops, added three times in the kettle, are Cascade, Centennial and Columbus, which create 60 bitterness units.

It is an immensely complex beer with spicy, herbal hops, cracker wheat grain and citrus fruits on the nose. Bitter hop resins and orange fruit dominate the palate, with toasted malt and a hint of butterscotch from the crystal malt. The long finish has massive hop bitterness, citrus fruit and nutty, sappy malt.

ABV	6%
First brewed	1998
Brewery	Sebago Brewing Company, Gorham, Maine
Website	www.sebagobrewing.com

Three Floyds, Dreadnaught Imperial IPA

Dreadnought is the name that has been given to several famous British naval battleships and a submarine. I don't know if the three Floyds – brothers Nick and Simon and their father Mike – had this name in mind when they launched their imperial IPA (note the slightly different spelling), but it certainly fires on all cylinders. The Floyds opened their brewery in Hammond in 1996 and success led to a move to Munster, where they also have a brewpub. The *Washington Post* says they brew 'the best beers on the planet'.

Dreadnaught has a hop recipe comprised of Amarillo, Cascade, Centennial, Chinook, Citra and Simcoe, creating a palate-blasting 100 bitterness units: the beer is dry hopped twice to ensure the maximum bitterness and aroma are squeezed from the plants. Pale malt is bravely the only grain to stand up to this onslaught of bitterness and citrus fruit.

The beer is exceptionally pale, with a mighty aroma of fruit – grapefruit, mango and peach to the fore – with spicy and floral hops and honey-sweet malt. Hops and fruit bounce off the tongue with a gentle biscuit malt note, while the finish has iodine and quinine notes from the extreme hop bitterness, with continuing bittersweet fruit and honeyed malt.

ABV	9.5%
First brewed	circa 2000
Brewery	Three Floyds Brewing, Munster, Indiana
Website	www.3floyds.com

Tree House, Julius

Amarillo, Centennial and Simcoe hops create 75 bitterness units in a beer brewed with pale, cara and honey malts. The aroma and palate are a delight, with honeyed malt vying for attention with passion fruit and mango. The finish is dry with a bitter, hoppy finale, but there are continuing notes of honey and fruit.

ABV	6.8%
First brewed	2012
Brewery	Tree House Brewing Company, Monson, Massachusetts
Website	www.treehousebrew.com

Victory, Hop Devil India Pale Ale

This is a rarity – an American IPA with a big malty character. There's no shortage of hops – Cascade, Centennial and Chinook – but Pilsner, cara and Vienna malts combine to give a 'malt loaf' and sultana fruit note to the beer. Spicy, floral hops balance the rich grain base and the beer ends with a complex bittersweet note.

ABV	6.7%
First brewed	1996
Brewery	Victory Brewing Company, Downington, Pennsylvania
Website	www.victorybeer.com

Weyerbacher, Last Chance IPA

The brewery has a number of seasonal and regular IPAs, with Last Chance offering an example of a beer that's well hopped but not dauntingly so and highly drinkable. It has 60 bitterness units from the use of Cascade, Centennial, Citra and Mosaic hops and it's also dry hopped with Citra and Mosaic. The malts are not listed, but the beer has a pale colour with tropical fruits and rich floral and herbal hops on the aroma with a good balance of lightly toasted malt. Hop bitterness builds in the mouth on a solid biscuit malt backbone with a continuing bittersweet fruit note. The finish is a fine, lingering balance of juicy malt, ripe fruit and bitter, spicy hops. A portion of the sales of the beer is donated to local animal rescue centres.

ABV	5.9%
First brewed	2012
Brewery	Weyerbacher Brewing Company, Easton, Pennsylvania
Website	www.weyerbacher.com

Wicked Weed, Freak of Nature Double India Pale Ale

This double IPA has 3 pounds of hops – Centennial, Chinook, Columbus and Warrior – in the kettle with the addition of Amarillo and Simcoe for dry hopping. Not surprisingly, the beer is all about hops, with aromas and flavours of pine, grapefruit and passion fruit bouncing off the nose and palate. The finish is bittersweet with an underpinning of toasted malt but hop bitterness prevails.

ABV	8.5%
First brewed	2012
Brewery	Wicked Weed Brewing Company, Asheville, North Carolina
Website	www.wickedweedbrewing.com

England

English IPA has been restored to its pedestal. It was a beer that, like Icarus, soared too close to the sun in the 19th century and crashed to the ground. The last rites were said during World War One, when government restrictions on brewing strong beer reduced IPA to a shadow of its former glory and made it indistinguishable from pale ale.

But, inspired to a large extent by the American experience, IPA is back on the agenda. English craft brewers have also been aided by the research conducted by historians and writers, along with the archives of the Brewery History Society, which have helped to unlock both the complex history of IPA and also some of the original recipes. Today there are more than 300 examples of the style being brewed.

American hops have found favour among English craft brewers who want to give their brews a rich and fruity twang. Others prefer to use English varieties to stay true to style and they have been supported by farmers who have energetically promoted traditional hops such as the Fuggle and the Golding. One brewer, Hogs Back in Surrey, has gone so far as to find seeds for a long-forgotten hop, the Farnham White Bine, and grown it in fields alongside the brewery. Farmers have also risen to the challenge of imported hops from the US, Europe and Australasia by developing new varieties such as Endeavour and Jester to give more of a citrus note to home-grown IPAs that drinkers savour.

The style has returned to Burton-on-Trent, the town that became the main centre of pale ale brewing in the 19th century. Marston's, with its vast pub estate and free trade muscle, has made Old Empire in bottle and cask available throughout the UK. It's been joined by smaller brewers in the town who have great pride in the history and traditions of Burton and have created thoughtful versions of IPA.

London will not be left out. The capital has seen a veritable explosion of new craft breweries in recent years. There are now 70, with new ones coming on stream almost every month. Several on both sides of the Thames claim the mantle of George Hodgson's Bow Brewery which exported pale ale to India in the late 18th and 19th centuries. Brewers in Bermondsey, Greenwich and Hackney produce versions of IPA that range from punchy West Coast-inspired beers to more traditional interpretations.

Burton and London are not alone. From Cornwall to Cumbria you will find superb IPAs. Raise a glass and welcome back an old friend.

Acorn Brewery, Endeavour IPA

Dave Hughes has, arguably, done more to boost the IPA revival in England than any other brewer. He has an unquenchable passion for the style and produces a new version on a monthly basis. To date he has brewed more than 120 IPAs using hops from around the world and has started a new series featuring English hops.

He opened his brewery in 2003 and his main beer is Barnsley Bitter, which is a frequent finalist in CAMRA's Champion Beer of Britain Awards. He started with a 10-barrel plant and success led to a move to a new site where he produces 160 barrels a week.

His range of IPAs brewed with English hops makes use of new varieties developed to meet the demands of craft brewers. The English hop industry went into crisis early in the 21st century as a result of so many craft breweries concentrating on American-style IPAs. The British Hop Association fought back by promoting its traditional varieties and developing new ones that offer the pungent citrus character demanded by both brewers and drinkers. This has been achieved in some cases by crossing American and New World hops with English ones. In a recent version Acorn used a new English variety called Endeavour: it's named in honour of Inspector Morse, who was known to enjoy a drop and once said 'beer is food'; in Colin Dexter's last Morse novel he revealed that Morse's first name was Endeavour.

For his IPAs, Dave Hughes uses the same malt backbone of Maris Otter pale malt and a touch of crystal, building hop aroma and flavour on this base.

The verdict

The version that uses Endeavour hops has a pale copper colour and a delightful aroma and palate of blood orange and lemon, balanced by a biscuit malt note. The palate is a fine balance of juicy malt, citrus fruit and spicy hops, with a lingering finish of tart fruit, spicy hops and biscuit malt. Units of bitterness are around 55 but will vary from brew to brew.

ABV	5%
First brewed	2017
Brewery	Acorn Brewery, Barnsley, South Yorkshire
Website	www.acorn-brewery.co.uk

Adnams, Innovation IPA

Adnams is a family-owned brewery that dates from 1872, based in the seaside town of Southwold with its famous multi-coloured beach huts and an inshore lighthouse. For many years Adnams built sales and popularity with its Bitter and stronger Broadside but it has reinvented itself in the new century to meet changing consumer demands.

A new warehouse is eco-friendly, with a grassed roof and tanks that catch rainwater for washing equipment, while new brewing vessels can recycle steam to provide motive power and use 58 per cent less gas than the kit it replaced. Adnams has added a small distillery for making gin, vodka and whisky.

Adnams has an enthusiastic young head brewer, Fergus Fitzgerald, who has added a range of new beers to the portfolio. When managing director Jonathan Adnams wanted to celebrate the new brewhouse, he said to Fergus: 'Make something to wow me.' Fergus responded with an IPA that is an American-English hybrid, using the Boadicea hop from England, Columbus from the US and the floral Styrian Goldings from Slovenia. The grains are pale and wheat malts.

Fergus also brews Ease Up IPA, a session beer (4.7 per cent alcohol) with an impressive blend of hops: Amarillo, Centennial, Chinook, Galaxy, Goldings, Mosaic and Simcoe.

The verdict

Innovation is a chestnut-coloured beer with spicy/peppery hops, candied fruits and gently toasted grain on the aroma. Bitter hops dominate the palate, but there's a good balance of toasted malt and pungent fruit. The finish has a fine balance of bitter hops, bittersweet fruit and biscuit malt.

ABV	6.7%
First brewed	2008
Brewery	Adnams Sole Bay Brewery, Southwold, Suffolk
Website	www.adnams.co.uk

Burton Bridge Brewery, Empire Pale Ale

They don't come much more authentic than this beer: brewed in the ancestral home of IPA, aged for six months and then bottled with live yeast. The aging process replicates the length of a sea voyage to India while bottle conditioning allows the beer to continue to improve for several months. It comes from a brewery founded in 1982 by Geoff Mumford and Bruce Wilkinson behind the Burton Bridge Inn – one of the earliest and most successful of the new small craft producers. Geoff and Bruce worked for a large national brewer, Ind Coope, in Burton and Romford before branching out on their own and they have built a large portfolio of beers, light and dark, all with great respect for the town's traditions.

Empire Pale Ale is never sold on draught. In the style of a Victorian IPA, it's brewed from pale malt and brewing sugar only, with no darker grains. The hops used are English Challenger and Styrian Goldings. If the use of a foreign hop seems odd in such a quintessentially English beer, it's worth noting that brewers in the 19th century often used both grain and hops imported from abroad. And the Styrian Golding is an off-shoot of the English Fuggle.

The verdict

Pale bronze in appearance, this has a pronounced orange fruit note from hops and house yeast dominate the aroma and palate. The fruitiness is balanced by biscuit malt and spicy and resinous hops, with a long and lingering finish that offers juicy malt, tart fruit and bitter hops.

ABV	7.5%
First brewed	1996
Brewery	Burton Bridge Brewery, Burton-on-Trent, Staffordshire
Website	www.burtonbridgebrewery.co.uk

Five Points, IPA

Five Points is a new and vigorous craft brewery that opened in 2013, taking its name from a busy road junction. The founders are from Hackney and are proud of their East End roots. The leader of the team is the experienced pub and bar owner Edward Mason who has a passionate belief in putting something back into the community and aiding the environment. Electricity for the brewery comes from 100 per cent renewable sources while 5 per cent of the profits are invested in local charities and community projects.

In spite of its London roots, Five Points IPA is inspired by the West Coast American styles. The hops are American Cascade and Australian Galaxy and the beer is dry hopped for additional flavour. It's neither filtered nor pasteurized and is available in keg, bottle and canned formats.

The verdict

Light copper in colour. Passion fruit, mango and peach leap from the glass, backed by delicious sappy malt and hop resin notes. There's a creamy note on the palate from the use of a touch of wheat, cutting the hop bitterness and bittersweet fruit. The finish is intensely hoppy but is beautifully balanced by creamy malt and rich fruit.

ABV	7.1%
First brewed	2014
Brewery	Five Points Brewing Company, Hackney, London E8
Website	www.fivepointsbrewing.co.uk

Fuller's, Bengal Lancer India Pale Ale

There's been brewing on this site alongside the Thames for more than 350 years and the present company, formed in 1845, is still owned by members of the founding families. Fuller's, with an estate of more than 200 pubs and hotels and selling beer throughout the UK, enjoys a fine reputation for dedication to beer styles and quality of the end product. It has added to such revered cask ales as London Pride and Extra Special Bitter an IPA that was launched in 2010 and immediately stood out from a crowded sector due to the sheer integrity of the beer.

It's named after a cavalry regiment formed by the Nawab of Awadh in the 18th century and which, by the following century, was under the control of the British Army in India: the name symbolizes the bamboo lances carried by the cavalry men. The officers were a mix of British and Anglo-Indian, partial to a glass of IPA.

Fuller's beer is bottle conditioned and is brewed with Fuggles and Goldings hops and dry hopped with Goldings and Target. Units of bitterness are 47. The grains are pale and crystal malts.

The verdict

A beer with a deep burnished gold colour and an inviting aroma of hop resins, sherbet lemon fruit and a caramel note from the crystal malt. Passion fruit and lemon jelly dominate the palate but they are balanced by a peppery and spicy Goldings hop note. The finish is long, with a bittersweet character from malt and fruit but with a massive hop presence: piny, spicy and peppery. A draught version, at 5 per cent alcohol, is available from October to January.

ABV	5.3%
First brewed	2010
Brewery	Fuller, Smith & Turner Griffin Brewery, Chiswick, London W4
Website	www.fullers.co.uk

Hardknott, Intergalactic Space Hopper

Dave Bailey is known as 'the hard nut from Hardknott'. He's a tough, outspoken and uncompromising artisan brewer with a passion for making beers he likes and which he hopes others will appreciate. And he makes them with 'bucket-loads of hops' for maximum aroma and flavour: they are not for the faint-hearted and he extols the health benefits of drinking well-hopped beers.

The brewery was launched in 2005 by Dave and his wife Ann at the Woolpack Inn in Boot, at the foot of the notorious Hardknott Pass in the Lake District. They moved to Millom in 2010 with a 16-hectolitre brewhouse with its own bottling line.

Dave doesn't shy away from the fact that he is based close to the nuclear plant at Sellafield: some of his beers – Katalyst, Nuclear Sunset and Dark Energy – make the connection clear.

His IPA takes the notion of 'hop foward' beers to a new level. It's brewed with 100 per cent pale malt and hopped with Cascade, Chinook, Citra and Pacific Jade varieties and then dry hopped with Chinook, Galaxy, Simcoe and Wakatu.

The verdict

As pale as a Pilsner, the beer has a massive attack of fruit: pear, lemon, lime, lychee, to name just a few, with a balance of honeyed malt and spicy hops. The palate is uncompromisingly bitter and hoppy, but mouth-puckering fruit and juicy malt add balance, before the finish kicks in with shattering bitter hops and only fading memories of fruit and malt.

ABV	5.2%
First brewed	2015
Brewery	Hardknott, Millom, Cumbria
Website	www.hardknott.com

Howling Hops, IPA West Coast Special No 2

Hackney is fast becoming a must-visit district to witness London's contribution to the IPA revival. Howling Hops – such a brilliant name – has brought a Czech dimension to enjoying beer. Its brews are served straight from tanks in the manner of Pilsner Urquell and Budweiser Budvar and served in the Tank Room where customers, sitting at long trestle tables, can enjoy them with imaginative food. The Tank Bar is open seven days a week from noon: Queen's Yard, White Post Lane, E9, a few minutes from Hackney Wick station.

The brewery started life in the cellar of a pub, the Cock Tavern in Mare Street, Hackney, and moved four years later in 2015 to a sprawling warehouse alongside a basin off the River Lea which once took supplies, including Hodgson's India Ale, to the East India Docks.

The impressive steam-heated brewing kit was built in Bavaria and can produce 15 barrels per batch. As well as the draught beers served from the tanks, Howling Hops also sells them in keg and bottle-conditioned formats.

The IPA is brewed with pale malt and generously hopped with Amarillo, Columbus, Mosaic and Simcoe varieties.

The verdict

Pale hazy gold colour with a big candied fruit aroma, a touch of lemon rind and coriander with a sweet grain note. Bittersweet fruit blends with herbal hops and biscuit malt on the palate followed by a lingering finish that is a fine balancing act of rich fruit, juicy malt and spicy hops.

ABV	6.9%
First brewed	2015
Brewery	Howling Hops, Hackney Wick, London E9
Website	www.howlinghops.co.uk

The Kernel, India Pale Ale

Bermondsey vies with Hackney as the in-place for craft beer in London: beer-lovers take the 'Bermondsey mile' on Saturday to visit all the new breweries in the district, although The Kernel no longer serves beer to drink at the brewery. High on the list is The Kernel, run by Evin O'Riordain, an Irishman with a great passion for IPA. He discovered American IPAs on a trip to New York City in 2007 and went home to start home-brewing. He also worked as a cheesemonger in Covent Garden and Borough Market and built strong links with upmarket restaurants in London, some of which were eager to take his beer when he set up on a commercial basis.

He opened The Kernel in 2009 under a railway arch, naming the brewery after the all-important seeds in a grain of barley. Demand forced a move to bigger premises in 2012.

While he does produce some draught beer, he concentrates on bottle-conditioned versions that suit the demands of bars, restaurants and drinkers keen to have good beer at home. A large proportion of his output is dedicated to IPA, which is a movable feast. There is no regular brew, just a rolling programme using different hops and varying the strength of each beer.

The only constant is a grain base of Maris Otter pale malt with cara and cara gold for a honey-coloured finish. To date, Evin has used, among many other hop varieties, Ahtanum, Amarillo, Centennial, Chinook, Citra, Columbus, El Dorado, Galaxy, Mosaic, Motueka, Nelson Sauvin, Pacific Jade, Rakau and Simcoe varieties.

The verdict

Two versions tasted for this book. The first, a blend of Centennial and Chinook, with spicy and peppery hops, mango, peach and raspberry fruit and an oatcake malt note. Palate and finish are intensely bitter and fruity. A second beer brewed with Citra has a pronounced grapefruit character with grassy hops and a creamy malt note.

ABV	6–7.5%
First brewed	2009 (recipe changes frequently)
Brewery	The Kernel Brewery, Bermondsey, London SE16
Website	www.thekernelbrewery.com

Little Valley Brewery, Python IPA

The brewery stands high above the town of Hebden Bridge, with superb views of hills and dales. Brewer Wim van der Spek is from the Netherlands, where he learned beer-making skills at the major Dutch independent, Gulpener; he co-owns Little Valley with his wife Sue Cooper. They use pure Pennine water to fashion organic beers: Wim not only uses organic malts and hops but also refuses to fine his beers with isinglass derived from fish. Power for the brewery comes from a wind turbine. Their beers, produced on a 10-barrel plant, are approved by the Soil Association and the Vegan Society.

Python takes its name from both the Indian snake and the water-cooled pipes used to keep cask beers at the correct temperature as they travel from pub cellars to bar. The beer is made with pale, Munich and wheat malts and is hopped with First Gold, Fuggles and Pacific Gem varieties. First Gold was the first 'hedgerow' variety developed in England: it grows to half the height of conventional hops and is easier to pick and less prone to pest and disease attack.

The verdict

A bright gold colour with sulphur on the nose, spicy hop resins, 'malt loaf' and a hint of butterscotch. Citrus fruit and bitter hops dominate the palate while the finish is long and complex with spicy hops, tart fruit, toasted malt and a continuing hint of butterscotch.

ABV	6%
First brewed	2011
Brewery	Little Valley Brewery, Hebden Bridge, West Yorkshire
Website	www.littlevalleybrewery.co.uk

Magic Rock, Cannonball India Pale Ale

Stuart Ross, the head brewer at Magic Rock, had an epiphany when he visited the US and tasted West Coast IPAs. 'I wanted to bring those wonderful flavours to our brewery and make a range of hop-forward, bold and exciting beers,' he says. Stuart earned his brewing spurs at Kelham Island in Sheffield and launched Magic Rock in 2011 with Richard and Jonny Burhouse. They have shaken up the brewing scene in Huddersfield with red ale, a powerful stout and a beer called Salty Kiss based on an obscure German style known as Gose, with salt added to malt and hops, but the IPA is the best-selling beer in the range.

Cannonball is brewed with extra pale Golden Promise malt and hopped with no fewer than six varieties: Amarillo, Centennial, Citra, Columbus, Magnum and Simcoe. It's available year-round in craft keg or can. It is occasionally joined in the brewery taproom by big brothers Human Cannonball Double IPA at 9.2 per cent and Un-human Cannonball Triple IPA, a 12 per cent beer that should be sipped with caution.

The verdict

The unfiltered, hazy gold beer has a big hit of citrus fruit on the nose, with lemon, lime, grapefruit and blood orange to the fore, balanced by honeyed malt and peppery hops. Honeyed malt builds in the mouth, forming a powerful backbone for bittersweet fruit and peppery hops. The finish is long and quenching, with juicy malt, citrus fruit and bitter hop resins, followed by a dry finale.

ABV	7.4%
First brewed	2011
Brewery	Magic Rock Brewing, Huddersfield
Website	www.magicrockbrewing.com

Marston's, Old Empire IPA

Marston's are a Burton legend, still using 'union room' wooden fermentation vessels, yet curiously they never produced an IPA in the 19th century. The reason is that Marston's used the railway to great effect, with their own sidings, and transported beer – mainly pale ale – around Britain without need for export trade.

The brewery filled the gap in 2003 with Old Empire. I was delighted to be involved, visiting Burton several times to taste sample beers, crying 'Use more hops!', until a satisfactory version was produced. The beer is fermented with yeast drawn from the unions. It's a true Burton IPA, brewed only with pale Optic malt and hopped with American Cascade and English Fuggles and Goldings. It has 40 units of bitterness. The beer is available in both bottled and cask-conditioned draught formats.

The verdict

A pale gold beer with the unmistakable 'Burton snatch': a sulphur note on the aroma from the sulphates in the water. Earthy and spicy hops, succulent malt, vanilla and a light citrus note quickly break through the sulphur, followed by juicy malt, peppery hops and bittersweet fruit in the mouth. The long finish is packed with biscuit malt, spicy hops and lemon fruit.

ABV	5.7%
First brewed	2003
Brewery	Marston's, Burton-on-Trent, Staffordshire
Website	www.marstons.co.uk

Meantime, India Pale Ale

Meantime has come a long way in a short time. It started as a small lock-up brewery opposite Charlton Athletic football ground, founded by Alastair Hook. He is a master brewer who trained at Heriot-Watt and Munich brewing schools. He quickly gained a reputation for quality, properly brewed ales and lagers and in 2010 moved to a new site near Greenwich with a modern plant that can produce 200,000 barrels a year.

Meantime was caught up a maelstrom of events in 2016. It was bought by global giant SABMiller, which in turn was taken over by even bigger colossus AB InBev. This mega brewer has since sold on Meantime to Asahi of Japan. In spite of the turbulence, its IPA remains superb.

It is brewed with a strong bow to tradition: English pale malt, a touch of crystal malt, and Fuggles and Goldings hops – the hop varieties would have been used by Victorian brewers. The beer is handsomely packaged in 750ml bottles with Champagne-style corks and wire cages.

The verdict

Golden beer with an inviting aroma of spicy hops, marmalade fruit and toasted grain. Orange fruit builds in the mouth on a solid backbone of toasted grain and bitter hops. The finish is long and quenching, with peppery and earthy hop resins balancing bittersweet fruit and toasted grain.

ABV	7.4%
First brewed	2005
Brewery	Meantime Brewing Company, London, SE10
Website	www.meantimebrewing.com

Moor, Return of the Empire

'Drink Moor Beer' is the slogan of this brewery that started life in the Somerset countryside and was bought in 2007 by Californian Justin Hawke; in 2014 he moved it to central Bristol, conveniently near Temple Meads station. Justin has a passion for hops, IPA and beer that is produced naturally without filtration, pasteurization or clearing agents such as finings, all of which, he believes, strip flavour from the end product. He was told he would never sell cloudy beer, but he says there has been no consumer resistance to his brews.

It was while he was serving in the US Army in Germany that he discovered cloudy wheat beer and he brought that experience to play with the beers he makes in Bristol. He is also well versed in West Coast IPAs back in his native San Francisco but in England he has fashioned beers that combine a good malt character with robust bitterness. For Return of the Empire he used the English-grown Jester hop that has been bred by crossing American Cascade with an unnamed English variety. The grains are pale malt and a touch of wheat. Moor also brews Hoppiness IPA, at 6.5 per cent alcohol.

As well as pioneering unfined beer, Justin has gone into canning and was delighted in 2016 when CAMRA gave the seal of approval to his canned ales, where the beers undergo a natural secondary fermentation.

The verdict

The pale gold beer has an enticing aroma of lime marmalade and biscuit malt, interwoven with powerful spicy hop notes. The palate is bittersweet with a good balance of bitter hops and a fruit character reminiscent of lychees, lemons, lime and grapefruit. The finish is dominated by cracker bread grain, tangy fruit and spicy, bitter hops.

ABV	5.7%
First brewed	2015
Brewery	Moor Beer Company, Bristol
Website	www.moorbeer.co.uk

Oakham Ales, Green Devil IPA

Production director John Bryan discovered the Citra hop while he was visiting the Yakima Valley area of Washington State in 2009. He was bowled over by the appealing fruit character of the hop – lychees, grapefruit, gooseberry and tropical fruit – and was determined to use it back home. When he was able to get a supply he launched Citra, a pale ale that has become Oakham's leading beer, and followed it with Green Devil IPA.

The brewery started life in the town of Oakham and moved to Peterborough in 1998, transforming a former employment exchange into the Brewery Tap, the biggest brewpub in Europe. Further expansion led to a move to a bigger plant on the outskirts of the city, but the original kit remains at the Brewery Tap for trial and seasonal brews.

John Bryan describes Green Devil as an 'American-English hybrid', with a solid malt backbone balancing the bitter and fruit character of the hops. The beer is brewed with pale malt only and Citra hops are used in both whole flower and pellet form: John adds pellets to the conditioning vessels following fermentation. The beer has around 65 units of bitterness. He has also adopted the German system of kräusening, which means adding some partially fermented sugary wort to the beer to encourage a strong secondary fermentation.

The verdict

Shining bright, pale bronze beer with lychees the most obvious fruit on the nose but with contributions from grapefruit and gooseberry and lightly toasted malt. Bittersweet fruit, juicy malt and tangy hops fill the mouth, with a long, lingering finish packed with rich fruit, spicy hops and mellow malt.

ABV	6%
First brewed	2010
Brewery	Oakham Ales, Peterborough, Cambridgeshire
Website	www.oakhamales.com

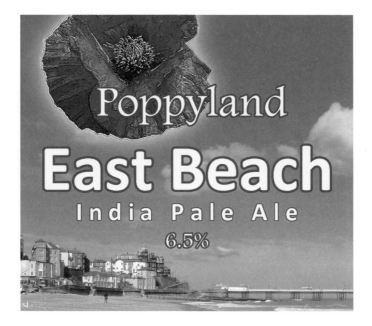

Poppyland, East Beach India Pale Ale

When Martin Warren brewed a beer called East Coast IPA, a tongue-in-cheek Norfolk version of the American West Coast style, he found a couple of years later that mighty Greene King had launched a beer with the same name. As the Suffolk brewer spills more beer than Martin makes, he thought it advisable to change the name of his beer to East Beach.

Martin is a forager brewer. He combs the cliffs, hedgerows and beaches in and around Cromer to add the likes of wild damsons, gorse and thorns to his beers, brewed on a 2½-barrel plant in a former car repair shop. One brew was a Belgian-inspired Crab Saison designed to drink with seafood, with apples added for the secondary fermentation.

His IPA is a more traditional beer, made with the finest East Anglia extra pale Maris Otter malted barley with the addition of American hops, such as Cascade, Columbus and Summit. The beer is late hopped with Cascade for additional aroma and flavour and the bitterness units are 70.

You will have to forage to sample the beers. One Cromer pub, the Red Lion, sells them, as do specialist beer shops in Norfolk. If the brewery at 44 West Street is closed, Martin's phone number is displayed in the window: phone him and he will be happy to come over from his house on the opposite corner to sell you some bottles.

The verdict

Hazy bronze colour with sulphur on the nose, floral, herbal and peppery hops and a 'malt loaf' grain note. Juicy malt on the palate is balanced by earthy and spicy hops and bitter orange fruit. The finish becomes increasingly bitter and hop-dominated, but a fine balance of biscuit malt and rich fruit is maintained.

ABV	6.5%
First brewed	2016
Brewery	Poppyland Brewery, Cromer, Norfolk
Website	www.poppylandbeer.com

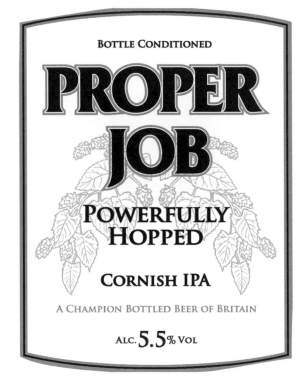

BOTTLE CONDITIONED

PROPER JOB

POWERFULLY HOPPED

CORNISH IPA

A CHAMPION BOTTLED BEER OF BRITAIN

ALC. 5.5% VOL

St Austell, Proper Job Cornish IPA

Proper Job is a Cornish expression meaning a task well done and it's a fitting name for one of the very best modern English IPAs: it was CAMRA's Champion Bottled Beer of Britain in 2011. It pays homage to the 32nd Cornwall Regiment that protected the British Residency in Lucknow during the Indian Mutiny of 1857.

Head brewer Roger Ryman goes to the Yakima Valley in Washington State every year to choose the best hops of the harvest for Proper Job. He blends the hops with Maris Otter malt; he so loves the oatcake flavours of the barley variety that he has encouraged Cornish farmers to grow it for the brewery; it's usually grown principally in East Anglia, but the Cornish version accounts for two-thirds of St Austell's grain supply.

Chinook and Willamette whole hops are added to the copper and following the boil the hopped wort rests on a bed of Cascade, Chinook and Willamette. Following fermentation the beer is conditioned for a couple of weeks and, to ensure maximum freshness of flavour, is filtered and re-seeded with fresh yeast.

A draught cask-conditioned version is 4.5 per cent alcohol.

The verdict

A bright gold beer that has a powerful fruit aroma of grapefruit, orange and mango, with oatcake grain and floral/spicy hop notes. Bittersweet fruit, chewy malt and bitter hops combine for a full palate while grapefruit comes to the fore in the finish but is well balanced by biscuit malt and bitter hops.

ABV	5.5%
First brewed	2006
Brewery	St Austell Brewery, St Austell, Cornwall
Website	www.staustellbrewery.co.uk

Sambrook's Brewery, Battersea IPA

Duncan Sambrook was so devastated by the closure of the much-loved Young's brewery in Wandsworth in 2006 that he abandoned a lucrative career in the City of London as an expert in business investment to open his own brewery in neighbouring Battersea. He was backed by the experience of David Welsh, who had followed a similar course, giving up the world of business to run the Ringwood brewery in Hampshire until he was bought out by Marston's. Their backgrounds meant they knew how to raise money and run an efficient company, not always the case with new craft breweries.

Sambrook's opened in 2008 and rapidly carved out a niche in the burgeoning craft beer scene in London. Wandle Ale, named after the river that gives Wandsworth its name, and Junction Bitter that celebrates Clapham Junction train station, have become big brands in a few short years. Duncan broadened the appeal of the brewery by adding a porter that recalls the historic London style of the 18th century, followed by an IPA with a big bow in the direction of Hodgson's across the Thames in Bow.

Battersea IPA is brewed with Maris Otter pale malt and a touch of cara malt, and is hopped with two American varieties – Chinook for bitterness and Citra for aroma.

The verdict

Dazzling gold colour with a delicious 'malt loaf' aroma with powerful hints of sultana fruit and floral hops. A rich, bittersweet palate is a superb blend of juicy malt, chewy fruit and bitter hops, while the finish lingers with a fine balance of malt, hops and fruit, and a bitter and hoppy finale.

ABV	6.2%
First brewed	2014
Brewery	Sambrook's Brewery, Battersea, London, SW11
Website	www.sambrooksbrewery.co.uk

Shepherd Neame, India Pale Ale

When Shepherd Neame, Britain's oldest brewery, recreates an IPA from the 1870s it should have the ring of authenticity – but it took skills similar to those of World War Two code breakers to bring the recipe for the beer to light. The brewery dates from 1698. It's still run by one of the founding families, the Neames, and stands at the heart of the local hop gardens, prized for their East Kent Goldings variety. John Owen is the company's archivist and when he came across some ancient leather-bound brewers' logs, covered in dust and cobwebs, in the cellars he found they contained the recipes for a range of beers, including stout and IPA. The recipes were written in code: Shepherd Neame was keen to brew an IPA with a genuine Victorian recipe, but first the code had to be cracked.

The reason for the secrecy was because the rival Rigdens brewery stood immediately opposite Shepherd Neame and they engaged in a daily battle to get pubs throughout Kent to take their beers. The Neames were worried that a disaffected member of staff could pop across the road and sell the brewery's recipes to their rival: hence the code.

John Owen spent several months working with brewer Stewart Main to decipher the recipes. The codes were written with a series of letters, such as GBX, JBX and SBX. Main's brewing experience told him the letters referred to the malts and hops used in the beers, along with the amounts for each brew. Painstakingly, Owen and Main chipped away at the letters, written in faded copperplate writing, and finally were satisfied they had an authentic recipe for the IPA.

The beer they recreated is brewed with pale and crystal malts. The hops are the prized local Fuggles and Goldings. The hops are added three times during the copper boil and create 40 units of bitterness. Brewing begins in old oak mash tuns still in use in the modern brewery.

A 4.5 per cent draught version is an annual seasonal beer.

The verdict

The beer has an orange/bronze colour and a big tart fruit aroma reminiscent of the sugary jelly sweets known as orange and lemon slices. Spicy hops and cracker-like malt are also present on the nose. Bittersweet citrus fruit, juicy malt and bitter hops combine in the mouth while the long finish is dominated by peppery hops and citrus fruit, with a solid underpinning of sappy malt.

ABV	6.1%
First brewed	2012
Brewery	Shepherd Neame Brewery, Faversham, Kent
Website	www.shepherdneame.co.uk

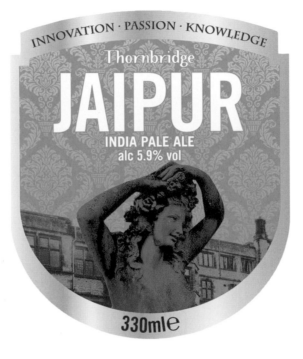

Thornbridge, Jaipur India Pale Ale

Thornbridge is a riches-to-riches story. The brewery started life in 2005 as a 10-barrel plant in garden buildings in Thornbridge Hall, a stately home in Derbyshire that had been bought by Jim and Emma Harrison in 2002. Its beers were so successful that in 2009 Thornbridge opened a new state-of-the-art brewery alongside the River Derwent near Bakewell in the heart of the Derbyshire dales. The brewery stands where Richard Arkwright harnessed the power of the river to invent the spinning frame, acknowledged as the launch pad of the Industrial Revolution in the 18th century.

A series of superb beers flow from Thornbridge, among them Jaipur, which has won more than 60 awards in brewing competitions and is widely regarded as one of the very best of the new IPAs. Jaipur, named after the Indian city with its famous pink walls, is inspired by American IPAs, even though the brewery is in the same region of England as Burton and enjoys similar salty water. Head brewer Rob Lovatt, who joined from Meantime in London, uses Ahtanum, Centennial and Chinook hops from the US and builds their hop flavours on a solid base of Maris Otter pale malting barley. The hops are added three times during the boil in the kettle to extract the maximum aroma and bitterness. It has 55–57 units of bitterness.

The verdict

Straw-coloured beer with a superb aroma of lychees and grapefruit with honeyed malt and floral hops. Bittersweet fruit, gently toasted malt and spicy, bitter hops fill the mouth, followed by a complex finish in which intensely bitter hops vie for attention with honeyed malt and ripe tropical fruits.

ABV	5.9%
First brewed	2005
Brewery	Thornbridge Brewery, Bakewell, Derbyshire
Website	www.thornbridgebrewery.co.uk

Westerham Brewery, Viceroy India Pale Ale

This IPA, brewed for the National Trust, celebrates the life of Lord Curzon, Viceroy of India. He may have been a controversial figure but he was admired as a restorer of great buildings: the Taj Mahal in India and several stately houses in England when he returned home.

Robert Wicks, who opened Westerham Brewery in 2004, is surrounded by history. Sir Winston Churchill's country home is close by at Chartwell, Scotney Castle at Lamberhurst is a historic estate where hops are grown, while Westerham was once home to the Black Eagle brewery. This substantial brewery had a sizeable estate of pubs stretching as far as London and supplied beer to troops fighting in France during World War Two.

Robert has restored these traditions. He has brought back the Black Eagle yeast culture stored in the National Collection of Yeast Cultures in Norwich and uses Kent hops in many of his beers. But there's a modern note at Westerham: Robert has installed a device called the Hop Rocket, which looks like the rocket used by the animated characters Wallace and Gromit. But this has a serious intent: the hopped wort rests on a bed of hops – as many as 15 kilos per brew – for maximum aroma and flavour. Viceroy IPA has 50 units of bitterness, from Progress and Target hops from Scotney, and uses Maris Otter pale malt.

The verdict

A honey-coloured beer with spicy hops, wholemeal biscuits and plum fruit on the aroma. Peppery hops, chewy malt and ripe plum fruit fill the mouth while the finish is bitter and spicy, with a good balance of juicy malt and tart fruit.

ABV	5%
First brewed	2009
Brewery	Westerham Brewery Company, Crockham Hill, Kent
Website	www.westerhambrewery.co.uk

Chapel Down, Curious IPA

Chapel Down is one of England's leading wineries and has won praise for its sparkling wines in particular. It added a small portfolio of beers and ciders in 2010, drawing on the company's wine-making skills. For example, its lager is brewed with a Champagne yeast. The beers are brewed for Chapel Down by commercial brewers, including Everards of Leicester and Hepworth in Horsham, Sussex. But in 2016 Chapel Down raised £1.7 million, mainly through crowdfunding, to build a state-of-the-art brewery in Ashford, close to the International Station on the Eurostar line.

Curious IPA is brewed with pale malt and is hopped with English Bramling Cross and Goldings, with American Chinook used as a late hop. It has a pale amber colour with a 'malt loaf' note on the aroma and a classic peppery attack from Goldings with a touch of blackcurrant from Bramling Cross. Hop bitterness builds in the mouth with bittersweet fruit and chewy biscuit malt. There's a delicious bittersweet finish with fruit, hops and biscuit malt in fine balance.

ABV	5.6%
First brewed	2010
Brewery	Chapel Down, Tenterden, Kent
Website	www.chapeldown.com

Cloudwater Brew Co, IPAs and Double IPAs

This is a difficult brewery to pin down. It brews a vast range of IPAs, but once a batch has been made and sold, the brewers move on. What links all the beers is the love of hops of founders James Campbell, former brewer at Marble (see page 208), and entrepreneur Paul Jones.

The brewery was founded in February 2015 and 22 months later they had produced 240 brews, using 145 recipes and 24 different yeast cultures from both the UK and the US. One double IPA, 9 per cent alcohol, used 140kg of New Zealand hops. The recipe for another beer was Maris Otter extra pale malt, glucose syrup, Pilgrim hops for the kettle boil, Centennial and Simcoe for late hopping, Ella and Pacific Jade in the hop back, and Centennial, Chinook, Citra, Nelson Sauvin and Vic Secret for dry hopping. Go and bag a brew! They can be sampled in a tap room opened in 2015, where visitors taste the beers and also enjoy conducted tours of the brewery (7–8 Piccadilly Trading Estate, Manchester M1 2NP).

ABV	Various
First brewed	2015
Brewery	Cloudwater Brew Co, Manchester
Website	www.cloudwaterbrew.co.

Concertina Brewery, Bengal Tiger

The brewery is in the cellars of a working men's club near Doncaster – the last club in England to make its own beer. It takes its name from a prize-winning concertina band that was based there in the early 20th century. The eight-barrel brewing kit produces Club Bitter as well as Bengal Tiger: the latter is brewed with pale and crystal malts and Fuggles, Styrian Goldings and Target hops. The amber-coloured beer has an aroma of biscuit malt, spicy hops and orange and lemon fruit, with a malty/hoppy palate underscored by citrus fruit. Sharp fruit, juicy malt and spicy and piny hops combine in the finish.

Visitors can enter the club for a small fee at 9a Dolcliffe Road, Mexborough. The beers are also available in a few pubs in the area.

ABV	4.6%
First brewed	1992
Brewery	Concertina Brewery, Mexborough, South Yorkshire
Website	None

Dominion Brewery, Pitfield's 1837 India Pale Ale

The brewery was founded in 1982 in the Pitfield Beer Shop in North London and led a peripatetic life before migrating to a farm in Essex. It's now owned by one of the original brewers, Canadian Andy Skene, who continues founder Martin Kemp's commitment to organic beer. The IPA is based on a Victorian recipe and Andy and Martin worked with the Durden Park Beer Circle, a group of home-brewers who recreate old beer styles, to formulate the recipe. It's brewed with organic pale malt and a touch of chocolate malt to give a true Victorian copper colour to the beer. It's hopped with just one variety, English Target, which creates 70 units of bitterness. The beer is certified as organic by the Soil Association and is suitable for vegans.

The amber/copper beer has a powerful aroma of spicy hop resins, orange fruit and lightly toasted malt. Hop bitterness builds in the mouth but is balanced by tart fruit and rich biscuit malt. The finish is long and packed with hop resins, orange and lemon fruit notes, toasted malt and a gentle hint of chocolate.

ABV	7%
First brewed	2002
Brewery	Dominion Brewery Company, Moreton, Essex
Website	www.dominionbrewerycompany.com

Fourpure, Shape Shifter West Coast IPA

Fourpure is one of the group of craft breweries that make up the 'Bermondsey mile' in south-east London – they are open to visitors at weekends. The brewery was founded in 2013 by Daniel and Thomas Lowe, who were inspired by West Coast IPAs in the US, and in Oregon in particular, where some of the finest American hops are grown. The Lowes were the first British craft brewers to can their beers; whether in can or keg the beers are not filtered, fined or pasteurized, to allow the natural ingredients to give full rein to their aromas and flavours.

Shape Shifter is brewed with pale malt and Centennial and Mosaic hops that create 68 units of bitterness. A pale bronze beer with a great burst of fruit on the nose: grapefruit, mango, orange, tangerine and pineapple, with powerful hints of pine and biscuit malt.

Bittersweet fruit and spicy hops dominate the palate with a solid backbone of rich juicy malt. The finish is long, complex, bitter, hoppy and fruity but with a continuing balance of biscuit malt.

ABV	6.4%
First brewed	2013
Brewery	Fourpure Brewing Co, Bermondsey, London SE16
Website	www.fourpure.com

Grain, Lignum Vitae

When Grain Brewery's IPA was named Overall Champion of the SIBA (Society of Independent Brewers) East of England beer competition in 2015, Phil Halls and Geoff Wright celebrated by changing its name to Lignum Vitae – 'wood of life', the most powerful wood in the world. The timing was perfect because the beer is brewed with Maris Otter Norfolk barley and it was the 50th anniversary of the variety first being grown.

Phil and Geoff set up their brewery in 2006 in a converted dairy in the Waveney Valley area and upgraded to 15 barrels a week in 2012. Lignum Vitae is a hymn to the hop, brewed with Fuggles and Brewers' Gold for bitterness and Cascade, Centennial and Citra for aroma. A bright gold beer with a big fruit hit in the aroma of orange, lemon and lime with a woody note from the hops and cracker biscuit malt. The bittersweet palate has a fine balance of citrus fruit, lightly toasted malt and herbal and spicy notes from the hops while the complex finish ends dry but is preceded by rich fruit, juicy malt and bitter hops.

ABV	6.5%
First brewed	2007
Brewery	Grain Brewery, Alburgh, Norfolk
Website	www.grainbrewery.co.uk

Greene King, IPA Reserve

Greene King is one of Britain's biggest independent breweries, founded in 1799 in the ancient town of Bury St Edmunds. It's one of the major producers of cask beers in the country but it has long been criticized for producing an IPA that weighs in at just 3.6 per cent. In 2012 the company responded to its critics by launching IPA Reserve, with a strength of 5.4 per cent. A second beer, IPA Gold, at 4.1 per cent, was launched at the same time and in total £4 million was spent on promoting the beers, including a TV commercial.

Reserve is brewed with Tipple pale malt, a new variety of malting barley grown close to the brewery, and the only hop used is the Styrian Golding from Slovenia that creates 36 units of bitterness. Deep bronze colour with grapefruit and orange notes on the aroma, gently toasted malt and hop resins reminiscent of fresh pine. On the palate, biscuit malt, citrus fruit and tart hops combine and lead to a long, dry and hoppy finish with continuing bittersweet fruit and toasted malt.

ABV	5.4%
First brewed	2012
Brewery	Greene King, Westgate Brewery, Bury St Edmunds, Suffolk
Website	www.greeneking.co.uk

Hawkshead, IPA

Alex Brodie is a rarity: a journalist with a head for business. He was a top BBC man – the Middle East correspondent and then an anchor on the Radio 4 *Today* programme – before deciding to spend more time with his family. A beer lover, he opened his brewery in 2002 in an old barn in Hawkshead in the Lake District. Success led four years later to a move to an old mill in Staveley, where custom-built brewing kit was installed. The complex is now called the Beer Hall and visitors can enjoy a beer and good food and see the brewery through a glass wall. Alex is a passionate supporter of cask ale but recognizes the demands of the modern market and also produces lager and craft keg beers at his ever-expanding site.

His IPA is American-influenced with a complex hop recipe of Cascade and Columbus from the US and Motueka from New Zealand. The beer is dry hopped following fermentation. The grains are Maris Otter pale, Vienna and crystal malts. A pale bronze beer with a pungent aroma of citrus and tropical fruits, and a hint of vanilla, sulphur and 'malt loaf' grain notes. Bitter hops build in the mouth with orange fruit, toasted malt and hints of vanilla and butterscotch. There's a quinine-like note in the finish from the hops, balancing tart fruit and juicy malt with a final flourish of vanilla.

ABV	7%
First brewed	2014
Brewery	Hawkshead Brewery, Staveley, Cumbria
Website	www.hawksheadbrewery.co.uk

Hook Norton, Flagship

Hook Norton is from a different world to modern craft brewing. The brewery dates from 1849 and is still in the hands of the founding family. The building is known as a 'tower brewery', with the brewing process flowing from storey to storey without the aid of pumps. Power comes from a 25-horsepower steam engine, high-sided wooden brewing vessels are used and beer is delivered to local pubs by horse-drawn drays with drivers in bowler hats and waistcoats. The beers are brewed with great devotion, using the finest natural ingredients.

Flagship was introduced as a bottle-conditioned beer in 2005 to mark the 200th anniversary of the Battle of Trafalgar: it's also occasionally available in draught form. It's brewed with Maris Otter pale malt and Admiral (a bow to Admiral Nelson), Fuggles and Goldings hops.

A gold-coloured beer with orange marmalade, caramel and peppery hops on the aroma. Honeyed malt builds in the mouth, balancing zesty fruit and bitter hop resins. The finish ends on a firmly bitter hop note, but there remains a good balance of tart fruit and rich malt and caramel.

ABV	5.3%
First brewed	2005
Brewery	Hook Norton Brewery, Hook Norton, Oxfordshire
Website	www.hooky.co.uk

Langton Brewery, Empress Ale

Empress Ale is brewed under licence by Langton for Surj Virk, who has a mission in life to bring good beer to Asian restaurants: 'Good Asian cooking deserves more than fizzy lager,' he says.

The beer, with its charmingly old-fashioned elephant print label, is called a golden ale, but it's firmly in the IPA category and perfectly fits Surj's mission. It's brewed with pale malt with a touch of wheat and hopped with Cascade and Fuggles. It has a woody, spicy and lemongrass aroma with biscuit malt. Peppery hops, juicy malt and lemon fruit combine on the palate with a hint of camomile. The finish is fruity and malty with earthy and woody hops dominating.

ABV	4.5%
First brewed	2016
Brewery	Langton Brewery, Thorpe Langton, Leicestershire
Website	www.empressale.com

Marble Brewery, Lagonda IPA/Earl Grey IPA

Marble started life as a microbrewery at the back of the Marble Arch pub on Rochdale Road. It quickly built a reputation for its beer, using top-quality grains and hops, and avoiding finings made from fish swim bladders to clear the beers of yeast. This means the beers are suitable for vegetarians and vegans. In 2011 a bigger brewery was installed in buildings inside a railway arch close to the pub.

Lagonda IPA is named after the classic car and is brewed with Maris Otter malt, cara malt and wheat malt with Centennial, Citra, Green Bullet and Simcoe hops. It has a big hit of grapefruit and orange on the aroma with pine and biscuit malt. Bittersweet fruit and leafy hops dominate the palate and lead to a long finish in which hops and fruit combine with biscuit malt.

Earl Grey IPA has been a sensational success and prompted other brewers to add unusual ingredients to their beers. In this case, a brew of Earl Grey tea is made, strained and cooled and the tea leaves are then placed in a muslin bag in the fermenting vessel. Earl Grey tea is made with the addition of bergamot, a citrus fruit grown mainly in the

Calabria region of Italy. The hops are Citra, Columbus and Goldings. Earl Grey has a powerful note from aroma to finish of bergamot, balanced by floral and peppery hops and honey malt.

ABV	Lagonda 5%/Earl Grey 6.8%
First brewed	2005/2012
Brewery	Marble Brewery, Manchester
Website	www.marblebeers.com

Peerless, Full Whack

Brewery owner Steve Briscoe describes his beer as 'a scouse IPA'. It's produced alongside a mighty river where in the 19th century IPAs set sail for India. Scouse can be used to describe anyone or anything relating to Liverpool and 'whack' or 'wack' is a form of Liverpudlian greeting similar to the Cockney 'mate'. The brewery opened in 2009 using kit from the now-closed Mash & Air restaurant-cum-brewery in Manchester.

Full Whack is brewed with Maris Otter pale malt and a touch of crystal, with First Gold and Fuggles and Cascade hops. The pale amber beer has a powerful aroma of spicy and floral hops, zesty fruit and 'fresh bread' malt. Hop bitterness builds in the mouth but is well balanced by juicy malt and tangy fruit. The finish ends dry and bitter, but there are continuing notes of honeyed malt and sharp fruit.

ABV	6%
First brewed	2012
Brewery	Peerless Brewing Company, Birkenhead, Merseyside
Website	www.peerlessbrewing.co.uk

St Peter's, India Pale Ale

The brewery has one of the finest locations for making beer, in a moated medieval hall near Bungay. It was established in 1996 by John Murphy and quickly achieved success with its beers in flagon-shaped bottles.

The IPA is brewed with pale malt from East Anglia, water from the brewery's own well drawn through chalk layers, and First Gold hops used for both aroma and bitterness. The pale gold beer has a tempting aroma of peppery and floral hops, orange and lemon fruit and sappy malt. There's a solid malt backbone on the palate, but bitter hops and zesty fruit dominate, with a finish that has a quinine-like bitter intensity, and fruit zest continuing to make its presence felt.

ABV	5.5%
First brewed	2006
Brewery	St Peter's Brewery, St Peter South Elmham, Suffolk
Website	www.stpetersbrewery.co.uk

Teignworthy, Edwin Tucker's East India Pale Ale

The brewery, founded in 1994, shares the Victorian stone buildings that make up Tuckers Maltings. The IPA is brewed in honour of Edwin Tucker, who set up his business in 1831; his successors continue the tradition of transforming grain into malt by spreading it on heated floors, turning it by hand and finally heating it in a kiln: modern revolving drums are not in favour. Tuckers supplied large amounts of malt to brewers during the heyday of IPA and is now the only major malting company in the West Country – it is open to visitors.

The IPA is brewed with lager malt, following another Victorian habit of importing this type of malt in order to produce a truly pale beer. A touch of wheat malt is added to give the beer a good collar of foam. The hops are Bramling Cross and Goldings and the beer is bottle conditioned. A bright golden beer with an aroma of lightly toasted malt, lemon fruit and peppery hops. Creamy malt, spicy hops and tart fruit fill the mouth while the finish becomes increasingly bitter, with earthy and peppery hop resins, tart fruit and a lingering 'fresh bread' malt note.

ABV	6.5%
First brewed	2013
Brewery	Teignworthy Brewery, Newton Abbot, Devon
Website	www.teignworthybrewery.com

Vocation Brewery, Heart & Soul

John Hickling ran the successful Blue Monkey brewery in Nottingham before selling up and moving to the outskirts of Hebden Bridge, with a stunning views of the moors. His aim was to make exceptional beers with the aid of pure water from the Pennines. He has a custom-built 15-barrel brewing kit.

Heart & Soul is a session IPA using pale malt and American hops, which create an aroma of passion fruit, grapefruit, mango and pineapple, with fruit, biscuit malt and spicy/floral hops in the mouth and a long, bittersweet finish that ends dry and bitter but with continuing rich fruit and biscuit malt.

ABV	4.4%
First brewed	2015
Brewery	Vocation Brewery, Hebden Bridge, West Yorkshire
Website	www.vocationbrewery.com

Wilde Child, HopStrosity Triple IPA

Keir McAllister-Wilde learned brewing skills at Elland and Saltaire breweries in Yorkshire before branching out on his own. His mission is to make beers full of uncompromising flavours, with American hops to the fore. HopStrosity is described as a triple IPA, with 62 units of bitterness contributed by Columbus, Galena and Summit in the kettle and then dry hopped with Galena and Summit. The grains are pale and crystal malt. The copper-coloured beer has a powerful aroma of raisin fruit, spicy hop resins and freshly baked bread, with rich malt dominating the palate but balanced by raisin fruit and spicy hops. The long and bitter finish becomes dry but with continuing dark fruit and biscuit malt notes.

ABV	10.5%
First brewed	2016
Brewery	Wilde Child Brewing Co, Leeds, West Yorkshire
Website	www.wildechildbrewing.co.uk

Windsor & Eton Brewery, Uprising Treason West Coast IPA

Windsor & Eton is a phenomenally successful brewery in sight of Windsor Castle. It was set up by experienced brewers in 2010, including former employees of the now-closed Courage plant in Reading. Head brewer Paddy Johnson invited his son Kieran to use the brewing kit to make his own beers under the Uprising name. Kieran calls them 'hipster beers' and is reaching out to younger drinkers. His IPA uses barley from the Crown Estate, with a touch of Munich and wheat malts. The hops are Chinook, Galaxy, Mosaic and Simcoe, with a new English variety called Olicana. The pale gold beer has a spicy and herbal hop aroma balanced by biscuit malt and orange fruit. The palate has a solid malt backbone with spicy hops and zesty fruit, followed by a quenching, hoppy and fruity finish.

ABV	5.8%
First brewed	2016
Brewery	Windsor & Eton Brewery, Windsor, Berkshire
Website	www.webrew.co.uk

Wold Top, Scarborough Fair IPA

The brewery is based on a farm where Tom and Gill Mellor use the finest grains and local chalk-filtered water to fashion their beers and employ careful husbandry to protect the environment. They are also conscious of the fact that many drinkers have a problem with beers that contain wheat, and this IPA is brewed with the addition of maize to barley malt. The grains are pale and Munich malts and maize, with three hops: Chinook, Mosaic and Simcoe. The beer is bright gold with a herbal, spicy and peppery aroma, tangerine fruit and rich malt. Bitter hops build in the mouth with juicy malt and zesty fruit, followed by peppery and herbal hops, tangy fruit and juicy malt in the finish.

ABV	6%
First brewed	2003
Brewery	Wold Top Brewery, Driffield, East Yorkshire
Website	www.woldtopbrewery.co.uk

Scotland

Scottish brewers have moved on from the Export ales of the 19th and 20th centuries, which were that country's version of IPA. Beers such as McEwan's Export are malt-driven and lightly hopped, but today's craft brewers are using hops and pale malts to bring new aromas and flavours to the style and give them appeal to younger drinkers.

Fyne Ales, Superior IPA

The brewery has an idyllic location on a farm at the head of Loch Fyne and has access to pure Highland water for its beers. Fyne Ales was founded in 2001 by Jonny and Tuggy Delap, whose family has been farming on the site for more than 100 years. The brewing operation is now run by their son Jamie, who has built Fyne into one of the major craft breweries in Scotland. In 2014 a £2 million expansion, part funded by Highlands & Islands Enterprise and the Scottish government, trebled production. Fyne Ales, in cask, keg and bottle, are now available throughout the UK and exported to several European countries.

If you call a beer Superior it has to be good and this double IPA is brewed with meticulous care and attention to detail. Along with Maris Otter pale malt, torrefied wheat and brewing sugar, two American hops are used, Cascade and Citra, which are added four times throughout the brewing process: in the kettle, as dry hops and in the conditioning vessel, where the beer is aged for four weeks before being bottled with live yeast. In order to give the finished beer a 'Champagne sparkle', as Jamie Delap says, the beer is kräusened. This is a German term used mainly in lager production and involves adding wort – unfermented sugary extract – in the conditioning vessel to encourage a strong secondary fermentation.

Superior IPA is packaged in an attractive 750ml bottle with a swing-top fastener. Superior is one of the attractions at the annual summer festival staged at the brewery, where good beer is matched with food – much of it made with ingredients from the farm – and live music. There is also a shop and a taproom where beers can be sampled.

The verdict

There's an encouraging pop as the swing-top is clicked open and then the golden beer foams into the glass with a lively head. There's a pungent aroma of fruit – apricot, peach and tangerine – with pine notes and biscuit malt. The palate brims over with tropical fruit, juicy malt and spicy/piny hops, while the long and lingering finish is bittersweet, a fine balance of rich juicy malt, ripe fruit and bitter hops. Superior indeed!

ABV	7.1%
First brewed	2014
Brewery	Fyne Ales, Cairndow, Argyllshire
Website	www.fyneales.com

Barney's Beer, Volcano IPA

Barney's is the only craft brewery in the centre of Edinburgh, based on the site of the former Summerhall brewery founded in the 18th century. Andrew Barnett was destined to make beer. The son of a brewery worker from the English Midlands, Andrew moved to Edinburgh in 1988 and studied for a degree on the brewing and distilling course at Heriot-Watt University. He worked for breweries and the revered Macallan single malt whisky distillery before launching his own small company in 2010. He has won many plaudits and awards for his beers, of which Volcano is his best-selling brand. The grains are Optic pale malt, cara malt and pale crystal malt and the beer is hopped with Cascade, Chinook, Bramling Cross and Perle. Volcano, available on draught as well as in bottle, has a pale chestnut colour and a rich and inviting aroma of freshly baked bread, hop resins, tropical fruit and pine. The palate is bittersweet, with biscuit malt and vanilla balancing bitter hops and fruit. The finish lingers and finally becomes dry and hoppy, but there are continuing contributions from malt, vanilla and tangy fruit.

ABV	5%
First brewed	2012
Brewery	Barney's Beer, Edinburgh
Website	www.barneysbeer.com

BrewDog, Punk IPA

BrewDog is a phenomenon, an often outrageous, publicity-seeking company that has taken not just Scottish but British brewing by the scruff of the neck and given it a mighty shake. The founders James Watt and Martin Dickie are unconventional and in-your-face, willing to dress up as penguins or drop mummified animals from a helicopter on London to gain attention. What is beyond dispute is that they have brought many young people into drinking beer and also investing in the brewery. Founded in 2007 near Aberdeen, BrewDog has grown as a result of crowdfunding, with supporters helping to raise the capital for investment and expansion. The brewery site is now enormous and a new brewery is being built in the United States to attack the American market. There are also BrewDog bars and bottle shops located throughout Britain.

The name Punk IPA sums up the operation: the British beer writer Adrian Tierney-Jones has compared the impact of Watt and Dickie on the beer scene to that of the Sex Pistols in the world of popular music. Punk was one of the first revivalist IPAs in

Britain and has inspired many craft brewers to follow the style. It's brewed with Maris Otter pale malt and hopped with Ahtanum, Chinook, Nelson Sauvin and Simcoe. The hops combine to give not only profound bitterness but herbal, floral, leafy, grapefruit and lemon zest notes. Lemon and lime dominate the palate with iron-like bitterness, balanced by juicy malt. The finish is packed with tart citrus fruit and an iodine-like note but with a good balance of rich sappy malt and a hint of caramel.

ABV	5.6%
First brewed	2007
Brewery	BrewDog, Ellon, Aberdeenshire
Website	www.brewdog.com

Caledonian Brewery, Deuchars IPA

If BrewDog is hipster beer, Caledonian is traditional to its fingertips. The brewery dates from 1869 and makes use of the hard water that bubbles up from the red sandstone underground strata known as Edinburgh's 'charmed circle'. Robert Deuchar's brewery closed in the 1960s and 'the Caly', as it's known, acquired the rights to IPA. If the strength is modest, it's a sign of the way in which IPA was hammered by government restrictions early in the 20th century. It still manages to be full-flavoured and it certainly pleases discerning beer drinkers. It's one of the top ten alcohol brands in Scotland and when it was named Champion Beer of Britain by CAMRA in 2002 it became available as far south as Cornwall.

The brewhouse is memorable, with gleaming copper vessels fired by direct flame, originally coal and now gas. The brewers say this method creates a good 'rolling boil' and avoids the hopped wort being stewed. Deuchars IPA is brewed with Golden Promise pale malt and a touch of crystal and it's hopped with Aurora, Cascade, Fuggles and Styrian Goldings. It has a luscious citrus fruit note balanced by spicy hops. Juicy malt, hop resins and bittersweet fruit coat the palate followed by a long finish in which peppery hops linger, with lemon fruit and biscuit malt. The beer is 3.8 per cent on draught and 4.4 per cent in bottle.

ABV	3.8%/4.4%
First brewed	1987, originally 1869
Brewery	Caledonian Brewery, Edinburgh
Website	www.caledonianbeer.com

Clockwork, Oregon IPA

When Robin and Gay Graham opened Clockwork in the Cathcart area of Glasgow in 1997 they introduced the concept of the brewpub to Scotland – a bar and restaurant with beer brewed on the premises which could be matched with food from the kitchen. Clockwork is widely copied but it's become a Glasgow institution. The beers are stored in cellar tanks beneath a blanket of carbon dioxide created by fermentation. Customers can see the brewhouse while they eat. Tours of the brewery (1153–1155 Cathcart Road) are available and the beers can be taken away for home consumption in mini-kegs.

Oregon IPA, as the name implies, is a Glaswegian version of a West Coast IPA, brewed with Centennial and Chinook hops that are added three times during the copper boil. The grains are Maris Otter pale malt and wheat malt. The pale gold beer has a lilting aroma of floral, herbal, grassy and cedarwood hops, with citrus fruit and honeyed malt. Hop bitterness builds in the mouth with a fine balance of bittersweet fruit and creamy malt, followed by a long, quenching finish with cedar notes, citrus and mellow malt and a bitter, hoppy finale.

ABV	5.5%
First brewed	2015
Brewery	Clockwork Beer Company, Glasgow
Website	www.clockworkbeercompany.co.uk

Innis & Gunn, IPA

Innis & Gunn is best known as the Edinburgh company that was the first to age beer in whisky casks. It was founded by Dougal Sharp, the head brewer at Caledonian Brewery, who left to start his own business following the interest created by a beer-infused whisky produced by distiller William Grant with casks Dougal had supplied. He imported bourbon barrels from Kentucky and infused them with beers, ranging from pale to stout, produced for him by brewers in the south of Scotland. In 2016 Innis & Gunn raised £3 million through a crowdfunding bond scheme and bought the Inveralmond Brewery in Perth, which will be expanded from 30 barrels to produce both Inveralmond and the full range of I&G beers.

This IPA is not oak-aged but is one of a new range of beers made possible by the move to Perth. It's brewed with extra pale malt and hopped with Cascade, Centennial and Mandarina hops. The pale bronze beer has a big kick of peppery and spicy hops with a pronounced cinnamon note and cracker biscuit malt. Rich biscuit malt fills the mouth but is balanced by bitter hops, a woody and herbal note, and fruit zest. The finish becomes increasingly bitter and hoppy but continues to be balanced by peppery hops and tart fruit.

Innis & Gunn beers can be enjoyed on tap in three Beer Kitchen bars and restaurants in Edinburgh, Dundee and St Andrews, with more planned.

ABV	5.6%
First brewed	2016
Brewery	Innis & Gunn, Edinburgh
Website	www.innisandgunn.com

Lerwick, IPA

Without fear of contradiction, this is the most northerly IPA brewed in the British Isles, unless the Valhalla Brewery on Unst joins the act. As a result of Shetland's remoteness, beer drinkers had to make do with mainstream keg beers imported from the mainland until Valhalla and Lerwick opened in 1997 and 2011 respectively, introducing cask-conditioned beer to astonished islanders.

Lerwick IPA is brewed with pale, crystal and a touch of chocolate malts, and is hopped with Cascade and Chinook, with Cascade also used as a dry hop. The copper-coloured beer has a big peppery aroma with a caramel hit and a hint of bitter chocolate alongside bitter hop resins and biscuit malt. There's a fine balance of toasted grain and bitter hops on the palate with notes of vanilla and chocolate, followed by a lingering and refreshing finish with sweet grain balanced by hops, caramel and spicy hops.

ABV	5%
First brewed	2015
Brewery	Lerwick Brewery, Shetland
Website	www.lerwickbrewery.co.uk

Stewart Brewing, Pentland IPA/Ka Pai

Steve Stewart believes passionately in putting something back into the community. His brewery not only produces his own range of beers but also has a smaller plant called the Craft Beer Kitchen, which is used by students at Heriot-Watt University's brewing and distilling course and members of the public, who can produce beers at weekends. Steve is a graduate of Heriot-Watt who worked for Bass in Britain, where he learnt all aspects of brewing and retailing. But after spending some time at the legendary Harpoon Brewery in Massachusetts he decided to open his own plant. In 2004, with his wife Jo and her father, he opened a 10-barrel plant where he brewed such traditional Scottish ales as Export and 80 Shilling. Within 10 years the Stewarts had to move to a bigger site to cope with demand and installed an impressive Bavarian-built plant capable of brewing both ale and lager.

Steve and his brewers produce, among other beers, two contrasting interpretations of IPA. Pentland, named after the hills in the Edinburgh area, is firmly rooted in the Scottish style but with a tad more hop character than traditional Export. It's brewed with Maris Otter pale malt and wheat malt and hopped with Challenger, Magnum and Styrian Goldings. It has a solid malt backbone from aroma to finish but with good contributions from spicy and fruity hops. It is only available as draught. Ka Pai (cask, keg and bottle) is described as a 'South Pacific hop bomb' and uses a variety of hops from Australia and New Zealand, including Green Bullet, Pacifica and Wakatu. The grains are extra pale and wheat malts that underscore a massive hit of passion fruit, lychee and mandarin fruit, with herbal and spicy hop notes.

ABV	Pentland IPA 3.9%/Ka Pai 5.2%
First brewed	2004/2013
Brewery	Stewart Brewing, Loanhead
Website	www.stewartbrewing.co.uk

Tryst, Raj IPA

Tryst was launched in 2003 by John McGarva at a spot where in past centuries drovers taking sheep and cattle to market would stop to rest, drink and converse: 'tryst' is an ancient word meaning 'meeting place'. John uses locally grown barley and wheat in his beers but goes far beyond Scotland in his search for hops. His Raj IPA, with a striking label recalling the time when the British ruled India, won the coveted title of CAMRA Champion Beer of Scotland in 2016, which led to the beer being stocked throughout the UK in cask and bottle. It's brewed with pale and wheat malts and hopped with Admiral, Challenger, East Kent Goldings and First Gold hops. It's a truly pale beer with a minty, herbal and spicy aroma with hop resins and fresh bread malt. Juicy malt combines with hops, juicy malt and orange fruit in the mouth, followed by a long finish that ends shatteringly dry and bitter but is preceded by continuing notes of sweet malt and orange fruit.

ABV	5.5%
First brewed	2005
Brewery	Tryst Brewery, Larbert, Falkirk
Website	www.trystbrewery.co.uk

Williams Brothers, Double Joker IPA

Bruce and Scott Williams achieved worldwide acclaim when in the 1980s they restored an ancient form of Scottish beer called Fraoch – pronounced 'frook' – which means heather ale. It was brewed with flowering heather, adding both flavour and wild yeast to the beer. In 2004 the brothers moved into the former bottling hall of George Younger's brewery in Alloa, once known as the 'Burton of Scotland' as a result of the number of breweries based there and the quality of the local water. The brothers installed a bigger brewery and now produce a wide range of beers, ranging from Fraoch and other restored ancient Scottish styles to conventional modern ones.

Double Joker, as the name implies, is a double IPA and is brewed with Amarillo, Centennial and Simcoe hops that create 65 units of bitterness. The grains are lager malt, pale crystal and Vienna malt. The golden beer has a big hop hit in the aroma of passion fruit, mango and lychee, balanced by toasted malt and woody hops. Rich, bittersweet fruit builds in the mouth against a solid toasted malt and spicy hop backbone. The finish is long and deep, ending dry, bitter and hoppy, but bittersweet fruit and toasted malt continue to offer balance and complexity.

ABV	8.3%
First brewed	2012
Brewery	Williams Brothers Brewing Company, Alloa
Website	www.williamsbrosbrew.com

Wales

IPA did not enjoy a major presence in Wales during the style's 19th-century heyday. The influence of church and chapel, with denunciations of the demon drink from the pulpit, restricted the availability of strong beer. And vast armies of coal miners and steel workers preferred to down pints of low-strength dark mild and light bitter to refresh them after long hours of toil. But the decline of both heavy industry and the church has led to greater interest in IPA, fuelled by the arrival of new craft breweries keen to produce full-flavoured beers for a modern audience.

OTLEY 11
MOTLEY BREW
ABV 7.5%

IIPA drenched in
American hops.

SIBA WALES & WEST
PREMIUM BITTERS /
SILVER 2013

Otley 11, Motley Brew

Otley is one of the pacesetters in the Welsh beer revival. The brewery, founded on an industrial estate just outside Pontypridd in Mid Glamorgan in 2005, is run by Nick, Charlie and Matthew Otley, whose family has run pubs in the area for many years. Nick Otley says he wanted to add a brewery because 'We couldn't find anyone brewing the type of beer we wanted to drink and sell. We wanted a bigger punch of hops and a cleaner, lighter beer than was being produced.'

The range of beers is impressive and much use is made of the letter O in the branding. A spiced wheat beer called O-Garden caused ripples due to its similarity to the Belgian Hoegaarden, while Oxymoron was tongue-in-cheek, knowing that black IPA is a controversial style. The Otleys are on safer ground with Otley 11 double IPA. The name Motley Brew comes from the generous use of New World hops – Centennial, Chinook, Columbus and Pacific Gem – that contribute fruity aromas and flavours to a beer brewed with pale, cara red and crystal malts with some torrefied wheat.

As well as the bottled beers, draught versions can be sampled in Otley's showpiece pub in Pontypridd, the Bunch of Grapes, with top quality cuisine and Beer Academy dinners where beer is matched with food.

The verdict

Bright amber beer with a caramel and cedarwood aroma from the slightly darker malts, with rich biscuit notes and pepper and spice. Bitter hops build in the mouth, but there's a rich toasted malt backbone with continuing notes of pepper and caramel, and bitter orange fruit making an appearance. The finish is long and complex with bittersweet fruit vying for attention with toasted malt, caramel and spicy hops.

ABV	7.5%
First brewed	2012
Brewery	Otley Brewing Company, Pontypridd
Website	www.otleybrewing.co.uk

Bluestone, Hammerstone IPA

This is brewing in the raw: the microbrewery is based on an organic hill farm in the Preseli Hills in the Pembrokeshire National Park, an area rich in history and legends of King Arthur as well as Neolithic standing stones of the local bluestone rock.

The Turner family has been farming at Cilgwyn for generations and in 2013 they installed a 10-barrel brewing plant in a 200-year-old stone barn. They thus restored an ancient tradition of farm brewing, when farmers' wives made ale to refresh the labourers. The Turners use pure spring water from the Preseli Hills and when brewing is complete they clean and recycle the water through a system of reed beds. The spent grain and hops are used as animal feed on the farm.

The IPA is made with pale malt and Cascade, Challenger, Chinook and Waimea hops. It has a luscious aroma of biscuit malt, spicy hops and citrus fruit, with hop bitterness building in the mouth on a solid malt backbone and continuing spice and fruit. The finish lingers with biscuit malt and bittersweet fruit giving way to a dry and hoppy finale.

ABV	4.5%
First brewed	2013
Brewery	Bluestone Brewing Company, Cilgwyn, Pembrokeshire
Website	www.bluestonebrewing.co.uk

Bragdy Dinbych/Denbigh Brewery, I Presume Ale IPA

The brewery, based in a Welsh-speaking area of the Vale of Clywd, opened in 2012 behind the Hope & Anchor pub in Denbigh; success led to a move to bigger premises in 2015.

The IPA is dedicated to Henry Morton Stanley, who was born in Denbigh, went to work in the United States as a journalist and famously found the missing explorer Dr David Livingstone in 1871 in Africa, where Livingstone had been searching for the source of the Nile. Stanley's greeting, 'Dr Livingstone, I presume', has gone down in history. The beer goes down equally well.

No ingredients have been revealed, but the pale bronze beer has a big spicy hop and juicy malt aroma with hints of cumin. The hops build in the mouth, but there's a good balance of sappy malt and lemon fruit. The fruit notes dominate the finish with spicy hops and biscuit malt. The brewery's beers are mainly sold in bottle-conditioned format for local fairs and markets but are available cask-conditioned for local pubs.

ABV	5.3%
First brewed	2012
Brewery	Bragdy Dinbych/Denbigh Brewery, Denbigh
Website	www.bragdydinbych.co.uk

Kingstone Brewery, Humpty's Fuddle IPA

The brewery is in an idyllic position, just over the River Wye's border with England and close to the ruins of Tintern Abbey. The abbey, the first Cistercian monastery in Wales, was built in the 12th century and closed during the reign of Henry VIII, after which it fell into disrepair.

Kingstone Brewery opened in 2005 with a four-barrel plant and has built a strong local following for its draught and bottled beers. Their IPA pays homage to a popular figure in British legend and nursery rhyme: Humpty Dumpty, the egg-shaped figure that fell from a wall and couldn't be put back together again by all the king's horses and men. Fuddled is an old term for inebriation: are they suggesting that Humpty had too much to drink? The IPA is brewed with just one English hop, the Fuggle, and a grain bill that includes pale and crystal malts and a touch of maize. The pale bronze beer bears the unmistakable imprint of the Fuggle: earthy, spicy and resinous. Hops are balanced on the aroma and palate with nutty malt and a hint of caramel, and a good balance of bitter, spicy hops, caramel and biscuit malt in the finish.

ABV	5.8%
First brewed	circa 2010
Brewery	Kingstone Brewery, Chepstow, Monmouthshire
Website	www.kingstonebrewery.co.uk

Monty's, EastBound Imperial India Pale Ale

Monty's opened in 2009; and within a few years the owner Pam Honeyman won major awards from both CAMRA and SIBA (the Society of Independent Brewers) There is a visitor centre in The Cottage close to the brewery, which has a small pilot brewery where trial brews are conducted. EastBound is a strong IPA brewed with Maris Otter pale malt, crystal malt and wheat and it has just one hop, the American Columbus. The bronze-coloured beer has an inviting aroma of honeyed malt, floral hops and citrus fruit, with hop bitterness building in the mouth but with a powerful backbone of rich malt and tangy fruit. The finish is long and complex, ending dry and bitter but with continuing contributions from biscuit malt and bittersweet citrus fruit.

ABV	7.3%
First brewed	2016
Brewery	Monty's Brewery, Montgomery
Website	www.montysbrewery.co.uk

Mumbles Brewery, India Pale Ale

Rob Turner started brewing in 2011 and other breweries until he was able to install a 10-barrel plant at Swansea's Enterprise Park. The brewery takes its name from the headland on Swansea Bay comprised of two hills. As well as his regular beers, Rob Turner carries out collaboration brews with other craft producers. His IPA is brewed with pale malt and is hopped with traditional English Fuggles and Goldings. Fuggles are also used as a dry hop in cask. The pale gold beer has a distinctive earthy and peppery aroma from the hops, with rich marmalade fruit and biscuit malt. Hop bitterness and ripe fruit build in the mouth on a solid malt platform. The finish lingers, ripe orange and lemon fruit balancing peppery hops and juicy malt.

ABV	5.3%
First brewed	2015
Brewery	Mumbles Brewery, Swansea
Website	www.mumblesbrewery.co.uk

Neath Ales, Green Bullet

When Jay Thomas was made redundant as a college lecturer, he turned his passion for beer from a hobby into a commercial pursuit. He opened Neath Ales in 2009 and concentrates on cask and bottle-conditioned beers: the beers are free from additives and are neither filtered nor pasteurized. Jay's IPA is named after the New Zealand Green Bullet hop, which is blended with Maris Otter malting barley. The beer has a massive aroma of vinous fruit and pine wood from the hop balancing rich and lightly toasted malt. Citrus fruit dominates the palate with a good balance of honeyed malt and bitter, hop resins. The finish ends dry and bitter.

ABV	6%
First brewed	2010
Brewery	Neath Ales, Port Talbot
Website	www.neathales.co.uk

Tiny Rebel, Hadouken

The impact of winning CAMRA's Champion Beer of Britain award in 2015 can be seen in full measure here. Bradley Cummins and Gareth Williams were astonished by the reaction, with pubs throughout the UK clamouring for the winning beer Cwtch, Welsh for 'cuddle'. Tiny Rebel opened in 2012 with a 12-barrel plant and in 2016 Brad and Gareth relocated to a new site with five times the capacity. Hadouken is brewed with pale and cara malt and wheat and is hopped with American varieties Cascade, Chinook and Columbus. The pale bronze beer has tropical fruit, apricot and tangerine on the aroma with a freshly baked bread note. Bittersweet fruit dominates the palate, with hop bitterness building but with a solid backbone of biscuit malt. The finish is a superb balance of ripe, bittersweet fruit, juicy malt and bitter hops.

ABV	7.4%
First brewed	2013
Brewery	Tiny Rebel, Newport
Website	www.tinyrebel.co.uk

Ireland

IPA was a beer style that passed Ireland by in the 19th century. In spite of its proximity to the rest of the British Isles, brewing followed a different course in Ireland. Ale made without hops persisted for many centuries and even when hops were introduced beers tended to be exceptionally malty, with red ale the main style. The big change came with the development of porter and stout in the 18th and 19th centuries. Irish brewers, with Arthur Guinness leading the way, adapted London's porter and stout and turned the style into an Irish icon. By the end of the 19th century, Guinness had overtaken England's Bass to become the world's biggest brewer, its Export Stout challenging the hegemony of IPA on the world stage.

Times, tastes and attitudes change. Many Irish drinkers consider that Guinness, part of global drinks giant Diageo, and Murphy's, owned by Heineken, have lost much of their Irishness and they are turning to the new wave of craft brewers. Most independent brewers produce stout, but they have widened their horizons and portfolios with pale and golden ales, giving IPA the opportunity to make a late entry to the island.

O'Hara's, Irish Pale Ale

Carlow Brewing Company is better known as O'Hara's because it was founded by Seamus and Eamonn O'Hara in 1996 and is still owned by the family, with Seamus in charge as chief executive. It has grown to become Ireland's leading independent brewery and its beers, O'Hara's Irish Stout in particular, are widely exported. In 2015, €1 million were raised to expand the brewery, which now has a staff of fifty. In common with other Irish craft breweries, Seamus and his team are not attempting to outflank Guinness – an impossible task in Ireland – but are offering a wide range of beers to appeal to discriminating drinkers, younger people in particular. Some of O'Hara's beers are even sold on draught in cask-conditioned form, which is rare in Ireland.

Irish Pale Ale is described as 'dry hopped IPA' and is brewed with locally grown barley malt, pure mountain water and hopped with Amarillo and Cascade: Ireland's damp climate makes hop growing difficult.

The verdict

An immensely complex and rewarding pale gold beer, with an aroma of fresh tobacco, biscuit malt, hop resins, herbs, spices and grapefruit. Fruit builds in the mouth – grapefruit, lemon and lime – with juicy malt and bitter hops. The finish is long with hop resins, citrus fruit, spices, tobacco and sappy malt.

ABV	5.2%
First brewed	2015
Brewery	Carlow Brewing Company, Muine Bheag, Co Carlow
Website	www.carlowbrewing.com

Blacks of Kinsale, Mosaic IPA

When Maudeline Black gave her husband Sam a home-brewing kit for Valentine's Day she launched a love affair with beer. Sam enjoyed brewing so much that the husband-and-wife team opened a brewery in 2013. Their aim, they say, is to 'escape the mundane of the mass market by producing beers with passion, personality – and lots of hops!'

The range includes a series of Discovery IPAs, highlighting specific hop varieties or styles. The Blacks call the series 'kick ass beers' and aim them at young drinkers who appreciate the powerful flavours of New World hops. Given the name of the brewery, the range includes a Black IPA. Mosaic is described as a West Coast IPA; it has an appealing bronze colour with orange and tangerine fruit on the nose with rich wholemeal biscuit notes from the grain and a hint of spice. Bittersweet fruit fills the mouth with spicy hop resins and juicy malt. The finish is dry and bitter, but there's a fine balance of ripe fruit and juicy malt.

The brewery is open to visitors in spring and summer. There is also a tap room and bar where the beers can be sampled.

ABV	6.5%
First brewed	2013
Brewery	Blacks of Kinsale, Kinsale, Co Cork
Website	www.blacksbrewery.com

Brú, Irish Craft IPA Rí

The brewery is based in the valley of the River Boyne, an area rich in history and legend, and ancient gods and warriors inspire the beers' names. This IPA is named in honour of Brian Boru, the last King of Ireland: Rí is an ancient Gaelic word for king. The brewery was founded in 2013 by Dave O'Hare, who is head brewer, and Daire Harlin, a law graduate and keen home-brewer. Daire says he was inspired by the success of quality wines in Ireland that had replaced the likes of Blue Nun and wanted to bring craft beer to the attention of younger drinkers: 'As people experience new tastes, they realize beer can taste like something other than cold fizzy water.'

His IPA is brewed with Irish-grown pale and Munich malts and hopped with Cascade, Citra, Goldings and Summit hops. The bronze beer has a toasted malt aroma with a peppery note from the Goldings and hints of citrus fruit. The palate is dry, with

Great Lakes, RoboHop Imperial IPA

Not to be confused with its namesake in the United States (see page 121), Great Lakes is considered to be one of the finest, if not the finest, brewer of modern IPAs in Canada. It has had a topsy-turvy history. It began life in the Toronto suburb of Brampton in 1987, brewing 'extract beer' – using malt and hop syrups in the manner of home-brewing. That business model folded in 1990 and was sold to Peter Bulut Senior, who had made money in the construction industry.

The brewery re-opened in the district of Etobicoke in 1991; it used full grain and hops, but at first it made forgettable ales and lagers, sold mainly as house beers for bars and restaurants. But as the new century dawned, Great Lakes reformulated with more characterful beers and became known as one of Canada's leading IPA specialists. RoboHop is brewed with two-row pale malt, carapils, flaked wheat and glucose. The hops are Citra, Columbus, Equinox, Mosaic, Nelson Sauvin and Simcoe.

The verdict

Hazy gold colour with a fruit cocktail aroma balanced by hop resins and pine. The palate begins sweet, with apricot fruit, pine notes, citrus hops and toasted grain. Hop bitterness builds but fruit and herbal notes offer balance with notes of apricot, peach and pear. The finish is big with hop bitterness dominating, but toasted malt and bittersweet fruit hold the balance.

ABV	8.5%
First brewed	2013
Brewery	Great Lakes Brewery, Toronto, Ontario
Website	www.greatlakesbeer.com

Black Bridge Brewery, IPA!

This microbrewery opened in 2014, the brainchild of husband-and-wife team Clayton and Kari Stenson. Clayton had been a dedicated home-brewer for 10 years and was keen to move up to commercial brewing. The 20-hectolitre brewery is named after a local landmark, a river crossing said to be haunted as a result of a murder there many years ago.

On a more cheerful note, the Stensons' beers can be enjoyed in their taproom alongside the brewery at 295 Alexander Drive. The IPA is brewed with pale, cara and Munich malts with an addition of honey and is hopped with Centennial, El Dorado and Simcoe varieties that create 62 bitterness units. It's very pale and crystal clear – a rarity in the world of modern IPAs, which are often hazy because they are unfiltered. It and has a delicate aroma of lime, with fresh pine needles and lemon. Bittersweet fruit builds on the palate with herbal, pine and biscuit malt, followed by a quenching finish in which malt, hops and fruit are in perfect harmony.

ABV	7%
First brewed	2014
Brewery	Black Bridge Brewery, Swift Current, Saskatchewan
Website	www.blackbridgebrewery.ca

Central City, Red Racer IPA

Central City, founded by Darryll Frost, started as a brewpub in a mall in central Surrey, a suburb of Vancouver, before moving to a much bigger, 65,000 square-foot plant in the downtown area, with both a brewery and a distillery, though the original pub is still in operation. The quality of the beers improved with the arrival of brewmaster Gary Lohin, who is regarded as one of the most talented brewers in British Columbia. Central City's beers are now sold from Victoria to Newfoundland as well as in the US.

Red Racer IPA is brewed with imported Maris Otter pale malt and crystal malt and hopped with Amarillo, Centennial, Magnum and Simcoe. The bright copper-coloured beer has peppery hops, grapefruit and hints of roasted malt on the aroma, with toffee malt to the fore in the palate, giving way to lemon and ruby grapefruit on top of a biscuit malt backbone. The finish is dry with peppery hops, biscuit malt, citrus fruit and hints of toffee and caramel.

ABV	6.5%
First brewed	2004
Brewery	Central City Brewing Company, Surrey, Vancouver, British Columbia
Website	www.centralcitybrewing.com

Collective Arts, State of Mind Session IPA

The beers at first were contract-brewed and given a highly visual marketing spin by using the work of independent artists for the labels. Success led to a bricks-and-mortar brewery being opened in Hamilton, which Collective Arts shares with another brewery, Nickel Brook.

Collective Arts has set out its stall by making hoppy pale ales with generous additions of late hops. It has followed the American trend of offering a session IPA that is less of a 'hop bomb' and can be consumed with both pleasure and comfort. It's brewed with two-row pale malt, cara malt, flaked oats and flaked wheat and is hopped with Amarillo and Centennial. It pours medium gold and hazy and has a fruity nose with peach, mango, lemon, dried apricot and grapefruit zest. Tropical fruit leads on the palate with additions of lychee and grapefruit, with a solid malt backbone and bitter hops. The finish is bitter but with compensating lush fruit and juicy malt.

ABV	4.4%
First brewed	2014
Brewery	Collective Arts Brewing, Hamilton, Ontario
Website	www.collectiveartsbrewing.com

Driftwood, Fat Tug IPA

Driftwood Brewery opened in 2008, founded by Jason Meyer and Kevin Hearsum, who had been brewers at the Lighthouse Brewing Company in Victoria, before setting up their own operation on Vancouver Island, where they were joined by Gary Lindsay. Their eclectic range includes porter, wheat beer, saison and sour.

Fat Tug IPA has won approval across Canada as one of the best new wave versions of the style and now accounts for around half the brewery's output. Fat Tug is brewed with Pilsner, crystal and carapils malts and the hop varieties used are Amarillo, Cascade, Centennial, Citra and Columbus. The golden beer has a citrus fruit aroma with a spicy and floral hops note and honeyed malt.

A cocktail of fruits builds in the mouth and is beautifully balanced by rich grain and floral hops, with a long finish that finally becomes dry but with preceding notes of fruit zest, gently toasted malt and spicy hop resins.

In 2015 a new 60-hectolitre brewhouse came on line with a state-of-the-art bottling facility. The brewery has a shop where growlers can be filled with fresh beer for home consumption.

ABV	7%
First brewed	2010
Brewery	Driftwood Brewery, Victoria, British Columbia
Website	www.driftwoodbeer.com

Garrison Brewing, Imperial IPA

Halifax was a garrison town as far back as the 18th century and brewers sprang up there to quench the thirsts of both soldiers and settlers. When Garrison Brewing, with Daniel Girard as brewmaster, opened in 1997, it concentrated, understandably, on an Irish red ale that had once been the predominant style in the province.

But the brewery has spread its wings and has opened up the market in New Brunswick to its beers, a bold step as before that beers from Nova Scotia were available only in that province.

The imperial IPA is brewed with Maritime pale malt, Munich and cara malts, with Amarillo, German Magnum and – according to Daniel Girard – 'a lot of Cascade'. It has a deep copper colour with fragrant floral notes of orange zest, lemon and grapefruit on the aroma with spicy and floral hops. There are rich citrus fruit notes on the palate, with sweet orange and apricot balancing rich malt. The finish is intensely bitter, with hops dominating the malt and fruit notes.

ABV	8%
First brewed	2007
Brewery	Garrison Brewing Company, Halifax, Nova Scotia
Website	www.garrisonbrewing.com

Le Castor, Yakima IPA

This is a brewery in the French-speaking region of Canada with a mixed Scottish and American pedigree. Daniel Addey Jibb and Murray Elliott worked as carpenters in Scotland before returning to Canada, where they used their skills to make timber-framed houses. But the economic crash of 2008–9 left them short of work and they decided to open a brewery in which they aged some of their beers in wood.

Their IPA makes a deep bow in the direction of the Yakima Valley in Washington State: Daniel and Murray use lashings of hops from the area in their IPA, which are added as kettle, late kettle and dry hops. The malts are all organic and include pale and Munich, with Cascade, Centennial, Citra and Palisade hop varieties. The beer is pale gold and cloudy with an explosion of fruit on the nose: lemon, pineapple, grapefruit and kiwi with toasted grain and floral notes. There are cocktail fruits on the palate with lemon, grapefruit and lime to the fore while the finish is dry, bitter and quenching, with citrus fruit, biscuit malt and spicy hops.

ABV	6.5%
First brewed	2013
Brewery	Microbrasserie Le Castor, Rigaud, Québec
Website	www.microlecastor.ca

Belgium and the Netherlands

Belgium is renowned worldwide for such remarkable beers as Trappist ales, spiced wheat beers, lambic beers produced by wild yeast fermentation, sour red beers and many more. But while British-inspired pale ales have been brewed in Belgium for many years, IPA has rarely featured.

The Netherlands has been dominated by Pilsner-style lagers from Heineken, Grolsch and other large companies, but now both countries are witnessing new craft breweries and a wider range of styles. IPAs have flourished as a result – but with a definable Low Countries character of strength and flavour.

Brasserie d'Achouffe, Houblon Chouffe IPA Tripel

This beer is a mouthful in every way and I will have to crack the Belgian beer code to make the name clear. Tripel or Triple means a beer high in alcohol: the most famous Belgian Tripel is brewed by monks at the Westmalle monastery near Antwerp and weighs in at 9.5 per cent alcohol. The use of 'tripel' by Achouffe is also a play on words as the beer is brewed with three hops. 'Houblon' is French for hop. Achouffe, in the beautiful rolling hills of the Ardennes, has brought new fame to Belgian beer. The founders, Pierre Gobron and Chris Bauweraerts, were passionate home-brewers who went the extra mile in the 1980s with a small commercial brewery. Their sales took off when they used a logo of the 'chouffe', a mythical gnome from the Ardennes. In 1986 they moved to early 19th-century farm buildings and installed modern brewing kit that has been regularly expanded and now produces 150,000 hectolitres a year. In 2006 Chouffe became part of the large Belgian Duvel Moortgat group that has busily grown sales of all the Chouffe beers, which now enjoy a cult following in France and French-speaking Canada.

Houblon Chouffe was introduced in 2006 when an American importer pointed out that nobody in Belgium knew what IPA was. Chris Bauweraerts, who is now a beer ambassador for Duvel Moortgat, researched the history of IPA and the first decision he made was to 'Burtonize' the soft water of the Ardennes with sulphates in order to make a beer true to style. Only pale Pilsner malt is used and the three hops are Amarillo, Saaz and Tomahawk that create 45 units of bitterness: the IBUs were originally 62 but have been scaled back. A fresh dosage of yeast is used for bottle conditioning and the beer will improve with age. The brewery stands in extensive grounds with a shop, restaurant and visitor centre: tours of the brewery are available.

The verdict

As pale as a Pilsner, the beer has a rich and full aroma of spicy, peppery and floral (elderflower) hops, lightly toasted malt, and fruit notes reminiscent of orange, lemon and peach. Oatcake malt dominates the palate but is challenged by spicy hops and ripe fruit, while the long finish is intensely bitter, dry and hoppy but with continuing notes of oatcake and bittersweet fruit.

ABV	9%
First brewed	2006
Brewery	Brasserie d'Achouffe, Achouffe, Belgium
Website	www.achouffe.be

Brussels Beer Project, Delta IPA

The Beer Project symbolizes the changing face of Belgian beer. It was set up in 2013 by Sébastien Morvan and a group of passionate beer lovers who felt the beer scene in their country was in danger of becoming hidebound and resting on its laurels. Their theme is 'leave the abbey, join the playground' – in other words, develop more modern styles than those offered by monks. Their project was created by crowdfunding, enabling them to install a substantial brewing plant at 188 Rue Antoine Dansaert in Brussels. It's a modern concept, with a bar and large tasting room where beers fresh from conditioning vessels can be sampled. The tasting room is open Thursday to Saturday, 2–10pm.

Sébastien and his colleagues create a number of collaboration brews: on my visit I sampled a Hot Rye IPA brewed with La Goutte d'Or in Paris (see page 247). The first beer – and still the most popular – is Delta IPA, which was chosen by 850 beer drinkers in Brussels asked to choose from four trial brews labelled Alpha, Beta, Delta and Gamma. Delta is brewed with 100 per cent pale malt and hopped with American Citra, English Challenger and German Smaragd varieties, giving 45 units of bitterness. The pale gold, unfined, hazy beer has an intensely peppery hop nose with floral and apricot notes and a solid underpinning of toasted grain. Dried fruits build in the mouth, with rich toasted grain and bittersweet fruit and hops, and a lingering finish offering a superb balance of biscuit malt, bitter and spicy hops and dried fruits.

ABV	6.5%
First brewed	2013
Brewery	Brussels Beer Project, Brussels
Website	www.beerproject.be

Duvel Moortgat, Vedett Extraordinary IPA

The brewery started life on a farm in 1871 and is still owned by the fifth generation of the Moortgat family. It has grown into a large company with an ever-expanding plant south of Antwerp. It owns breweries in the United States, the Czech Republic and the Netherlands as well as Achouffe, De Koninck and Liefmans in Belgium but has resisted takeovers from global giants and remains committed to quality, well-made beers. It's so famous for its Duvel strong golden ale that it has incorporated the name into the company title.

IPA was added to the range in 2014 and has become widely available in bottle and on draught: the packaged version is bottle conditioned. It's brewed with pale malt and hopped in the kettle with Cascade and Simcoe and dry hopped after fermentation with Centennial and Chinook. The beer conditions for two weeks in warm cellars, followed by four to six weeks of cold conditioning. It's extremely pale with a honeyed malt aroma balancing spicy hop resins and lemon fruit. Bitter hops build in the mouth with honeyed malt and sharp fruit, followed by a dry and hoppy finish with a continuing balance of juicy malt and tart fruit. Perhaps not extraordinary, but the beer is meticulously made and refreshing.

ABV	5.5%
First brewed	2014
Brewery	Brouwerij Duvel Moortgat, Breendonk-Puurs
Website	www.duvel.be

'tIJ, IPA

This is the brewery that proved there was more to Dutch beer than Heineken. It opened as a small brewpub in 1984, funded by songwriter Kaspar Peterson, and caught the imagination of beer drinkers throughout Europe as a result of its image and position. It's based in an old public bathhouse next to a windmill alongside the IJ River in Amsterdam at 7 Funenkade. The pronunciation of IJ – 'ay' – is almost identical to the Dutch word for egg and many of the labels feature an ostrich and an egg. The brewery and range have grown over the years, but there's still an emphasis on quality and organic ingredients. It's now part of the Belgian Duvel Moortgat group and the relationship has allowed 'tIJ beers to reach new markets in Europe and North America.

IPA was introduced in 2015 and rapidly became one of the brewery's most popular beers. It's brewed with pale malt and hopped with American Cascade and Citra varieties, which are added in both the kettle and the conditioning vessels. It's unfiltered and bottle conditioned. It's a shame that it has a label showing a topless woman which demeans the history of the style, but let's judge the contents of the bottle. The beer has a pale bronze colour and a herbal, grassy, floral and orange/tangerine aroma with honeyed malt and peppery hops. The palate starts bittersweet with rich orange fruit to the fore, but oatcake malt and spicy hop resins kick in. The finish is dry with citrus fruits mingling with smooth malt and hops: the hops finally dominate in an intensely bitter finale.

ABV	7%
First brewed	2015
Brewery	Brouwerij 'tIJ, Amsterdam
Website	www.brouwerijhetij.nl

Brouwerij Kompaan, No.58 Handlanger Imperial IPA

The brewery has grown quickly since it was set up in 2012 by Jasper Langbroek and Jeroen van Ditmarsch in The Hague. It has moved twice and in 2015 €50,000 were raised by crowdfunding to build a craft beer bar next to the brewery (55 Saturnusstraat, Den Haag). The brewery produces 8,000 hectolitres a year with room to grow. The

Imperial IPA is made with three malts – pale and two darker varieties – and is hopped with Amarillo, Cascade and Simcoe, with Amarillo also used for dry hopping: the beer has 60 units of bitterness. It has a cloudy chestnut colour with a big peppery/spicy aroma and a fresh bread malt note and raisin fruit. Malt leads the palate, but there are good contributions from spicy hops and dark fruit. The finish is dry and malty with pronounced burnt fruit and hop notes.

ABV	8.2%
First brewed	2013
Brewery	Brouwerij Kompaan, Den Haag
Website	www.kompaanbier.nl

Leffe, Royale Cascade IPA

The beer, the name and the brands are an object lesson in the way in which global corporations work. The large range of Leffe beer is resplendent in bottles with designs suggesting history, craft and a connection to the monastic brewing tradition. In fact they are all produced in a vast Stella Artois beer factory that's now part of the world's brewing colossus AB InBev.

The website will tell you in glowing detail about the beer's roots in a monastery near Dinant founded in 1152 and where beer was brewed from 1240. But the monastery was sacked during the Napoleonic period and Leffe brands have been made by commercial brewers for many years. I first encountered them at Mont St-Guibert, but Stella Artois closed that facility and moved the beers to Hoegaarden and finally to Leuven.

Let's put aside the politics and judge the beer. It's based on Leffe Royale, which is brewed with several hops, while the IPA, as the name implies, has just Cascade. It's dry hopped and has a pale gold colour topped by a thick collar of foam. It has a distinctive Belgian aroma, perfumy with peach-like fruit. The palate is dominated by sweet fruit and malt with only gentle hop notes. The finish is short, bittersweet with fruit and malt to the fore and only limited hop notes. It won a silver award in the 2015 World Beer Awards, but the judges said, 'It's not an IPA'.

ABV	7.5%
First brewed	2014
Brewery	Leffe/AB InBev, Leuven
Website	www.leffe.com

Martin's, IPA

John Martin was an Englishman from Newmarket who opened a beer import business in Antwerp in 1909 and turned both Bass pale ale and Guinness stout into popular brands in Belgium. The company is run today by his grandson Anthony Martin, who has expanded into brewing. He runs Timmermans, Belgium's oldest lambic brewery, built a new brewery in Waterloo and in 2015 restored an ancient tradition to Bruges when he re-opened the Bourgogne des Flandres brewery there.

The company also owns a pale ale brand that was originally called Courage Bulldog in England. It's brewed for Martin's by Palm, the specialist ale brewery, and Anthony Martin added an IPA that he says is true to the English rather than the modern American style. He thinks the yeast used to brew both his Pale Ale and IPA may be the original Courage culture. Pale and crystal malts are joined by Kent and Styrian Goldings whole hops: the beer is dry hopped with Dana following fermentation and is bottle conditioned. It has a pale chestnut colour with a herbal, spicy and fresh tobacco aroma with rye bread malt and a powerful sulphur note: the brewing water is Burtonized. The palate is bittersweet with rich biscuit malt, bitter hop resins and spices and pine notes. A blood orange fruit note emerges in the finish, which is dry and hoppy but balanced by juicy malt. One version comes in a handsome 75cl bottle with a Champagne cork and wire cage.

ABV	6.9%
First brewed	2015
Brewery	John Martin, Genval
Website	www.martinsbeers.be

St Feuillien, Green Flash
West Coast IPA

Described as a double IPA, the beer is a collaborative brew with the Green Flash brewery in San Diego, California. Saint Feuillien dates from 1873, closed for a period in the 20th century and re-opened in 1988. Green Flash exported beer to Europe but was concerned about freshness and teamed up with the Belgian brewery to replicate the beer and deliver it fresh to European destinations. The beers are identical save for the fact that the Belgian version is bottle conditioned. St Feuillien also produce their own Belgian Coast IPA at 5.5 per cent alcohol, using seven varieties of hops, both Belgian and American, for a full-flavoured fruity beer.

West Coast IPA is brewed with pale malt and hopped with Cascade, Centennial, Citra and Simcoe varieties that create a mighty 95 bitterness units. The beer has a bright amber/bronze colour, fluffy foam and an aroma reminiscent of sherbet lemons, with additions of lemon, lime and lychee and a crispbread malt note. Bitter hops develop on the palate with spicy and herbal notes and continuing tart fruit, all on a solid toasted malt spine. The units of bitterness express themselves in a shatteringly bitter finish with a quinine-like intensity, but honey malt and fruit linger to provide balance.

ABV	8.1%
First brewed	2005
Brewery	Brasserie Saint Feuillien, Le Roeulx
Website	www.st-feuillien.com

Siphon, Damme Nation

A five-hectolitre microbrewery opened in July 2016 at an ancient inn, Gasthof Siphon, alongside two canals that were once vital arteries linking Belgium with France and the Netherlands. The brewery is run by Franklin Verdonck and Breandán Kearney: Breandán is from Northern Ireland but is now resident in Ghent where he runs Belgian Smaak or Taste, writing and lecturing about beer … and now brewing it.

As well as a traditional Belgian saison and an oyster stout, the brewery produces a West Coast-inspired IPA brewed with pale and cara Munich malts and hopped with Amarillo, Cascade and Citra hops; the beer is also dry hopped. It's quite dark for the style, amber/chestnut in colour, with a big spicy and caramel aroma with toasted malt and pine-like hops. Hop bitterness builds in the palate and the finish, balanced by caramel, pine and rich biscuit malt. The beer is available on draught as well as bottle: at the inn – 1 Damse Vaart-Oost, 8340 Damme – you can enjoy it with excellent food, including traditional beef stew and dishes with eel, a local delicacy.

ABV	7%
First brewed	2016
Brewery	Siphon Brewing, Damme
Website	www.siphonbrewing.be

France

France is the world's greatest producer of fine wine, and it also has a tradition of brewing beer. If you sip a glass of either wine or beer in a brasserie, you are enjoying it in a bar or café that takes its name from the French for brewery. A powerful brewing tradition thrives in the north in the Pas de Calais region, with a style known as bière de garde. The Strasbourg region, as a result of its Germanic connections, is a major producer of lager, dominated by Kronenbourg. But now beer is widening its reach. Inspired by the Belgians to the north and the impact of pale ale from across the Channel and beyond, a number of microbreweries have opened in recent years, while Paris has both a new brewery and a number of specialist beer shops.

Goutte d'Or, Ernestine IPA

The brewery opened in 2012, restoring a long-lost brewing tradition to Paris. Thierry Roche gave up his day job to raise money from crowdfunding and launched the first new brewery in the capital for decades. It's based in the 'drop of gold' area of the 18th arrondissement and Thierry draws the inspiration for his beers from a variety of styles along with ingredients from market stalls in a working-class district with large Arab and North African populations. He brews Myrha – named after a local street – with the addition of date sugar; Charbonnière, a smoked amber beer; a Belgian-style saison with the addition of spices; and beers made with tea and coffee alongside malts and hops. Thierry's beers are neither filtered nor pasteurized: he has made some collaborative brews with the Brussels Beer Project (see page 240), including Stereo Lips, which has the addition of Ugandan vanilla beans and Mexican chipotle.

Ernestine is brewed in homage to the Chapelloise Brewery that was once located in Rue Ernestine. Pale and cara malts are balanced by Centennial, Chinook and Columbus hops that create 44 units of bitterness.

The brewery and its shop are open on Thursday and Friday between 5 and 7pm and Saturday 2–7pm: 28 Rue de la Goutte d'Or, Paris 75018.

The verdict

An amber beer with a rich biscuit malt aroma, a caramel note, grapefruit and spicy hop resins. The palate has bittersweet fruit, toasted grain and spicy, bitter hops followed by a long and complex finish where toasted malt and caramel interweave with ripe fruit and bitter, spicy hops.

ABV	7%
First brewed	2013
Brewery	Brasserie la Goutte d'Or, Paris
Website	www.brasserielagouttedor.com

Craig Allan, India Project 'Ale

Craig Allan is a Scot who has taken British ales to northern France and built a good reputation in bars and specialist beer shops. He has also persuaded the owners of fine restaurants to offer beer as well as wine with their dishes. Craig studied brewing at Heriot-Watt University in Edinburgh and worked for several British craft breweries before branching out into wine in the Burgundy region. He then settled with his family in a small village in the Picardie region where he started to brew. His first three beers were made by De Proef brewery in Belgium but Craig was able to open his own plant in 2015.

He calls his IPA a project as every batch uses different hops: some brews are single hop, others have two. The hops used have included Ahtanum, Citra, Columbus, Equinox and Nugget. Batch L12 2016, tasted for this book, was comprised of pale malt, rye malt (30 per cent) and wheat malt and was hopped with Mosaic and Simcoe, delivering 70 IBU. The unfiltered beer has a hazy gold colour, a dense head of foam, and a big spicy aroma that comes from the rye malt as well as the hops: the hops also deliver pungent notes of pine and citrus. Bitter hops dominate the palate with rye adding a spicy note alongside honeyed malt and tart fruit. The finish is intensely bitter, but the hops are well balanced by rye, pine and citrus fruit.

ABV	5.5%
First brewed	2015
Brewery	Brasserie Craig Allan, Plessis-de-Roye
Website	· www.craigallan.fr

La Brasserie du Mont Salève, Amiral Benson Nelson Sauvin IPA

Michaël Novo was a keen home-brewer who decided to go the extra kilometre in 2009 and planned his own small brewery, which opened a year later. He's based in a stunning area of the Alps overlooking Lake Léman and his beers' 1930s-style labels show a woman against a backdrop of a cable car in the Alps. He uses fine Alpine water and sources his grain from the region. His range of beers includes porter, stout and wheat beer and several feature the Nelson Sauvin hop variety from New Zealand, which has a fruity character reminiscent of Sauvignon grapes.

His IPA is named after a character in the comedy film *Hot Shots*, who endlessly repeats the same hilarious clangers: it's not a comment on Michaël's beers! Amiral Benson has 70 bitterness units and has a fine, fruity, vinous aroma with honeyed malt and spicy hops. Fruit and hops build in the mouth, balanced by juicy malt and bittersweet fruit, followed by a long finish that ends dry but with preceding notes of rich, vinous fruit and creamy malt. The brewery also produces a 6.7 per cent India Pale Ale brewed with Amarillo and Simcoe hops.

ABV	6%
First brewed	2010
Brewery	La Brasserie du Mont Salève, Neydens
Website	www.labrasseriedumontsaleve.com

Ninkasi, IPA

You have to take seriously a brewery named in honour of the goddess of beer in ancient Sumeria, though she would be hard pressed to recognize modern styles of beer made with hops. The brewery was founded in 1997 in Lyon, restoring the city's 19th-century brewing traditions. But it outgrew the site and in 2012 moved to nearby Tarare with new plant able to produce 18,000 hectolitres a year. The group has grown impressively, owns several restaurants and has a concert hall alongside the brewery, which also has a distillery for making vodka. The beers have won medals in the French Agricultural Awards, World Beer Awards and Brussels Beer Challenge.

IPA is made with Pilsner, cara and Munich malts and is hopped with Cascade, Galena and Palisade varieties. It has an amber colour and a rich and inviting aroma of toasted grain, ripe citrus fruits and floral and herbal hops. Biscuit malt is balanced by grapefruit and bitter hops in the mouth followed by a complex finish with biscuit malt interweaving with bittersweet fruit and hop resins.

ABV	6%
First brewed	2012
Brewery	Fabrique Ninkasi, Tarare
Website	www.ninkasi.fr

Brasserie de la Pleine Lune, Aubeloun IPA

Beer is spreading south through France from its natural heartland in the north-east of the country: the Full Moon brewery in the Drôme department of south-eastern France was launched in 2011 by Benoît Ritzenthaler. He started as a keen home-brewer, then worked with an artisan brewer in the region before building his own plant. He has widened his skills by creating collaborative brews with Pays Flamand, Le Paradis and Vallée du Giffre.

At his own brewery Benoît makes rich-tasting beers using natural ingredients and ages some of the beers in wood. He creates great hop character in the beers, as can be seen in his IPA, which uses Centennial, Citra, Green Bullet, Pacific Gem and Simcoe varieties and has 50 units of bitterness. The grains are pale, Pilsner, Munich and cara malts. The deep bronze beer has a massive hit of fruit on the aroma, with grapefruit to the fore but with notes of lemon, lime and lychee, along with toasted malt. Bittersweet fruit dominates the palate, but there's a good balance of caramel, toasted malt and spicy hops. The big finish has bittersweet fruit, bitter and spicy hops and finally a lingering caramel note.

Benoît works with other French craft brewers to make collaborative beers, including Brasserie du Pays Flamand.

ABV	7%
First brewed	2011
Brewery	Brasserie de la Pleine Lune, Chabeuil
Website	www.brasserie-pleinelune.fr

Brasserie Saint-Loupoise, Titanic IPA

The brewery is based in old farm buildings where tobacco used to be dried. Ludovic Dez has not attempted to follow traditional brewers in the Pas de Calais region with *bières de garde*; instead, he looks across the Channel for inspiration. Ludovic loves British beers and brews stout and barley wine as well as IPA.

The IPA is brewed with two English and two American hops and is unfiltered and conditioned in the bottle. It's matured for three weeks before being released. It has a hazy amber colour and a rich aroma of toasted malt, berry fruits and bitter hop resins. Dark fruit builds in the mouth on a solid backbone of toasted malt with growing hop bitterness. The finish is long and complex, hop bitterness growing but balanced by toasted malt and over-ripe fruit. Titanic goes down well!

ABV	7%
First brewed	2012
Brewery	Brasserie Saint-Loupoise, Huby-Saint-Leu
Website	www.brasserie-saint-loupoise.fr

Brasserie De Sutter, Crazy IPA

The brothers Antoine and Frédéric De Sutter have won two major awards for their IPA: a gold medal in 2014 at the French Agricultural Fair in Paris and another gold in the World Beer Awards the following year. Based in Normandy, they are committed to the region's traditions and they brand their beers with the image of a cow to stress their local roots.

Crazy IPA has a cartoon of the Statue of Liberty with a cow imposed on the face: in the present political climate, that's not too wide of the mark. The brothers studied beer-making at the renowned brewing faculty of Leuven University in Belgium before returning home to build a 40-hectolitre plant at Gisors in 2012. They rapidly won a reputation for their beers. The brothers do not reveal full details of their recipes. The beers are unfiltered and unpasteurized and the IPA is hopped with three American varieties that create 35 units of bitterness. The pale gold beer has biscuit malt, citrus fruit and peppery hops on the aroma. Juicy malt, tart fruit and bitter hops dominate the palate. The finish is bittersweet to start, with citrus fruit and biscuit malt, but the hops take over in the bitter and peppery finish.

ABV	6.5%
First brewed	2012
Brewery	Brasserie De Sutter, Gisors
Website	www.brasseriedesutter.com

Italy

It's difficult to believe, but Italy, one of the world's great wine-producing nations, has around 900 small craft breweries. There has been a veritable explosion of craft brewing in recent years as younger Italians, concerned with 'bella figura' – looking trendy and modern – turn away from traditional food and drink, and look for inspiration to other European countries and to the United States.

Most of the breweries are small and in many cases are no more than micros, but they have brought a sense of excitement to a beer scene that has been dominated for decades by pale lagers such as Peroni and Moretti. Some breweries, such as Baladin in Piedmont, are growing fast: Baladin now supplies its own specialist beer bars and restaurants in most major cities. Lacking a beer culture in Italy, many of the artisan breweries, including Baladin, turn to Belgium for styles and recipes. But a growing number of brewers are now producing pale ales and IPAs, and importing hops from Europe and the US to give them the correct aromas and flavours.

Birrificio Lambrate, Gaina IPA/ Quarantot Double IPA

Lambrate is a district of Milan and the brewery based there has grown rapidly since it was launched in 1996. It has expanded several times to keep up with demand and now produces 4,000 hectolitres per brew. It has added a pub (5 Via Adelchi) and a restaurant (60 Via Golgi). It has a laid-back, modern style: the key people are Alessandro, Fabio, Paolo, Davide and Giampaolo – with no surnames required. They call themselves the pioneers of craft brewing in Milan and work with the hopeful slogan 'Who drinks beers lives 100 years'.

All their beers are unfiltered and unpasteurized. Gaina means 'chicken' and is Milanese slang for the way drunk people walk: presumably they won't make it to 100. The beer is brewed with Pilsner, CaraMunich and carapils and hopped with Cascade, Centennial, Simcoe and Zeus varieties that create 60 bitterness units. Quarantot means 'forty-eight' and refers to a saying meaning 'to make a mess': this in turn refers to the uprisings in 1848 that led to the first Italian War of Independence. The beer is not a mess: it's brewed with pale Pilsner malt and hopped with Cascade, Centennial, Chinook, Equinox, Mosaic and Summit varieties that produce a resounding 140 units of bitterness.

The verdict

Gaina is pale bronze in colour and has an aroma of fresh chestnuts, fruity hops and freshly baked bread. The palate offers ripe malt, citrus fruit and bitter hops followed by a bittersweet finish that becomes dry and hoppy but has a fine balance of biscuit malt and ripe fruit. Quarantot is extremely pale with a big aroma of herbal and spicy hops, orange and lemon fruit, and honeyed malt. Lemon fruit builds in the mouth with pine-like hops and toasted grain. The finish is long and complex, bittersweet initially with ripe fruit notes and honeyed malt but ending dry and intensely bitter.

ABV	6%/8%
First brewed	circa 2000
Brewery	Birrificio Lambrate, Milan
Website	www.birrificiolambrate.com

'A Magara, Mericana India Pale Ale

Eraldo Corti discovered good beer when he drank English bitter during a trip to the UK in 1999. When he returned home he started to brew in his kitchen with a group of friends and then made the step up to commercial production in 2014. 'A Magara is Calabrian dialect for 'witch' and Eraldo hopes he has brought some magic to the region, with beers that are unfiltered and conditioned in the bottle. His IPA is brewed with unnamed hops, but the aroma and flavour suggest they are New World varieties. The beer has a hazy bronze colour, with pine kernels, lemon zest and toasted malt on the aroma. The palate is fruity and herbal with biscuit malt and spicy hops, followed by a dry, fruity, herbal and pine-like finish with a good balance of toasted malt.

ABV	6.7%
First brewed	2014
Brewery	A Magara, Nocera Terinese
Website	www.alchimiacalabra.it

Brewfist, Spaceman West Coast IPA

This brewery in Lombardy, founded in 2010, is making a good name for itself among beer lovers with a range that is mainly inspired by the craft brewing scene in the United States. Spaceman is its best known and biggest-selling beer. It's brewed with Pilsner malt and hopped with Citra, Columbus and Simcoe varieties that clock up 70 units of bitterness. The beer is not pasteurized and has a pale gold colour with a big hit of grapefruit and peach on the aroma, with biscuit malt and peppery hops. Bittersweet fruit and bitter hops dominate the palate but with a good balance of toasted grain. The finish is dry, hoppy and bitter, with continuing notes of peach, toasted malt and peppery hops, leading to a better climax.

ABV	7%
First brewed	2010
Brewery	Brewfist, Codogno
Website	www.brewfist.com

Birrificio La Ribalta, Falstaff Double IPA

There's a rare sight on the bar at La Ribalta in Milan – British handpumps. The microbrewery opened in 2015 and the founders – Alessandro Meco, Riccardo Berenato and Davide Bottini – brew several beers inspired by British pale ales and bitters. They import specialist British and American yeast cultures to obtain the correct balance of flavours for their beers and they say the hard water in Milan is ideal for brewing pale ales.

Their strong IPA has an American twist, using Cascade, Chinook, Columbus and Simcoe hops. As a result of adding cara malt to pale malt, the beer has a chestnut colour with a 'malt loaf' aroma and a raisin fruit note along with spicy hops. There's a massive hit of dark fruit on the palate, with toasted malt and spicy, herbal and floral hops. The finish lingers, toasted malt and dark fruits balancing an increasing bitterness.

ABV	7.5%
First brewed	2015
Brewery	Birrificio La Ribalta, Milan
Website	No website

Birrificio Otus, Lolipa IPA (BS4.7)

'Otus' means 'owl' and the name was chosen to emphasize the founders' commitment to the environment and using local ingredients as far as possible. Some of the beers have the addition of herbs and plants plucked from the countryside.

The company was created by a group of beer lovers who pooled their resources and sought further financial backing from kindred spirits in the area who became small shareholders. The brewery is run by Anna Cremonesi, Raoul Tiraboschi and Ruben Agazzi, with experienced head brewer Mauro Bertolini. They are currently brewing 100,000 litres a year but plan to grow that figure to one million. Each brew has a batch number, hence BS4.7, as well as a descriptive name. It's brewed with pale and crystal malts and hopped with El Dorado, Mosaic and Sorachi Ace varieties. In spite of the crystal malt, it's an extremely pale gold beer with lemon fruit and woody hops on the nose and a cracker-like malt note. Intensely bitter hops build on the palate, with light biscuit malt and tart fruit. The finish has some fruity sweetness to start but the hops take over, sidelining the malt and ending bitter and spicy.

ABV	4.5%
First brewed	2016
Brewery	Birrificio Otus, Seriate
Website	www.birrificiootus.com

Birrificio Rurale, Hop Art/Scarliga European Double India Pale Ale

As the name suggests, this is a brewery in the countryside in Lombardy but close to Milan. It was opened in 2009 by Beppe Serafini, Silvio Copelli, Lorenzo Guarino, Stefano Carnelli and Mark Hunt and they have quickly built a strong following in the region for their wide range of beers. Hop Art uses different hops each year: the beer tasted for this book is hazy and pale, with pine kernels, spicy hops, a hint of liquorice, juicy malt and lemon fruit on the aroma. The palate is bittersweet with lemon fruit, spicy hops and juicy malt to the fore. The finish has a good balance of biscuit malt, spicy hops and tart fruit. The double IPA is labelled 'European' because it uses hops from Europe – Dana and Kazbek – in preference to New World varieties. It's pale gold with a surprising note of nutmeg on the nose, and woody hops and toasted malt. The palate is fruity – pears, tangerine and apricot – with juicy malt and spicy hops. The finish is bittersweet to start, with a powerful presence of ripe fruit, pear, but biscuit malt and woody hops combine to make a dry conclusion.

ABV	Hop Art 4.4%/Scarliga 8.5%
First brewed	circa 2012/13
Brewery	Birrificio Rurale, Desio
Website	www.birrificiorurale.it

Toccalmatto, Skizoid American IPA

Bruno Carilli describes his brewery as The Beer Freak Show and says his beers are for hop freaks: you get the message. He worked in the food and drinks industry for several years before setting up his brewery in 2008. He has a vast range of beers, drawing on brewing experience from all round the world: they include Russian Imperial Stout, English barley wine, Belgian saison and gruit, an ancient style made with herbs and spices and without hops.

His IPA, on the other hand, doesn't lack hops. They are all American: Centennial, Chinook and Columbus, combining with pale and cara malts to produce a copper-coloured beer with apricot, peaches and pine on the aroma, 'malt loaf' grain and herbal, grassy hops. Bitterness builds on the palate with a superb balance of chewy grain and herbs and spices. The finish is intensely bitter and hoppy.

ABV	6.2%
First brewed	2008
Brewery	Birra Toccalmatto, Fidenza
Website	www.birratoccalmatto.com

Vale la Pena, Amarafemmena IPA

This has to be the most unusual IPA brewed anywhere in the world – by prisoners in a jail in Rome. The project is supported by a number of Italian craft brewers and is financed by the government. The aim is to give prisoners training with a view to working as brewers when they leave jail. They are allowed out on day release to use a small brewing plant in Rome, where they are joined by professional brewers.

The IPA, for example, is made in collaboration with Francesco Amato of Birrificio del Vesuvio, a brewery near Naples. The ingredients are not revealed, but the bottle-conditioned beer has a hazy gold colour and a herbal and spicy aroma with hints of cinnamon and toasted malt. Toasted malt dominates the palate, but there's a good balance of bitter and spicy hops with a continuing cinnamon note. The finish is dry, spicy and malty, but the herbal and cinnamon note continues to the end.

ABV	6.1%
First brewed	2015
Brewery	Birra Vale la Pena, Rome
Website	www.valelapena.it

Switzerland

Switzerland has played a long and important role in brewing. The abbey of Saint Gallen, founded in the eighth century, was one of Europe's greatest brewing monasteries, and historians have used its archives to describe malting and brewing techniques in the medieval period.

The Hürlimann brewery in Zurich was established in 1836 and used ice cut from the foothills of the Alps to develop modern lager brewing. Its scientists carried out a long analysis of yeast which enabled lager beers of up to 12 per cent alcohol to be developed: the brewery's yeast was made available to other brewers and led to the strong Bock beers in Germany. Hürlimann's own Samichlaus (Santa Claus) beer, lagered for a year, was for a period the strongest beer in the world, though it's long been overtaken. While the country is best known for its lager beers, young brewers are now casting their net wider and are taking inspiration from abroad.

Bière Trois Dames, Pasionaria IPA Double

Raphaël Mettler and his wife Sylvie set up their brewery in 2008: they mastered brewing techniques, studied opportunities in the local beer market, and developed a distribution system throughout Switzerland. They teamed up with an American company to make their beers available in the US. In 2009 they were joined by experienced brewer Mike Vermeulen and the brewery now employs a sizeable staff. The range includes oak-aged and fruit-based beers. The brewery is named in honour of Sylvie and her two daughters, but the woman on the label of the double IPA salutes the memory of Dolores Ibárruri, a leading Republican in the Spanish Civil War who was known as La Pasionaria – passion flower. She was celebrated for her slogan 'No pasarán!' – 'they shall not pass' – during the battle of Madrid in 1936. She lived in exile and returned to Spain in 1977 when she was elected to parliament. She died in 1989. The beer brewed in her honour is produced with Pilsner, crystal and wheat malts and hopped with Columbus and Simcoe, which create 80 bitterness units.

The verdict

A deep bronze/amber beer with a deep fluffy collar of foam, followed by a big aroma of peppery and woody hops, dark sultana-like fruit and rich, toasted malt. Bitter and spicy hops build in the mouth, but there's a solid backbone of toasted malt and burnt fruit. The finish is deep and complex, dominated by rich toasted malt and dark fruit, but peppery hops provide balance as the beer finally ends dry.

ABV	9%
First brewed	2010
Brewery	Brasserie Trois Dames, Sainte-Croix
Website	www.brasserie3dames.ch

Kitchen Brew, Session IPA

Fabian Ehinger was bitten by the beer bug on a long trip to the United States and he returned home with a mission to brew commercially. He set up a 25-litre micro-plant in a disused kitchen and produced his first beer in 2013. He then used the plant of the Saint Louis Brewery in Basel until he was able to open his own micro-brewery in 2016 where he produces 2,000 litres a year.

The IPA is brewed with German Pilsner and cara malts and hopped with Mosaic from Washington State. Fabian uses an American yeast culture. The bronze coloured beer has a floral, herbal and spicy hop aroma with lightly toasted malt. Bitter hops dominate the palate with juicy malt and orange and lemon fruit notes. The tart fruit carries over into the finish, with malt fading as bitter hops increase their presence, leading to a dry finale. The brewery has a tap room for visitors.

ABV	4.5%
First brewed	2016
Brewery	Kitchen Brew, Allschwil, Basel
Website	www.kitchenbrew.ch

Germany

Germany is renowned and revered throughout the world for its magnificent traditional lagers and wheat beers that are carefully made from the finest natural ingredients and allowed to age without rush. Brewing adheres to the 16th-century Reinheitsgebot, or purity law, that allows only malted grain, hops, yeast and water to be used. But in 2016, when there were celebrations to mark 500 years of the law, a number of young craft brewers started to rebel against its restrictions and challenged it with beers using other ingredients.

Other brewers have started to look abroad for the inspiration for new beers. This has led to pale ale and IPA making an appearance in Germany, and one major California brewery has set up shop in Berlin to deliver fresh IPAs to Europe. It will be fascinating to follow the impact of Stone in Berlin.

The great revival

And Union, Friday/Handwerk

In the modern parlance of the brewing world, And Union is a 'gypsy' or 'cuckoo' brewery, which has no brewery of its own but works on a co-operative basis with a number of independent producers in Bavaria. The springboard for the company was in South Africa, where beer lovers Rui Esteves and Brad Armitage were frustrated by the lack of good beer in the country and the high start-up costs of launching a brewery there. In Bavaria in 2007 they teamed up with beer expert Axel Ohm and gastronomist Patrick Rüther to plan beers that were made in small batches and properly matured. The majority of the beers are produced by Arcobräu, which has been brewing in Moos, Bavaria, since 1567. Using that experience, the And Union IPAs are aged for between eight and ten weeks – Germans would call that 'lagering'. They are not filtered or pasteurized and are faithful to the Reinheitsgebot (beer purity law). Friday is described as 'Über IPA', which suggests it's more than a traditional IPA, though it's not exceptionally strong by modern American standards: And Union says, in English, that it's 'not for woosies'. It's brewed with pale malt and hopped with Chinook and Hallertau Aroma varieties that create 55 bitterness units. Handwerk is called an 'every day' IPA or session beer. It has the same malt and hop recipe as Friday and the hops reach 40 bitterness units. And Union has an aggressive export policy and its beers are available in Britain, Ireland, other European countries, the Baltic States and South Africa.

The verdict

Friday has a fruity – tangerine and peach – aroma with spicy and herbal hop notes and rich toasted malt. Honeyed malt combines well in the mouth with tropical fruits and grassy and peppery hops. The finish is long, with toasted malt interweaving with bittersweet fruit and grassy hops, but finally ending dry. Handwerk has a honeyed malt aroma with herbal hops and apricots on the nose. The palate balances dry fruits, creamy malt and herbal, grassy hops, with a bittersweet finish in which herbal hops blend well fruit and toasted malt.

ABV	Friday 6.5%/Handwerk 5.5%
First brewed	circa 2010
Brewery	And Union, Munich
Website	www.andunion.com

BrauKollektiv, Dolly India Pale Ale

The name of the beer allows the owners of BrauKollektiv scope for jokes. They say it's 'an IPA so good that it can't be cloned' and 'it's unlike the rest of the flock'.

You will gather that this is not an entirely German operation. It was founded in 2014 by keen home-brewers Gil Scheuermann, James Tutor, Chris Murphy and Bernhard Frenzel: Murphy is from Melbourne, Australia, while Tutor hails from Long Beach, California. The beer is named in honour of Dolly (1996–2003), from Scotland, the first sheep to be cloned.

The IPA has a complex recipe of Pilsner, pale ale, Munich and Vienna malts and is hopped with Amarillo, Simcoe, Magnum and Tettnang varieties. The unfiltered beer has a hazy bronze colour and a tempting aroma of floral/herbal and spicy hops balanced by rich biscuit malt. Bittersweet citrus fruit builds in the mouth with creamy malt and spicy hops. The finish is quenching and finally dry but with notes of creamy malt, bitter and spicy hops and continuing tangy fruit.

BrauKollektiv also brews Jacques West Coast IPA with 7.9 per cent alcohol.

ABV	6.9%
First brewed	2014
Brewery	BrauKollektiv, Freiburg
Website	www.braukollektiv.com

Riedenburger Brauhaus, Dolden Sud IPA

This is a traditional family-owned Bavarian brewery, founded in 1866, and run today by Max and Katrin Krieger, the fifth generation of the family.

Since 1989 they have added to the usual range of Bavarian beers – Helles lager, dark or Dunkel and wheat beers – an IPA that uses a blend of local, American and English hops: Amarillo, Cascade, Centennial, Chinook, Hallertau Mittelfruh, Pilgrim and Spalter. The beer has 55 units of bitterness and is brewed with locally grown summer barley.

The pale, hazy gold beer has an intense, spicy and herbal aroma with lightly toasted malt and woody/cedar hops. Hop bitterness grows on the palate against a toasted malt backbone with tart lemon fruit notes. The finish is bitter, with hops dominating but with continuing contributions from lemon fruit and biscuit malt. All in all, it is an outstanding beer.

Since 1989 the brewery has made only organic beer according to Bioland guidelines and its beers are not filtered. Much of the grain comes from the gardens of the Plankstetten monastery.

ABV	6.5%
First brewed	circa 1989
Brewery	Riedenburger Brauhaus, Riedenburg
Website	www.riedenburger.de

Schönramer, India Pale Ale

Schönram brewery is more than 230 years old and brews a typical range of German beers: Helles lager, dark or Dunkel beer and wheat beer. It has added an IPA due to the influence of brewer Eric Toft, who looks every inch a Bavarian in his lederhosen but is from the United States and has a mission to stir up the conservative Bavarian brewing scene.

His IPA is high in alcohol and uses local pale malt and the Hallertau Mandarina hop, fermented with an American yeast culture. The beer is pale gold in colour and has an entrancing aroma of toasted malt, spicy, peppery and herbal hops, and a note of fresh tobacco. Bitter hops build in the mouth, with sappy malt and orange fruit. The finish is dry and bitter with a growing fruit note and continuing spicy and herbal hops.

ABV	7.8%
First brewed	2015
Brewery	Braurerei Schönram, Petting
Website	www.brauerei-schoenram.de

Stone, Ruination Double IPA

What is a brewery based in California doing in Berlin? The answer is offering IPA to Berliners and also distributing its beers fresh and unpasteurized from the plant to other European countries. Greg Koch, founder and chief executive of Stone, checked 130 sites in Europe before settling on Berlin. The full title of the complex is Stone Brewing World Bistro and Gardens and it is based at Marienpark. The plant can produce 45,000 hectolitres or 38,000 barrels a year, with space to expand to 150,000hl. The site opened in the summer of 2016 and as well as several restaurants there are plans for a bakery and art galleries. Stone will test the German Beer Purity Law with a vanilla porter but is concentrating on IPA. The full range of its pale ales is reproduced here and it will be interesting to see how Berliners react to Ruination, a beer that has 100 units of bitterness from Azacca, Centennial, Citra, Chinook, Magnum and Simcoe varieties. The pale gold beer has a massive aroma of citrus and tropical fruits balanced by pine-like notes and juicy malt. Hop bitterness and bittersweet fruit build in the mouth, and the finish starts bittersweet but ends with a shatteringly dry and iodine-like hop character.

ABV	8.5%
First brewed	2016
Brewery	Stone Brewing, Berlin
Website	www.stonebrewing.eu

Vagabund, Double IPA

Americans David Spengler, Tom Crozier and Matthew Walthall opened their bar in the Wedding district of Berlin in 2013; a year later they added a microbrewery, producing just 200 litres or 350 pints per brew. They came to Berlin by different routes but joined forces in a band and enjoyed brewing their own beer so much that they decided to turn their hobby into a commercial operation. The pub is small but spacious, dominated by a large bar with a notice announcing 'Our beers are brewed from malt, hops, yeast and water and are unpasteurized, unfiltered and unhomogenized': an American interpretation of the Reinheitsgebot. The bar at 3 Antwerpener Strasse opens at 5pm weekdays and 1pm Saturday and Sunday and 'we close when we close'. Beer is available for take-home.

The double IPA is brewed with pale malt and Cascade, Centennial and Columbus hops and dry hopped with Simcoe. It has a cloudy bronze colour and a big elderflower and cinnamon aroma with biscuit malt and spicy hops. The palate is intensely dry with hints of lemon fruit, cracker-like malt and peppery hops. The finish has a challenging bitterness with powerful notes of crackers, lemon fruit and peppery hops.

ABV	7.5%
First brewed	2014
Brewery	Vagabund Brauerei, Berlin
Website	www.vagabundbrauerei.com

Scandinavia

In spite of the cold climate, Scandinavia is dominated by lager beer, with the tentacles of Carlsberg and its many subsidiaries gripping production and supply. But there is an older tradition of brewing *øl*, meaning 'ale'. With the exception of a few hardy independents, ale brewing slipped below the ice floes in the 19th and 20th centuries.

But, aware of the significant developments in the United States and Europe, new brewers have appeared to restore the ale tradition, but with a modern and hoppy twist. IPA is the vogue beer, but in many cases the artisans producing IPAs are known as 'gypsy' or 'cuckoo' brewers because they use other companies' equipment in a variety of countries to make their beers.

Mikkeller, Session IPA

Mikkeller is a phenomenon. It started in a kitchen in Copenhagen in 2006 and today its beers are brewed in many countries, with bars in several more. The beers are unconventional and often use unexpected ingredients, but they are made with serious intent by a restless and iconoclastic lover of grain, hops and anything else he can lay his hands on. Mikkel Borg Bjergsø taught maths and physics in Copenhagen, and brewed beer at home in his spare time. As his interest grew, he was determined to offer a better choice in a country dominated by Carlsberg and its Tuborg subsidiary. He said he wanted to take drinkers on an 'intense taste adventure' and began to experiment with different ingredients: to date he has brewed beers with avocados, chillies, chocolate, beans, syrups, epazote (a herb often used to make tea in Central and South America) and coffee beans.

Brewing takes place around the world as Mikkel travels to work with kindred spirits. In the early days, he worked regularly with De Proef in Belgium – the beer described here was brewed at De Proef – but he has created beers in the United States, Britain and the Far East. He has built a specialist small plant in Copenhagen to make oak-matured beers. When I asked him how many IPAs he produced, he said bluntly: 'Lots – and all the time.' The beer chosen for this book offers no more than a glimpse of his work. There will be many more to enjoy in the future: you can follow his journey on the brewery's website that also lists the growing number of Mikkeller bars in the US, Europe and the Far East. The session IPA is simple and straightforward by Mikkeller standards, brewed with pale malt and Citra hops. It's somewhat different to an earlier interpretation, Invasion Farmhouse IPA, which was brewed at Anchorage Brewing in Alaska and fermented with the wild yeast culture Brettanomyces.

The verdict

This really is pale ale, just a hint of colour in its cheeks. Tart lemon fruit dominates the aroma with floral/herbal/elderflower notes and honeyed malt. Bitter hops make their presence felt on the palate with continuing lemon fruit and creamy/honeyed malt. The finish is quenching, a fine balance of tart fruit, creamy malt and bitter hop resins.

ABV	4.5%
First brewed	2015; beers change frequently
Brewery	Mikkeller, Copenhagen, Denmark
Website	www.mikkeller.dk

Gotlands Bryggeri, Sitting Bulldog IPA

Gotland is Sweden's biggest island and was once best known for mead, a honey-based drink, and Gotlandsdricka, a type of beer similar to Finnish sahti, made with rye and filtered through juniper twigs. The island now has a brewery producing a wide range of more modern beer styles, including IPA. Johan Spendrup is the son of a brewer and had beer in his blood when he opened his brewery in 1994. He has the advantage of top quality, locally grown barley and fine water filtered through limestone. His Sitting Bulldog IPA has a label with an image that is cross between the breed of dog and Sir Winston Churchill, who is a folk hero in Scandinavia for helping to defeat Germany in World War Two: Carlsberg Special Brew was produced to mark his visit to Copenhagen in 1950.

The Gotlands beer is brewed with pale ale, cara and crystal malts and is hopped with Cascade, Centennial and Chinook: all three hops are used to dry hop the beer, which has 60 units of bitterness. In common with all the brewery's beers, it's suitable for vegans. It has a copper/chestnut colour with an aroma like Dundee cake – raisins, sultanas and cherries with a marzipan topping. Some peppery hops peep through all this richness. Fruit and toasted malts dominate the palate with only a walk-on role for hops, but they make their presence felt in the finish, which ends dry but is preceded by more rich, dark fruit, nuts and toasted grain.

ABV	6.4%
First brewed	circa 2000
Brewery	Gotlands Bryggeri, Visby, Sweden
Website	www.gotlandsbryggeri.se

Omnipollo, Nebuchadnezzar Imperial India Pale Ale

Henok Fentie and Karl Grandin started making beer in 2011 and in just a few years they have built up an international reputation and now export to 20 countries. Henok was a keen home-brewer who wanted to turn commercial and 'change people's perceptions of beer', while Karl had worked in the clothing industry. Henok says he writes the recipes while Karl designs the labels for the beers. They are gypsy brewers: their imperial IPA was brewed at De Proef in Belgium, but the duo travel widely. They have brewed in the

United States at Prairie Artisan in Oklahoma and Tired Hands in Pennsylvania. Henok and Karl have opened Omnipollos Hatt at 1a Hökens Gata in Stockholm, a specialist pizza restaurant that serves their beers and other craft brews.

Their imperial IPA was named the Best Beer in Sweden in 2012 and 2013. It is brewed with Pilsner, carapils and wheat malts and hopped with Amarillo, Centennial, Columbus and Simcoe. The pale gold beer has a delightful, nose-tingling aroma of eucalyptus, freshly baked bread and spicy hops. The palate is superb: a fine balance of juicy malt, bitter hop resins and lemon, lime and grapefruit. The finish is intensely bitter, but biscuit malt and bittersweet fruit take the edge off the bitterness. It is deceptively drinkable.

ABV	8.5%
First brewed	2012
Brewery	Omnipollo, Stockholm, Sweden
Website	www.omnipollo.com

To Øl, First Frontier IPA

There's a close link between To Øl and Mikkeller (see page 269): Tore Gynther and Tobias Emil Jensen were studying in Copenhagen and their teacher was none other than Mikkel Borg Bjergsø. The three spent some time brewing beer in the college kitchen and when Mikkel went on to found his brewing business the other two followed in his footsteps in 2010. They have a similar model to their teacher: they are gypsy brewers, using other brewers' facilities to fashion their beers – First Frontier was produced at De Proef in Belgium. The duo has also opened BRUS bars in Copenhagen and Reykjavik.

First Frontier is modelled on the American IPA style and the label shows images from the old Wild West and the warning that 'We all got pieces of crazy in us, some bigger pieces than others.' It's brewed with Pilsner, pale ale, cara malt and Munich grains with flaked oats, and is hopped with Centennial, Simcoe and Warrior varieties. The beer has a hazy gold colour and a dried apricots and ripe pears aroma with woody hops and toasted grain. Bitter hops build in the mouth, but there's a good balance of nutty/toasted grain and ripe fruits. The finish is long and complex, bitter hops interweaving with cracker-like malt and ripe fruit.

ABV	7.1%
First brewed	2011
Brewery	To Øl, Copenhagen, Denmark
Website	www.to-ol.dk

Australia

For decades, beer was dominated by mass market lager brands such as Foster's, Castlemaine XXXX and VB Bitter – which is not a bitter – all owned by global companies. The ale flag was kept flying by Coopers of Adelaide, with their sparkling ale and stout. Derided by mainstream drinkers as hopelessly old-fashioned, Coopers has had the last laugh and has become a cult producer, making more beer than all the other new craft breweries combined. Frustratingly, given Coopers' English origins, it's disappointing to find it hasn't added an IPA but, in its defence, it's hard pressed to keep up with the demand for its regular portfolio.

Australia has also responded with the highly prized Galaxy hop that creates more modern citrus character than the long-standing Pride of Ringwood. While none of the beers listed here use Galaxy it is being taken up by a growing number of craft brewers in the region.

Little Creatures, IPA

Little Creatures is the most talked-about and prize-winning of the new craft breweries in Australia, the one that was the touchpaper which ignited the brewing renaissance. Its rise has been spectacular, starting – inauspiciously – in a building that was once part of a crocodile farm; today it has smart modern breweries on both sides of the vast continent, in Fremantle and Geelong. It was the dream of Howard Cearns, Nic Trimboli and Phil Sexton, who had been inspired by American pale ales and launched their own version in 2000. They have added IPA and other styles, but it's their Pale Ale that remains the major product and the one that is most widely exported. The name of the brewery is derived not from the many furry creatures that inhabit Australia but from the Talking Heads album *Little Creatures* – which could refer to the yeast cells that transform malt sugars into alcohol.

There was consternation in 2013 when Little Creatures was taken over by the giant Lion Nathan group, which in turn is owned by Kirin of Japan, the biggest player in the beer markets of the Far East and Australasia. But unlike Europe and North America, the global brewers in the southern hemisphere are less concerned with cost-cutting and centralization, and Lion Nathan invested $60 million in the new Geelong complex. The breweries are now producing 10 million litres a year. In 2016 Little Creatures won the trophy for Champion Australian Craft Beer.

IPA is brewed with pale, carapils, Munich and cara rye malts and is hopped with varieties from both north and south: East Kent Goldings from England for bitterness, local Vic Secret in the whirlpool, New Zealand Southern Cross for aroma and American Amarillo for dry hopping. Bitterness units are 60.

The verdict

The amber/copper beer has a big hit of grapefruit and passion fruit on the aroma with peppery hops and rich biscuit malt. Bittersweet fruit coats the palate, but there's a solid malt backbone of chewy malt balanced by bitter hop resins. The finish is long, with continuing ripe fruit, bitter and peppery hops and nutty malt.

ABV	6.4%
First brewed	2013
Brewery	Little Creatures, Fremantle and Geelong
Website	www.littlecreatures.com.au

Feral Brewing Company, Hop Hog

Feral started life in 2002 surrounded by wineries in the Swan Valley region of Western Australia near Perth. Brewer and founder Brendan Varis quickly built a big following for his beers and he has won a shelf-load of awards in Australian competitions. Demand led to a move to a new plant in Perth where five million litres a year are now produced. A brewpub, which also offers excellent Australian cooking, has an experimental micro-plant for testing new brews and producing barrel-aged beers.

Hop Hog is brewed with pale and cara malts and is hopped and dry hopped with all-American varieties: Amarillo, Cascade, Centennial and Magnum, which create 48 bitterness units. The golden beer has a big citrus attack on the nose, with biscuit malt and pine-like hop notes. Hops explode on the tongue, but there's a solid malt backbone and bittersweet fruit. The finish is a tantalizing blend of bitter hop resins, rich fruit and juicy malt leading into a hoppy finale.

ABV	5.8%
First brewed	circa 2009
Brewery	Feral Brewing Company, Perth, WA
Website	www.feralbrewing.com.au

Fixation, IPA

'We're obsessed with great IPA,' says founder and brewer Tom Delmont and he proved the point by winning gold medals for Fixation at both the Australian International Beer Awards and the Craft Beer Awards for his interpretation of the style.

The brewery is an offshoot of Stone & Wood Brewing, which helped fund Tom when he said he wanted to make beer – but only IPA. He fell in love with the style on a lengthy tour of craft breweries in the United States and returned home with a mission to deliver beer with a profound hop character for Australian drinkers.

His IPA is made with pale malt and a dash of speciality grains and is hopped with Amarillo, Citra, Mosaic and Simcoe varieties that create 65 bitterness units. The beer has a pronounced grapefruit aroma, balanced by lightly toasted malt and floral and herbal hop notes. The palate is rich in bittersweet fruit, intensely bitter hops and rich malt, characteristics that follow through into the finish, which finally ends with a quinine-like bitterness. Fixation also makes a Double IPA.

Tom believes that IPAs are best drunk when young and fresh, so, going against the received wisdom of storing IPAs for several months, you won't find any aged IPAs at his brewery.

ABV	6.4%
First brewed	2015
Brewery	Fixation Brewing Company, Byron Bay, NSW
Website	www.fixationbrewing.com.au

Holgate Brewhouse, Hopinator

Paul Holgate from Manchester in England brought a love of good beer with him to Australia; his wife Natasha is from Sri Lanka and has an equal passion for good food. They combined their skills by building their microbrewery alongside a restored 19th-century hotel where guests can match beers with delicious meals. Paul even brings a touch of the Old Country to the bar, with hand pumps dispensing cask-conditioned ales, something of a rarity down under.

Hopinator, Paul's double American IPA, is amber-red thanks to an addition of Vienna red malt to pale. He adds hops no fewer than six times during the copper boil and the whirlpool stages. The varieties are American Centennial, Citra, Chinook, Mosaic and Simcoe. The finished beer has 65 to 66 units of bitterness and has a massive blast of fruit on the aroma and palate: grapefruit, orange, lemon and passion fruit, balanced by biscuit malt with hints of caramel and butterscotch. The long finish is bitter and hoppy with a continuing influence of toasted malt and caramel. The finale is dry and intensely hoppy.

ABV	7%
First brewed	2002
Brewery	Holgate Brewhouse, Woodend, Victoria
Website	www.holgatebrewhouse.com

Murray's, Icon 2 IPA

Murray's shares its home with vineyards and eucalyptus trees. It was founded in 2005 by Shawn Sherlock who had a passion for hops, to such an extent that he added them not only in the boiling copper but also in the mash tun and during the 'run off', when the sweet wort leaves the tun: this is a rare if not unique system.

Shawn left to open the Foghorn brewhouse in Newcastle and his work at Murray's has been carried on by Sean Costigan and Alex Tucker. For their strong IPA they use Maris Otter pale malt imported from England, with crystal and Vienna malts for colour and flavour. The hops are all American: Amarillo, Cascade and Equinox, which create 80 units of bitterness. The beer has a burnished copper colour and an aroma of passion fruit and tangerine, with peppery hops and a caramel note from the darker grains. The palate is a fine balance of biscuit malt, bitter hop resins and tart fruit followed by a dry finish dominated by bitter and spicy hops but with a good balance of rich malt and fruit.

ABV	7.5%
First brewed	2006
Brewery	Murray's Craft Brewing, Port Stephens, NSW
Website	www.murraysbrewingco.com.au

Newstead Brewing Company, Two to the Valley IPA

Mark Howe's brewery and pub stand in the shadow of the mighty Castlemaine Brewery of XXXX fame in the Newstead district of Brisbane, but he draws large crowds of drinkers and diners to his place at 85 Doggett Street. Mark studied for a PhD in molecular bioscience, which led to a keen interest in brewing. With financial support from his parents, he went into partnership with restaurateur Michael Conrad and their IPA won a gold medal in the Australian International Beer Awards.

The name of the beer stems from not-too-friendly relations between locals and American troops quartered in Newstead during World War Two: the Aussies would tell the soldiers that the local tram cost 'two pence to the valley', backed with an appropriate hand gesture. The beer is brewed with pale and cara malts and hopped with Cascade, Centennial, Citra and Simcoe, with 75 units of bitterness. The deep gold beer has a big hit of citrus fruit on the aroma with toasted malt and spicy hops. Grapefruit, peach, lychee and mango dominate the palate with a good balance of biscuit malt and bitter and spicy hops. Malt, fruit and hops combine in the long finish, but the finale is all about intense hop bitterness.

ABV	5.9%
First brewed	2014
Brewery	Newstead Brewing Company, Brisbane, QLD
Website	www.newsteadbrewing.com.au

Pirate Life, IIPA

Perhaps Coopers – Adelaide's large and long-established family-owned brewery – doesn't feel the need to add IPA to its range because Pirate is making the running with what one writer calls a 'monstrous' version, an imperial IPA high in alcohol and with a mighty 120 units of bitterness.

Pirate Life was founded in 2014 and had built up such a head of steam that it was named Champion Small Brewery in the 2016 Australian International Beer Awards, with a similar prize in the Craft Beer Awards that year. The style of the brewery founded by Jack Cameron and Red Proudfoot owes a lot to the fact that the duo worked for a while with BrewDog in Scotland (see page 216): as a result, they have a nonconformist approach to brewing and publicity but with less of the BrewDog bombast.

The imperial IPA is brewed with pale, cara and wheat malts and is hopped to the gunwales with all-American Centennial, Columbus, Mosaic and Simcoe varieties. The bronze beer has a mighty blast of every citrus aroma you can think of, with a rich biscuit malt note and woody and peppery hops. Bittersweet fruit coats the mouth with a solid honeyed malt backbone and bitter and resinous hops. The long and complex finish has bittersweet fruit and honeyed malt at first, but the hops and intense iodine bitterness take over in the finale.

ABV	8.8%
First brewed	2015
Brewery	Pirate Life Brewing, Hindmarsh, Adelaide, SA
Website	www.piratelife.com.au

New Zealand

New Zealand's craft brewers have had a long struggle and many didn't survive due to the awesome power of Steinlager, owned by Kirin of Japan since 2009. But Kiwi microbreweries are now flourishing, helped to a large extent by the worldwide demand for the country's magnificent new hop varieties, including Nelson Sauvin, Motueka and Riwaka that are grown without pesticides and chemical fertilizers.

Epic, Armageddon IPA/Hop Zombie

Epic was founded by Luke Nicholas in 2008; he had lived for several years in California, where he acquired a taste for strongly hopped pale ales and IPAs, Sierra Nevada's beers in particular. When he returned to New Zealand he teamed up with Kelly Ryan, who had also been travelling and had brewed with Thornbridge in Derbyshire, where he helped formulate the highly praised Jaipur IPA (see page 199).

The duo not only launched Armageddon but, in the finest traditions of IPA, put two oak casks of the beer on the ferry between the North and South Islands. The casks made 126 crossings, and when tasted the beer was not only deemed to be magnificent but had increased in strength to 7.2 per cent as a result of activity by wild yeasts in the wood. They have repeated the experiment several times and offer the version of the beer as a seasonal one. The regular beer is brewed with English pale malt and a light touch of cara malt while four American hops – Cascade, Centennial, Columbus and Simcoe – create 66 units of bitterness. Hop Zombie is a more recent addition to the range and is described as a double IPA. It's brewed with pale and Pilsner malt, but Luke and Kelly have gone all shy and say the hops are a secret. But they do reveal the bitterness units are 90.

The verdict

Armageddon has a pale copper colour with an enormous blast of lemon and grapefruit on the nose along with bitter hop resins and toasted malt. Bittersweet fruit, an oatcake-like grain note and intensely bitter hops fill the mouth while the long finish has tangy fruit, bitter hops and biscuit malt. Hop Zombie is as pale as a Pilsner with a rich and alluring aroma of sherbet lemons and pine kernels, with toasted malt and peppery hops. Ripe fruit coats the tongue with malt and hops adding balance, and there is a long, deep finish of bittersweet fruit, juicy malt and woody hops.

ABV	Armageddon 6.6%/Hop Zombie 8.5%
First brewed	2008
Brewery	Epic Brewing Company, Otahuhu, Auckland
Website	www.epicbeer.com

8 Wired Brewing, Hopwired IPA

Søren Eriksen is a wandering Dane who lived in Perth in Australia, where he drank Little Creatures and found that beer didn't have to be pale, fizzy stuff. His wife Monique bought him a Coopers home-brewing kit and when they moved to New Zealand they decided to brew on a commercial basis. Søren wanted to make IPA and he and Monique felt strongly that they should use all New Zealand ingredients and give IPA a Kiwi rather than an American hop character. For several years Søren used other brewers' kit but in 2009 he was able to open his own plant at Warkworth and two years later 8 Wired was named Champion Brewery of New Zealand.

The name of the brewery comes from a type of wire used in electric fencing; drinkers will certainly get an electric kick from an IPA with a distinctively different character to American-inspired ones. It's brewed with Gladfield pale malt with cara, crystal and Munich malts and the hops are Motueka, Nelson Sauvin and Southern Cross. The pale bronze beer has an aroma of passion fruit, limes, oranges, gooseberries and Sauvignon Blanc grapes, with cracker-like grain and hop resins. Toasted malt, ripe fruit and bitter hops dominate the palate followed by a long, complex finish that has bittersweet fruit interweaving with toasted grain and spicy hops.

ABV	7.3%
First brewed	2010
Brewery	8 Wired Brewing Company, Warkworth
Website	www.8wired.co.nz

Liberty Brewing, C!tra Double IPA

Joseph and Christina Wood are keen that you spot the use of the exclamation mark in the name of their beer, as they think it's rather special.

They have had a peripatetic life as brewers. Joseph brewed at home because he couldn't find any decent beer in West Auckland. When the Woods moved to New Plymouth they found it was even more of a beer desert until they discovered an online ingredients supplier called Liberty Brewing. The Woods not only bought the business but took the next logical step of building a small plant to use the malts and hops available. That proved such a success that they had to extend the plant more than once before moving back to the Auckland area, where they now have plant capable of producing 4,000 litres per brew.

C!tra is brewed with pale, crystal and Munich malts and 'secret hops' – not much of a secret given the beer's name. It has 90 units of bitterness. The pale gold beer has a pungent aroma of tropical fruits and grapefruit, with a fresh-bread grain note and herbal hops. Lemon and grapefruit dominate the palate, but there's a growing biscuit malt note along with bitter hop resins. The finish is bittersweet to start, but lemon fruit and hops start to dominate, leading to a quenching and bitter finale.

ABV	9%
First brewed	2013
Brewery	Liberty Brewing Company, Helensville, Auckland
Website	www.libertybrewing.co.nz

Panhead, The Vandal New Zealand Pale Ale

In 2013 Mike Neilson moved into an old Dunlop tyre factory and opened a brewery dedicated to both good beer and hot rod cars. His huge success resulted in the brewery being bought by the international Lion group in 2016. He uses New Zealand hops to give his beers a distinctively Kiwi character.

The Vandal is named after a legendary hot-rodder called John Reid, who burned rubber back in the 1960s with an ancient Dodge called the Vandal, which features graphically on the label. The beer is brewed with pale malt and Motueka, Nelson Sauvin and Riwaka hops. The straw-coloured beer has a characteristic Sauvignon Blanc wine aroma from the Nelson Sauvin hops, with rich biscuit malt and woody notes from the hops. The palate is a teasing blend of bitter hops, tart fruit, honeyed malt and woody hops with a long finish in which hop bitterness grows, but is balanced by vinous fruit and juicy malt.

ABV	8%
First brewed	2013
Brewery	Panhead Custom Ales, Upper Hutt, Wellington
Website	www.panhead.co.nz

Weezledog, Hopster New Zealand IPA

Mark Jackman is from Yorkshire, with a great love of English bitter; when he arrived in New Zealand he was dismayed to find there was so little good beer with hops to drink in his new country. So he started to brew at home and when he met his wife-to-be Marie he discovered her family were keen home-brewers, too. Fired with the brewing bug, they went the extra mile and started to brew commercially: they are gypsy brewers, using the plant of the Black Sands Brewery in Kelston, Auckland. Mark, who also runs the BeerGeek website, uses only New Zealand malts and hops, with Nelson Sauvin the dominant variety. For Hopster he adds hops in the copper and the whirlpool and also dry hops the beer, which has a healthy 100 units of bitterness. It is neither filtered nor pasteurized. It's a hazy gold colour with a ripe pineapple and apricot aroma backed by rich toasted malt and floral hops. The palate is dry from fruit and hops with a good toasted malt backbone. The finish takes no prisoners: it's intensely bitter and hoppy with biscuit malt and ripe fruit providing a much-needed balance. This one's not for the faint-hearted.

ABV	6.7%
First brewed	2014
Brewery	Weezledog Brewing Company, Auckland
Website	www.weezledogbrewing.co.nz

China and Japan

China and Japan have come to beer by different routes. Some 9,000 years ago a type of beer, made without hops, was produced in China but it disappeared during the Han Dynasty (206BC–AD220) when it was replaced by a drink called *huangjiu*, a type of rice wine. Beer didn't reappear until the late 19th and early 20th centuries when 'treaty ports' were built to encourage foreign trade and breweries were established in China by Czech, German and Japanese companies. China's best-known beer, Tsingtao, came from a German brewery in Qingdao province, while the biggest-selling brand, Snow, was first brewed by a Japanese company. In recent years, as the economy has grown and with it a rising middle class, China has become more open to western influences. As a result of the size of the country and its vast population, it's now the world's biggest beer-producing nation although per capita consumption is low.

Japan had no brewing tradition at all until the mid-19th century. Until then, sake or rice wine was the drink of choice. In 1853 an American naval commander, Matthew Perry, arrived with four frigates in Tokyo Bay and invited local dignitaries on board. They were given beer and, according to legend, one of the locals discovered a handbook on brewing, which was translated, enabling beer-making to make a late appearance in the country. As a result of bizarre government legislation in the 20th century, breweries were allowed to operate only if they made upwards of 200,000 hectolitres year. But in 1994, the ceiling was lowered to 600 hectolitres, enabling a raft of new breweries to open up. This has led to rather more interesting beers being made than the thin lagers of the major breweries.

IPA has become a cult beer in China following the visit of President Xi Jinping to the UK in 2015. David Cameron took the president to the 16th-century Plough pub at Cadsden in Buckinghamshire, close to Chequers, the prime minister's official country residence. They had lunch of fish and chips, washed down with Greene King IPA. As a result of blanket TV coverage at home, a large number of Chinese tourists have since made their way to the Plough to enjoy a similar pub lunch. It has become such a popular venue that the pub was bought in 2016 by SinoFortune, a Chinese investment company. And Greene King has seen sales of its IPA increase by 1,600 per cent in China.

Sourcing beers from China is difficult, but the following breweries produce IPAs: Boxing Cat, Great Leap, Jing A and Slow Boat.

Nanjing Craft Brewing Company, Baby IPA

Brewing in China is not easy. Gao Yan, a pioneer of the craft brewing movement, has been closed down twice by the government as a result of red tape and restriction on importing such materials as hops. Hops are grown in the country but the industry is small and doesn't produce the varieties artisan brewers are looking for.

But Gao Yan is determined to go on: 'Challenge everything, see how much of my behaviour the government will tolerate,' he says. He lived in the United States for fourteen years, where he acquired a taste for craft beer and returned home to open his brewery in 2007. He produces 100,000 cases a year and, as well as brewing, he has written a manual, *Get Your Own Brew*, to encourage others to follow his path. The label of his IPA, depicting a baby holding a fish, is a traditional image heralding the Lunar New Year. The recipe is not detailed, but the colour of the beer suggests some crystal or cara malts are blended with pale malt. It's known that Gao Yan has used Cascade and Willamette hops from the US, but the hops may vary depending on availability.

The verdict

A copper-coloured beer with a malt-led aroma of toasted grain and sultana fruit, and some spicy hop notes. The palate has toasted grain and burnt fruit with gentle hop bitterness, followed by a rich malt finish that has a rye bread note, dark fruit and woody, spicy hops.

ABV	5.4%
First brewed	2007
Brewery	Nanjing Craft Brewing Company, Nanjing
Website	No website

Baird Beer, Teikoku IPA/Suruga Bay Imperial IPA

Bryan and Sayuri Baird's brewery has an idyllic location on the banks of the Kano river. They have such a passion for beer that they gave up their university courses in the United States to move to the Pacific North-west to study brewing in the heart of the American hop fields. They moved to Japan in 2000 and opened the country's smallest brewery, producing just 30 litres per batch. Two years later they upgraded to 250 litres and by 2006 the demand for their beers led to them moving to their current site with new kit that can produce 1,000 litres per brew. They are also opening taprooms where drinkers can sample the beers with good food; one taproom is in Tokyo.

IPA aficionados will be intrigued by Baird's interpretations, as they have a surprisingly Scottish Export air about them. Roasted barley is added to the malts and the beers are fermented with a Scottish ale yeast culture. Teikoku has 55 bitterness units and is brewed with Maris Otter pale malt with amber and cara malts along with the roast. 'Various hops' are used. Suruga Bay Imperial IPA weighs in with 90 bitterness units and is made with Maris Otter, Pilsner and cara malts and candy sugar. Again the hops are 'various varieties'. Both beers are unfiltered and condition in the bottle.

The verdict

Teikoku has a deep bronze colour with peppery hops and roasted grain on the nose with powerful notes of caramel, vanilla and cinnamon. A bittersweet palate is dominated by toasted grain, with dark berry fruits and woody hints from the hops. The finish is richly malty with continuing notes of caramel and vanilla but ends dry with woody and peppery hops. Imperial IPA is a pale bronze colour with a strong note of eucalyptus on the aroma along with spicy hops and cracker-like malt. The palate is bittersweet with herbal and spicy hops to the fore along with juicy malt. The finish is juicy and malty to start with herbs and spices adding balance but it ends bitter and hoppy.

ABV	Teikoku 6.5%/Suruga Bay 8.5%
First brewed	2006
Brewery	Baird Brewing Company, Shuzenji
Website	www.bairdbeer.com

Nanto Brewery, Okinawa Sango IPA

Brewmaster Ganaha Seigo opened the brewery in 2001 and fashions the beers with the aid of pure water filtered through limestone. The beers are gluten free and suitable for vegetarians and vegans, and organic ingredients are used when they can be obtained. For the IPA, malt is imported from Canada and unspecified German hop varieties are used. The beer has a pale gold appearance with a herbal and floral aroma and notes of pine wood and cracker-like malt. Bitter hops build on the palate with biscuit malt and lemon fruit. The finish is dry and bitter, but there's good balance from biscuit malt and tart lemon fruit.

ABV	5%
First brewed	2001
Brewery	Nanto Brewery, Nanjo-shi, Okinawa
Website	www.nantosyuzo.com

Overleaf, clockwise from top left: drying hops; ripe barley ready for harvesting; a traditional Yorkshire pub; casks of beer ready for distribution; dried hops being added to the copper; the Beer-Ritz shop in Leeds, northern England.

New beers on the block

How far can you push the boundaries of IPA? At the risk of sounding trite, the acronym stands for India Pale Ale. As we have seen, it was the first pale beer brewed in the world, at a time when even lager beers were dark. It revolutionized brewing practice and led not only to such styles as pale ale and bitter but also golden lager. So how can IPA possibly be black?

Beginning, inevitably, in the United States, craft brewers have 'pushed the envelope'. On the back of the clamour for IPA, American brewers devised a beer they called black IPA. Not wishing to be left behind, British brewers hurried to emulate their cousins across the pond and the trend was picked up in other countries. 'Craze' would be an exaggeration, but for a while black IPAs featured heavily in brewers' portfolios and in specialist beer shops. The style – some would say aberration – proved controversial. Brewing historians pointed out there was no historical validation for such a beer. In the United States, the revered brewmaster at Brooklyn Brewery, Garrett Oliver, who also edits the seminal *The Oxford Companion to Beer*, says bluntly and pithily when asked about black IPA: 'Don't get me started.' I am firmly in the Oliver camp. The British beer writer Adrian Tierney-Jones has suggested a compromise: why not call such beers Black India Ale, with no mention of pale?

But it seems the tide is turning. Early in 2017, a market report in the US said black IPAs were losing their lustre and were declining in popularity – although you would not guess it from looking at the websites of many breweries. Nonetheless, they exist and it would be churlish to ignore them completely, so I include some examples in this section. They are excellent beers. Whether they are IPA is another matter.

The new fad is fruit IPA. When you consider the rich, fruity notes that New World hops offer, is it necessary to add citrus fruits? Perhaps not, yet I will cheerfully admit that my first taste of Beavertown's Bloody 'Ell Blood Orange IPA, in a backstreet pub in Norwich, was one of my finest taste experiences of 2016.

And where will IPA go next? One or two spiced IPAs have been spotted. Sour IPA? Don't hold your breath ...

Black IPAs

21st Amendment Brewery, Back in Black

The name of the brewery celebrates the 21st amendment to the American constitution which repealed Prohibition in 1933. Nico Freccia, writer, actor and home-brewer, teamed up with photographer Shaun O'Sullivan in 2000 to open their brewpub in the South Park area of San Francisco, close to the financial district. Success demanded a bigger production facility and in 2015 they opened a new brewery and tasting room in San Leandro. Their black IPA is brewed with pale, crystal, Munich and black malts and hopped with Centennial and Columbus which create 65 bitterness units. The beer has a luscious aroma of roasted dark grain, liquorice, espresso coffee and spicy hops. Dark grains, bitter fruit and coffee dominate the palate, but the hops add spice and woody notes. The finish is long, refreshing and bitter from hops and dark malts, with continuing notes of coffee and liquorice.

ABV	6.8%
First brewed	2008
Brewery	21st Amendment Brewery, San Francisco, California, USA
Website	www.21st-amendment.com

By the Horns Brewing Co., Bastard Brag

The brewery was opened in 2011 by Alex Bull, hence its name. Alex started with a 5.5-barrel plant, since upgraded to 12 barrels. The plant is based in an industrial unit near Wimbledon Stadium in south-west London and has a taproom, open Tuesday to Sunday, where regular beer-related events are held. The events include a type of poker called Bastard Brag, where three threes are the highest hand. The beer named after it is brewed with Maris Otter pale, crystal and cara malts and hopped with Columbus,

Crystal and Summit varieties, with 80 bitterness units. It has a rich butterscotch and toffee aroma with cappuccino coffee notes, nutty malt and peppery hops. The palate has creamy malt, toffee and coffee, balanced by an increasing bitter hop note, followed by a finish in which coffee begins to dominate but with continuing contributions from roasted grain and woody, resinous hops.

ABV	7.2%
First brewed	2014
Brewery	By the Horns Brewing Co, Summerstown, London SW17, England
Website	www.bythehorns.co.uk

Evil Twin Brewing, Femme Fatale Noir

Jeppe Jarnit-Bjergsø is a member of the Danish gypsy brewing fraternity – he is the identical twin of Mikkel Borg Bjergsø of Mikkeller (see page 269), but they are not the best of friends. Jeppe is also a former schoolteacher and home-brewer, and he started making beer commercially in 2010, using, he says, 'ten of the best breweries in the world'. He has been so successful that he now works from offices in Brooklyn, though he also has an office in Copenhagen. He is able to produce a wide range of beers with his brewing associates and they include several IPAs under the Femme Fatale label, including Mango and Blanc de Blanc. This black IPA is brewed at Westbrook Brewing in Mount Pleasant, South Carolina, and stands out from the IPA crowd by being fermented with a *Brettanomyces* 'wild yeast' culture that gives a distinctive funky character to the finished beer. The grains are two-row pale malt, wheat malt, Carafa (a dark-roasted malt) and roasted barley. The hop range is complex: Citra, Chinook, CTZ and Nelson Sauvin, with Citra and Nelson Sauvin also used for dry hopping. Units of bitterness are 30. The beer is deep ruby/black in colour and has an earthy, musty, 'horse blanket' aroma from the Brett. Roasted grain, dark fruits and spicy and peppery hops are also present on the nose. The palate is tart and acidic with hops building along with bitter fruit and roasted grain. The acidity declines in the finish as roasted grain, burnt fruit and spicy hops dominate and lead to a dry finale.

ABV	6%
First brewed	2013
Brewery	Evil Twin Brewing, Brooklyn, New York City, USA
Website	www.eviltwin.dk

Indeed, Midnight Ryder

Indeed was founded in 2012 by beer geeks Rachel Anderson, Nathan Berndt and Tom Whisenand in the artists' area of Minneapolis. They now employ 50 staff and invested $250,000 in 2013 to expand the brewery to a capacity of 6,400 barrels a year. They have two taprooms in the city and export widely. Experienced head brewer Josh Bischoff has developed an interesting range of beers, including some that are barrel-aged. Midnight Ryder is one of Indeed's most popular beers and is brewed with pale, black and pale crystal malts and caramel. The hops include Apollo and Cascade and bitterness units are 80. The beer has a big aroma of roasted grain, burnt fruit and bitter chocolate. Peppery hops break through in the mouth, balancing the dark malt and fruit notes. The finish is long and finally bitter, but there are continuing rich notes of roasted grain, dark fruits and chocolate.

ABV	6.5%
First brewed	2012
Brewery	Indeed Brewing Company, Minneapolis, Minnesota, USA
Website	www.indeedbrewing.com

Kitchen Brew, India Dark Ale

Kitchen Brew (see page 260) declares the beer is their take on the American interpretation of black IPA and proves the point by using Amarillo, Cascade and Citra hops. The grains are Pilsner, Munich, cara and roasted malts. The beer conditions in the bottle and has a bright amber/russet rather than black colour. The aroma is woody/piny with roasted grain, blackberry fruit and gentle spicy hops. The palate is sweet to start, with fruit to the fore, but bitter hops start to build, with a continuing note of roasted malts. The finish is a fine balance of woody, bitter and spicy hops, dark fruits and roasted malts, with the hops having the last say in the bitter finale.

ABV	5.8%
First brewed	2015
Brewery	Kitchen Brew, Allschwil, Basel, Switzerland
Website	www.kitchenbrew.ch

Northern Monk, Dark Arches Black IPA

Russell Bisset and his team started out as gypsy brewers but founded their own 10-barrel plant in 2014 in a Grade-II listed mill in the centre of Leeds. They claim to be restoring Yorkshire's ancient monastic tradition of brewing at such abbeys as Fountains and Kirkstall. As well as the brewing kit, the site includes a refectory with a Grub and Grog kitchen that specializes in food made with organic ingredients plus a bottle shop. The black IPA, fashioned by head brewer Brian Dickson, is made with pale and roasted malts and hopped with Mosaic and Simcoe varieties that create 50 bitterness units. It has a deep brown/black colour with liquorice and molasses on the aroma along with roasted grain, intense peppery hops and dark, burnt fruit. Creamy malt is joined on the palate by peppery hops, liquorice and dark fruit, while a bittersweet finish has creamy malt, burnt fruit, liquorice and peppery hops.

ABV	6.7%
First brewed	2014
Brewery	Northern Monk Brew Co, Leeds, England
Website	www.northernmonkbrewco.com

Birrificio Rurale, Castigamatt Black India Pale Ale

The brewery in rural Lombardy in north-eastern Italy (see page 256) brews a strong black IPA using pale and black malts and American hops. The beer is neither filtered nor fined and conditions in the bottle.

Rich roasted and toasted grains dominate the aroma with powerful notes of woody and resinous hops and dried apricot fruit. The delicious palate has creamy malt, mocha coffee, dried fruit and bitter hops, followed by a long and lingering finish with bitter, woody hops building but balanced by continuing notes of coffee, creamy malt and ripe fruit.

ABV	7.5%
First brewed	2011
Brewery	Birrificio Rurale, Desio, Italy
Website	www.birrificiorurale.it

Staggeringly Good, Dawn Stealer Noire IPA

The brewers are obsessed with dinosaurs, which feature on the beer labels, and are also passionate about not using any animal products, especially finings, the clearing agent made from fish swim bladders. As a result their beers are suitable for vegans and vegetarians, and they mature in the bottle with live yeast.

Brewing started in 2014 using spare capacity at other breweries, but a 10-barrel plant was built in 2015.

The Noire IPA is brewed with pale and cara special malts and hopped with Amarillo, Cascade, Chinook and Galena varieties that create 26 bitterness units. Deep russet rather than black, it has a big espresso coffee hit on the nose with raisin fruit, toasted grain and spicy hops. Creamy malt builds on the palate with bitter hops beginning to make more of a presence along with dark, burnt fruit. The finish is bittersweet, with herbal hops beginning to dominate but also with continuing notes of creamy malt and dark fruit.

ABV	5.2%
First brewed	2015
Brewery	Staggeringly Good Brewery, Southsea, Portsmouth, Hampshire, England
Website	www.staggeringlygood.com

Two Roads, Route of All Evil

Master brewer Phil Markowski is a philosopher as well as a beer-maker. He says life offers two directions and he prefers to take the road that's less travelled. This means he brews some pretty way-out beers, including some that are barrel-aged, others that are sour. There's good humour too: a French-style bière de garde is called the Road 2 Rouen. He launched the brewery in Stratford, Connecticut in 2013 and he must have done something right because in 2017 he was able to invest $12 million in a new brewery that will come on stream in 2018.

Route of All Evil is called a Black Ale, which will please the pedants, but in 2015 it won a gold medal in an international beer competition in the Black IPA class. Phil keeps his ingredients close to his chest but says the hops come from the Pacific Northwest. The black beer has a delightful and inviting aroma of dark chocolate, molasses and dark fruits with fruity hops peering through the gloom. Hops start to build in the mouth, then chocolate and roasted grains lead the charge towards a finish that begins with bittersweet molasses and chocolate, but roasted malts and bitter hop resins have the last word.

ABV	7.5%
First brewed	2013
Brewery	Two Roads Brewing Company, Stratford, Connecticut, USA
Website	www.tworoadsbrewing.com

Fruit IPAs

Beavertown, Bloody 'Ell Blood Orange IPA

This is a remarkable beer from an equally remarkable brewery that is one of the spectacular success stories in the craft brewing movement. Logan Plant, son of Led Zeppelin front man Robert Plant, started brewing in 2011 in the kitchen of his home in De Beauvoir town in Hackney, East London. Cockneys have no truck with fancy French names and call the area 'Beavertown', hence the name of the brewery.

When beer sales took off, he moved to bigger premises in Hackney and was then forced to move again to an industrial site in Tottenham. He now produces 40,000 barrels a year, much of it in the form of IPAs such as Lupuloid IPA, 8 Ball Rye IPA and Neck Oil Session IPA.

Bloody 'Ell, London-speak for something amazing, is the result of brewing two batches of beer and adding 18 tons of Sicilian blood oranges. The fruit is crushed and added to the whirlpool when the hopped wort has been boiled with Amarillo, Citra, Magnum and Simcoe hops (55 bitterness units). The beer is available when there's a supply of oranges. A pale beer with a massive hit of tart orange fruit, spicy hops and juicy malt on the aroma and palate. The finish is long and complex, bittersweet citrus fruit interweaving with juicy malt followed by a bitter finale with spicy hops lingering on the palate.

ABV	7.2%
First brewed	2013
Brewery	Beavertown Brewery, Tottenham, London N17, England
Website	www.beavertownbrewery.co.uk

Coronado Brewing Co., Guava Islander

Ron and Rick Chapman have become major West Coast brewers but have stayed true to their roots and beliefs. They started out in 1996 with a small brewpub on Coronado Island and a modest 10-barrel kit. In 2006 they expanded to 4–5,000 barrels a year but the growing demand for their beers forced a move to the mainland to a new facility in the Tecolote Canyon area of San Diego. They now brew 60,000 barrels a year, and also have a taproom alongside the brewery, but they have also kept their original brewpub on the island.

Guava Islander is described as a 'Tropical IPA' with guava purée added to pale malt and Centennial, Chinook and Columbus hop varieties that create 65 units of bitterness. The exceptionally pale beer has a rich and inviting aroma of pungent perfumed fruit, woody and spicy hops and honeyed malt. The bittersweet fruit coats the mouth, but there's room for creamy and honeyed malt and spicy hops. The finish is shatteringly dry from both the fruit and the spicy hops, but there's a fine, lingering balance of biscuit malt to tame the bitterness.

ABV	7%
First brewed	2016
Brewery	Coronado Brewing Company, Coronado, California, USA
Website	www.coronadobrewing.com

Dieu du Ciel, Disco Soleil

The brewery name means 'God in Heaven' and is used in French-speaking Canada to signify something exceptional. Founder Jean-François Gravel was a keen home-brewer who was inspired by Belgian beers and the success of Unibroue – the innovative Montreal brewery that opened in 1992 – to start his own small brewery in 1998. The Belgian influence can be seen in such beers as Blanche du Paradis and Blanche Neige. Jean-François achieved success and notoriety with a black pepper beer and he has now reached out to Canadians with an IPA brewed with Pilsner, wheat and a touch of cara hell: cara hell is a lightly toasted malt used in the Helles lagers in Germany. There's a definite Belgian influence with the addition of fruit, in this case kumquat. The hops are Amarillo, Bravo, Citra and Nugget. The pale gold beer has an intensely fruity aroma of kumquat, mango, orange and peach, with sweet tangerine on the palate combining with dry kumquat notes, floral and spicy hops and toasted grain. The finish is complex, bittersweet, with tropical fruits, spicy hops and toasted malt.

ABV	6.5%
First brewed	2013
Brewery	Brasserie Dieu du Ciel, Montréal, Québec, Canada
Website	www.dieuduciel.com

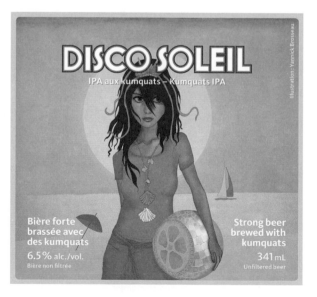

Schlafly, Grapefruit IPA

I wonder how mighty Anheuser Busch, brewers of Budweiser, feel about this successful pipsqueak in their town? Dan Kopman and Tom Schlafly had a different attitude to beer when they launched their brewpub, the Schlafly Tap Room, at 2100 Locust Street in 1991: their emphasis was on small-batch brewing using the finest raw materials. The official name is the Saint Louis Brewery, but the beers are branded Schlafly. The brewery has grown and now has a large production facility with restaurant at Maplewood.

The Grapefruit IPA is one of the company's most popular beers, with grapefruit purée added to the mash. Along with pale malt, the hops are Cascade, Chinook and Citra, with 40 units of bitterness. The hazy gold beer has a surprisingly restrained aroma, the fruit well balanced by juicy malt and peppery hops. Fruit from both the purée and hops build in the mouth, but there's also pepper and spice from the hops and lightly toasted malt. The finish is bittersweet, with a pronounced grapefruit note but balanced by biscuit malt and black pepper notes from the hops. Enticing and delectable.

ABV	5%
First brewed	2015
Brewery	The Saint Louis Brewery, Saint Louis, Missouri, USA
Website	www.schlafly.com

BY THE HORNS BREWING CO. LONDON

BASTARD BRAG BLACK IPA
7.2% ABV

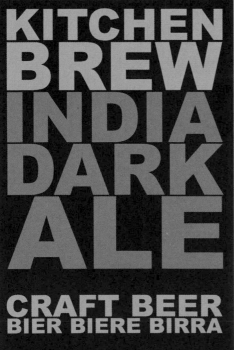

KITCHEN BREW INDIA DARK ALE

CRAFT BEER
BIER BIERE BIRRA

33CL   ALC. 6.5% VOL.

BACK IN BLACK

12 FL OZ. ALE 6.8% ALC./VOL. 65 IBUS

AMERICAN IPA BREWED WITH HIGH DARK MALTS

BLACK IPA

21 AMENDMENT BREWERY
21ST-AMENDMENT.COM

BEAVERTOWN
BLOODY 'ELL
BLOOD ORANGE IPA

EVILTWIN
BREWING

FEMME
FATALE
NOIR

Glossary

ABV (alcohol by volume)
International method for measuring and declaring for tax purposes the strength of beer. In the United States, a system known as Alcohol by Weight is used: 5% ABV is 4% ABW. But the American brewing industry now also declares beer by ABV to avoid confusion in export markets.

Adjuncts Cereals and sugars added to beer, often as a cheap substitute for malted barley but sometimes used by brewers to achieve special flavours. Producers of mass market lagers often dilute the barley mash with corn (maize) or rice. Invert sugar – sucrose converted to fructose and glucose – is commonly used alongside malt as it is easily converted into alcohol during fermentation. The early IPAs of the 19th century were often brewed with a blend of pale malt and sugar, with sugar making up around 10 per cent of the recipe. Adjuncts are not permitted in Germany under the terms of the Reinheitsgebot Purity Law (qv).

Ale Beer produced by warm or top fermentation. The term covers such styles as IPA, pale ale, bitter, porter, stout, old ale and barley wine in Britain and the US; in the Low Countries it covers Abbey and Trappist ales and some types of Bock or Bok. German and Belgian wheat beers are members of the ale family.

Alpha acid The natural acid in hop that gives bitterness to beer.

Aroma The 'nose' of a beer that gives an indication of the malty, hoppy and possibly fruity characteristics to be found on the palate.

Attenuation If a beer is 'fully attenuated', most or all of the malt sugars will have turned to alcohol. In some styles, such as English mild ale, some malt sugars are left in the beer for fullness of palate. Such beers are said to be 'not brewed out' or not fully attenuated.

Barley The main grain used to make beer. Barley has to be converted into malt (qv) before it can be used in the brewing process. Brewers call barley 'the soul of beer'.

Barrel In the brewing industry a barrel is a specific measurement of 36 imperial gallons (43 US gallons/164 litres) or, in the United States, 31.5 US gallons (26 imperial gallons/119 litres). Often used to describe a brewery's capacity: a microbrewery might typically start with a 10-barrel plant and produce 2–3,000 barrels a year.

Beer Generic term for alcoholic drinks made from grains. It includes ale, lager and Belgian lambic.

Bière de garde French 'keeping beer', a style associated with French Flanders and similar to saison (qv) produced in neighbouring Wallonia.

Bitter Draught English beer that developed from IPA and pale ale. It may range in colour from gold through amber to copper. The name 'bitter' indicates a generous amount of hop bitterness.

Bitterness see IBU.

Bottle conditioned/bottle fermented A beer bottled with live yeast that allows the beer to mature in the bottle, gaining condition ('sparkle') and additional alcohol. Strong bottle-conditioned beers can be laid down for several years.

Brettanomyces Wild yeast found in the atmosphere or buried deep in oak containers that attacks sugars in beer and develops a 'funky' or 'horse blanket' character. The name means 'British fungus' and was present in oak-aged IPAs in the 19th century.

Brewpub A pub that brews beer on the premises.

Burtonization Addition of such sulphates as gypsum (calcium sulphate) and magnesium to replicate the hard brewing waters found in wells and springs in Burton-on-Trent, the ancestral home of IPA and pale ale.

Burton snatch Term used to describe the sulphury aroma of a beer brewed with Burton or Burtonized water.

Campaign for Real Ale (CAMRA) Beer drinkers' organization founded in 1971 to protect cask-conditioned beer, which it dubbed 'real ale'. Highly influential, it has helped transform the British brewing industry and now has 185,000 members. It organizes beer festivals throughout the country, including the annual Great British Beer Festival in London that hosts the Champion Beer of Britain competition.

Cara malts Malts that undergo an extra stewing process that turns starch into a sugary liquid trapped under the husk. Stewing and drying causes the liquefied sugar to caramelize into dextrin, which cannot be fermented by brewers' yeast. Cara malts add colour and flavour to beer. They come in different varieties such as CaraMunich, carapils and, in Britain, crystal malt. Cara malts must be used sparingly or the beer will have an overwhelming 'barley sugar' flavour. Cara malt should not be confused with caramel, liquefied burnt sugar that can also be used in brewing: some English mild ales, for example, are made with a small amount of caramel. Confusingly, some American brewers who list 'caramel' in their recipes usually mean cara malt not caramel.

Carbon dioxide (CO2) Gas naturally produced during fermentation, creating carbonation ('sparkle'). Cask-conditioned and bottle-conditioned beers contain only natural gas. When beers are filtered in the brewery, applied CO2 may be used as part of the dispense system to deliver the beer in a pub or bar.

Cask Generic term for a container used to serve cask-conditioned beer. The sizes are pin (4½ gallons); firkin (9 gallons); kilderkin (18 gallons); barrel (36 gallons); and the rarely seen hogshead (54 gallons). A cask has two openings, one – the tap – for serving the beer, the second where 'shives' or wooden pegs are inserted to control the escape of CO_2 during secondary fermentation. See Keg.

Cask ale/cask-conditioned ale
Also known as cask beer or real ale. A draught beer that is neither filtered nor pasteurized and which undergoes a secondary fermentation in the cask. The style is associated with Britain, where it is a major style in pubs.

Condition(ing) Maturation of beer in either bottle or cask, during which the beer undergoes a secondary fermentation, adding a refreshing sparkle and more complex flavours.

Copper Vessel used to boil the sugary wort (qv) with hops. Traditionally made of copper but more often today of stainless steel. Known as the kettle or brew kettle in the US.

Double IPA Term used to describe stronger modern versions of IPA. It is not distinguished from imperial IPA: the two terms are interchangeable and strengths vary.

Draught Beer served from a bulk container and drawn to the bar. Spelt 'draft' in the US.

Dry hopping The addition of a small amount of hops to a cask or keg of beer to improve bitterness and aroma. Mainly associated with cask beer in Britain but now used more widely in hoppy beers such as IPA.

EBC European Brewing Convention. A scale that measures the colour of beer. A Pilsner may have 6–8 units, an English pale ale 20–40, porters and stouts 150–300 or more.

Esters Flavour compounds produced by the action of yeast as it turns sugars into alcohol and CO_2. Esters are often similar to fruits but can also resemble tobacco and leather. Lager brewers are careful to keep esters to a minimal level in their beers whereas ale brewers like the additional character they deliver.

Export Term used in Scotland for beers, IPAs in particular, that were developed in the 19th century for the export trade. McEwan's Export is one of the most famous examples.

Fermentation Turning malt sugars into alcohol and carbon dioxide by the action of yeast.

Filtration Removing yeast cells and other solids from finished beer. Neither cask-conditioned nor bottle-conditioned beers are filtered; cask beer naturally 'drops bright' after a few days, with yeast settling at the base of the cask. A growing number of craft keg brewers are moving away from filtration as they feel it strips flavour from beer and there seems to be little consumer opposition to beer that has a slight haze.

Fining Clarifying beer with the addition of clearing agents, often isinglass made from fish swim bladders. Caragheen or Irish moss can also be used and is preferred by vegetarians and vegans. Many brewers are looking at new ways to clarify beer to avoid using isinglass.

Finish The aftertaste of beer: the impression left at the back of the tongue and in the throat.

Grist Brewers' term for the milled grains to be used in the brewing process. The word comes from 'grind' and is still used in the ancient expression 'all grist to the mill'.

Hogshead Large (54-gallon) cask traditionally used in the brewing industry but now rarely seen.

Hop back Vessel used to settle and clarify hopped wort after the boil in the copper or kettle. Used in the main by brewers who prefer whole hop flowers to pellets. See Whirlpool.

Hops Climbing plant with cone-like flowers containing acids, resins and tannins that give aroma and bitterness to beer and help prevent bacterial infection.

IBU Abbreviation for International Bitterness Units. A measure of the acids in hops that create bitterness in beer. IBUs can range from 10–15 in international lagers to more than 40

in pale ales and bitters. Some modern interpretations of IPA have IBUs of 100 or more, but less bitter Session IPAs are increasingly popular.

Imperial IPA See Double IPA.

Infusion System of mashing beer, usually ale. The grain is left to stand in pure hot water in a mash tun at a constant temperature while enzymes in the starch convert the starch into fermentable sugar. Traditional lager brewers use a longer mashing regime, known as decoction, with the mash pumped from one vessel to another at higher temperatures.

IPA Short for India Pale Ale, the first pale beer in the world, was made in England towards the end of the 18th century and then in large volumes in the 19th century. The style was originally developed for export to India and became closely associated with Burton-on-Trent where the local water in the Trent Valley was ideal for making pale beer. IPA spawned both pale ale and bitter beer in England. The style is now brewed throughout the world.

Keg Sealed metal container that holds draught but not cask-conditioned beer. Keg beer is usually filtered and kegs are connected to cylinders of CO2 or mixed gas that drives the beer to the bar. A recent development, the key keg, is a plastic, one-trip container. New 'craft keg' beers are often unfiltered.

Kettle See Copper.

Kräusen German term for adding some partially fermented wort (qv) to beer to encourage a second fermentation during aging. Usually associated with lager production but used by some brewers of IPA.

Lambic Belgian beer produced by wild yeast fermentation. It has a distinctive acidic taste, which many people find refreshing. Some brewers are experimenting with 'sour IPA', made by adding wild beer yeast cultures.

Liquor Brewers' term for the pure water used in the mashing and boiling process.

Malt Grain – usually barley – that has been partially germinated, dried and cured or toasted in a kiln. The grain contains starches that will be converted by natural enzymes into fermentable sugar (maltose) during the mash (qv). The colour of the malt is determined by the level of heat in the kiln. All beers are made primarily from pale malt, which has the highest level of enzymes. Colour and flavour are the result of higher temperatures in the kiln that produce darker malts such as amber, brown or chocolate.

Mash The mix of malted grain and pure hot water or 'liquor', the first stage of the brewing process, when sugars are extracted from the malt.

Mash tun Vessel in which malted grain is mixed with 'liquor' to start the brewing process. Also known as the mash mixer.

Microbrewery A small brewery, often called a craft brewery, producing beer in small batches for local distribution – and many now sell their beer online. 'Micros' in Britain, the US and Australasia have been at the forefront of brewing innovation in the past 20–30 years. In Britain, the Society of Independent Brewers (SIBA) has a direct delivery distribution system that gives its members' beers greater presence throughout the country.

Mouth-feel The sensation that beer and its constituent parts – malt, hops and fruity esters – make in the mouth. The tongue is a highly sensitive organ that can detect sweetness, sourness, saltiness and bitterness as the beer passes over it.

Pasteurization Heating process developed by Louis Pasteur in the 19th century that kills bacteria and stabilizes beer. Many brewers now prefer to sterile filter beer to avoid the 'cardboard' flavour that can result from pasteurization. One leading opponent of the system was Pasteur himself, who developed it for wine and said beer was too delicate to withstand it. Cask-conditioned and bottle-conditioned beers are unpasteurized.

Porter Brown, later black, beer first brewed in London early in the 18th century. Its name came from its popularity with porters working in markets and docks. The strongest porters were called 'stout porters', later shortened to just stout. Dublin porter was famously known as 'plain'.

Priming The addition of sugar to encourage a strong secondary fermentation in beer.

Racking Running beer from a conditioning tank into a cask or keg, leaving behind some of the yeast sediment.

Real ale See CAMRA.

Reinheitsgebot Bavarian 'Purity Law' from 1516, decreeing that only malted grain, hops, yeast and water can be used to make beer.

Roasted barley Barley (or other grain such as wheat) that is not malted but heated at a high temperature. Such grain contains no fermentable sugars and is used for colour and flavour. Its main use is in dark beers such as porter (qv) and stout but is also used in some pale ales and IPAs such as Scottish Export.

Saison A 'farmhouse' beer from Wallonia in Belgium. Originally made to refresh farm workers during the harvest, it is now brewed commercially and has become popular with craft brewers in Britain and the US.

Shilling 19th-century Scottish designation for ales that indicated the price payable on a cask of beer, ranging from 60 shillings to 90 shillings and sometimes higher. The strongest Scottish beer is 'Wee Heavy'.

Sparge Rinsing the grain after mashing to flush out any remaining malt sugars from the mash tun: from the French *esparger*, 'to sprinkle'.

Stout See Porter.

Torrefied grain Grain – usually wheat – that has been heated or 'scorched' at a high temperature until it pops. Similar to popcorn, it is used by brewers to give a good head of foam to finished beer.

Wheat beer Beer made from malted wheat but usually blended with malted barley. Mainly associated with Bavaria, where it's known as weizen or weiss, and in Belgium where the beers often have the addition of spice, but wheat beers are now brewed in many other countries. Traditionally served unfiltered and naturally cloudy.

Whirlpool Vessel where hopped wort is clarified by centrifugal force to remove dead yeast cells and protein prior to fermentation. Whirlpools are used by brewers who use hop pellets in preference to whole hop flowers.

Wort Sweet, sugary extract produced by mashing malt and water.

Yeast A natural fungus that attacks sweet liquids, turning malt sugars into alcohol and carbon dioxide. Brewers' yeasts are either warm-fermenting cultures for ale brewing or cold-fermenting for lager brewing. Belgian brewers of lambic beer use wild yeasts such as *Brettanomyces* in the atmosphere or trapped in wooden aging vessels.

Resources

Beer festivals

USA
Chicago Beer Festival
thechicagobeerfestival.com – March

Great Arizona Beer Festival, Phoenix
www.azbeer.com – March

Los Angeles IPA Fest
www.laipafestival.com – March

Philly Craft Beer Festival, Philadelphia
www.phillycraftbeerfest.com – March

New York City Craft Beer Festival
www.nyccraftbeerfest.com – March

World Beer Festival, Raleigh, NC
allaboutbeer.com/gather-for-beer/world-beer-festival/raleigh-nc – April

Los Angeles Beer Festival
www.drinkeatplay.com/labeerfest – April

Great American Beer Festival, Denver
www.greatamericanbeerfestival.com –
October

UK
Craft Beer Rising, London
craftbeerrising.co.uk – February

National Winter Ales Festival
nwaf.org.uk – February (various cities;
moves every few years)
Great British Beer Festival, London
www.gbbf.org.uk – August
Indy Man Beer Convention, Manchester
www.indymanbeercon.co.uk – October

CAMRA regional and local beer festivals
throughout the year
www.camra.org.uk/events

Ireland
Irish Beer & Whiskey Festival, Dublin
secretsession.ie – March

Irish Craft Beer Festival, Dublin
www.irishcraftbeerfestival.ie – August/
September

Canada
Great Canadian Beer Festival, Victoria,
BC
www.gcbf.com – September

Belgium
Bruges Beer Festival
www.brugsbierfestival.be – February

Zythos Beer Festival, Leuven
www.zbf.be/en – April

Bierpassieweekend, Antwerp
www.bierpassieweekend.be – June

Belgian Beer Weekend, Brussels
www.belgianbrewers.be/en/ – September

Netherlands
Bier Festival, Groningen
bierfestivalgroningen.progressevents.nl/
en – April

Dutch Craft Beer Festival, Enschede
www.atak.nl/agenda/craft-beer-festival –
May

Italy
Italia Beer Festival, Milan

www.italiabeerfestival.it – March and November

Italia Beer Festival, Rome – May

Italia Beer Festival, Bologna – August

Fermentazioni Italian Craft Beer Fest, Rome
www.fermentazioni.it – September

Germany
Stuttgart Craft Beer Festival
www.craftbeerfestival-stuttgart.de – April

Craft Bier Fest Munchen, Munich
craftbiermuc.com – May/June

Berlin Beer Week
www.berlinbeerweek.com – July

Braufest, Berlin
www.braufest-berlin.de/en – September

Oktoberfest, Munich
www.oktoberfest.de/en – September

Volksfest, Stuttgart
cannstatter-volksfest.de/en – September/October

Norway
Oslo Håndverksølfestivalen
https://www.facebook.com/events/1843346612568049/ – June

What's Brewing, Stavanger
whatsbrewing.no – October

Sweden
Stockholm Beer & Whisky Festival
www.stockholmbeer.se – September/October

Spain
Barcelona Beer Festival
barcelonabeerfestival.com – March

Mash Craft Beer Festival, Barcelona
mash.beer – September

Australia
Great Australian Beer Spectacular, Melbourne and Sydney
www.gabsfestival.com – May

New Zealand
Great Kiwi Beer Festival, Christchurch
greatkiwibeerfestival.co.nz – January

Kegkoura Craft Beer Festival, Kaikoura
www.emporiumbrewing.co.nz/kegkoura-2017.html – March

Great Australian Beer Spectacular, Auckland
www.gabsfestival.com – June

Beervana, Wellington
www.beervana.co.nz – August

Japan
Great Japan Beer Festival, various cities
www.beertaster.org (don't forget to click on 'English') – April to September

Kyushu Beer Festival
yokanavi.com/en/event/64476/– October

Websites and blogs

US
AllAboutBeer.com online magazine

Jay R Brooks
brookstonbeerbulletin.com

John Holl
johnholl.com

Zymurgy online magazine
homebrewersassociation.org

UK
Brewery History, The journal of the
Brewery History Society online
www.breweryhistory.com/journal/index.
html

Pete Brown
petebrown.blogspot.com

Campaign for Real Ale
camra.org.uk

Melissa Cole
www.letmetellyouaboutbeer.co.uk

Jeff Evans
insidebeer.com
Roger Protz
protzonbeer.co.uk

Adrian Tierney-Jones
maltworms.blogspot.com

Belgium
Breandán Kearney
belgiansmaak.com

Canada
Stephen Beaumont
beaumontdrinks.com

Australia
Australian Brews News
brewsnews.com.au

craftypint.com

New Zealand
Beer & Brewer
www.beerandbrewer.com
Neil Miller
http://themalthouse.co.nz/blog

Books

A Barnard *Noted Breweries of Great
Britain and Ireland*, 4 vols (1889–91)

Pete Brown *Hops and Glory*
(PanMacmillan, 2010)

Martyn Cornell *Beer: The Story of the
Pint* (Headline, 2003)

Gilbert Delos *101 Bières* (Dunod, 2015)
T R Gourvish and R G Wilson *The
British Brewing Industry 1830–1980*
(Cambridge University Press, 1994)

Stan Hieronymus *For the Love of Hops*
(Brewers Publications, 2012)

Peter Mathias *The Brewing Industry
in England, 1700–1830* (Cambridge
University Press, 1959)

The Oxford Companion to Beer, edited by
Garrett Oliver (Oxford University Press,
2011)

Ron Pattinson *The Home Brewer's Guide
to Vintage Beer* (Quarry Books, 2014)

Roger Protz *The Story of Brewing in
Burton-on-Trent* (History Press, 2011)

Mitch Steele *IPA: Brewing Techniques,
Recipes and the Evolution of India Pale Ale*
(Brewers Publications, 2012)

Author's acknowledgements

Thanks

Principally and primarily to Mark Dorber, now at the Anchor, Walberswick, Suffolk, previously of the White Horse, Parsons Green, London, who made everything possible.

Historians Martyn Cornell and Ron Pattinson for sharing their knowledge. Stephen Beaumont in Canada and Matthew Kirkegaard in Australia for help with IPAs from their respective countries.

Jon Morris-Smith in London for bringing samples of Ballantine's IPA from the United States.

Breandán Kearney in Ghent, Belgium, for finding samples of Pliny the Elder. Claire-Michelle Pearson of St Albans for bringing samples of Asian IPAs on her travels.

Nigel Stevenson of James Clay for generously supplying samples of imported IPAs.

And to brewers around the world for answering queries about ingredients and recipes.

Roger Protz is a beer writer with an international following. He has written more than 20 bestselling books and writes for many magazines in the UK, US and Australia. He edits the annual *Good Beer Guide*, published by CAMRA, the Campaign for Real Ale. He stages talks and beer tastings in a number of countries, including Friends of the Smithsonian in Washington DC and the World Beer Festival in Durham, North Carolina, at the Great British Beer Festival and the BBC Food Show in the UK, and Beer Expo in Melbourne, Australia. He judges at the Great American and Great British festivals and the Brussels Beer Challenge.

His awards include Drink Writer of the Year (twice) in the Glenfiddich Awards and gold and silver awards from the British Guild of Beer Writers. He has been given lifetime achievement awards from the British Guild of Beer Writers and the Society of Independent Brewers.

His website is www.protzonbeer.co.uk

Picture acknowledgements

The author and publishers would like to thank the many breweries featured in the book for their help with supplying images.

Front cover artwork Matthew Allen
2 Mark Newton
19 UBREW/Stu Sewell
22-23 Tower Hamlets Local History Library and Archives
26-27 Private Collection/ Photo © Bonhams, London, UK/Bridgeman Images
30 © National Portrait Gallery, London
32 Private Collection/ Bridgeman Images
34-35 Mary Evans Picture Library
36-37 Private Collection/ Photo © Liszt Collection/ Bridgeman Images
39 Private Collection/© Look and Learn/Bridgeman Images
40 Private Collection/© Look and Learn/Bridgeman Images
42 M&N/Alamy Stock Photo
44-45 SSPL/Getty Images

48 © Illustrated London News Ltd/Mary Evans Picture Library
53 Collection of the Newark Museum #1172
56-57 Simon James/Hop & Barley
58-59 Mark Newton
60-61 Mark Newton
63 Florilegius/SSPL/Getty Images
64-65 Lander Loeckx/Alamy Stock Photo
66 Thomas Hanks/Hop & Barley
68-69 Universal History Archive/UIG via Getty Images
71 Print Collector/Getty Images
73 Oxford Science Archive/ Print Collector/Getty Images
76 Marston's Brewery
79 Matthew Allen
80 top left Mark Newton/ Hop & Barley
80 centre Mark Newton
80 below Roger Bacon/ REUTERS/Alamy Stock Photo

81 top right Mark Newton
81 below Roger Bacon/ REUTERS/Alamy Stock Photo
85 The Advertising Archives
87 The Advertising Archives
89 M&N/Alamy Stock Photo
90-91 The Keasbury-Gordon Photograph Archive/Alamy Stock Photo
92 Roger Protz
94-95 Grenville Collins Postcard Collection/Mary Evans Picture Library
97 Tegestology/Alamy Stock Photo
99 Malcolm McHugh/Alamy Stock Photo
288 above Norbert Schaefer/ Getty Images
288 below Mark Newton
288 below centre Mark Newton
281 above left Simon James/ Hop & Barley
281 above right Mark Newton
281 below Mark Newton
314 Ben Jacobs

Index

2x4 DIPA 155
4 Hop IPA 135
6 Hop IA 135
7 Hop IPA 135
8 Ball Rye IPA 298
8 Hop IPA 135
8 Wired Brewing Company 280
11th Hour IPA 150
21st Amendment Brewery 292, 302
90 Minute IPA 114-15

'A Magara 254
AB InBev 153, 156, 185, 243
Abbott's Brewery 24
Achouffe, Brasserie d' 239, 241
Acorn Brewery 162-3
adjuncts 72
Adnams Sole Bay Brewery 149, 164-5
ageing in wood 8, 14, 17, 24, 41, 52, 84, 86, 167, 219
The Alchemist Brewery 146
alcohol by volume see ABV
All Day IPA 118-19
Allsopp, Samuel 28, 29, 31, 33, 37, 40, 42, 43, 46, 49, 74, 96
Allsopp's Brewery 36
Alpha Dog Imperial IPA 126-7
Amarafemmena IPA 257
Amiral Benson Nelson Sauvin IPA 248-9
Anchor Brewing Company 16, 55, 105, 108-9
Anchorage Brewing 269
And Union 262-3
Anderson Valley Brewing Company 146
Anheuser Busch 301
Arcobräu 263
Armageddon IPA 279
Asahi 185
Aubeloun IPA 250
Australia 7, 8, 9, 16, 103, 272-7

Baby IPA 284-5
Back in Black 292, 302
Baird Brewing Company 286-7
Baladin 252
Ballantine, P., and Sons Brewing Company 83-7
Ballantine, Peter 52, 83
Ballantine India Pale Ale 15, 83-7
Ballantine's XXX 84
Ballast Point Brewing Company 147
barley 55, 59, 287
Barney's Beer 101, 216
Bass Brewery 8, 13, 31, 33, 37, 38, 42, 45, 46, 70, 71, 77-8, 88, 92, 96
Bastard Brag 292-3

Battersea IPA 194-5
Beavertown Brewery 291, 298, 303
Belgium and the Netherlands 9, 16, 103, 238-45
Bell's Brewery 147
Bengal Lancer 16, 170-1
Bengal Tiger 203
Black Bridge Brewery 234
Black Eagle Brewery 201
black IPAs 7, 105, 223, 291, 292-7
Blacks of Kinsale 230
Black Sands Brewery 282
Blimey That's Bitter IPA 156
Bloody 'Ell Blood Orange IPA 291, 298, 303
Blue Monkey Brewery 211
Bluestone Brewing Company 100, 224
Boddingtons 38
Bombay Bomber 14
Boston Beer Company 107
Boulevard Brewing Company 148
Bourgogne des Flandres Brewery 244
Bow Bridge Brewery 14, 23, 24, 37-8, 161, 195
Boxing Cat Brewery 284
Bragdy Dinbych 224-5
BrauKollektiv 264
Breakside Brewery 148
Breakside IPA 148
BrewDog 100, 216-17, 277
Brewery History Society 161
Brewery Yard Stock Ale 41
Brewfist 254
brewing processes 17-18, 67, 75-9, 78, 79, 93, 115, 189, 215
brewing sugar 72, 93
Brooklyn Brewery 9, 14, 103, 110-11, 291
Brooklyn East IPA 110-11
Brú Brewery 230-1
Brussels Beer Project 240, 247
Brutal IPA 134-5
Budweiser 83, 153, 301
Burghers' Brewery 45
Burton Ale 29
Burton Bridge Brewery 16, 166-7
Burton-on-Trent 8, 13, 17, 28, 29, 31, 34, 36, 37, 38, 43, 68-9, 73, 161
Burton snatch 183
Burton Union fermentation 75-8, 98, 151, 183
Burtonization 43, 69, 239, 244
By the Horns Brewing Company 292-3, 302

Caledonian Brewery 16, 98,

217
Campaign for Real Ale (CAMRA) 88, 93, 98, 187, 193, 217, 221, 226, 227, 305
Canada 9, 16, 232-7, 300
Cannonball India Pale Ale 180-1
Cannonball Triple IPA 181
Captain Lawrence Brewing Company 149
Carlow Brewing Company 229
Carlsberg 70, 268, 269, 270
casks 28, 32, 33, 38, 43, 75, 76, 287
Castigamatt Black India Pale Ale 296
Castle Eden Brewery 14
Castlemaine Brewery 276
Catalyst IPA 8, 16-18
Central City Brewing Company 234-5
Chapel Down 202
Chapelloise Brewery 247
Charles Wells 16, 98, 99
Charrington 38
China and Japan 9, 16, 103, 283-7
Christian Feigenspan Brewery 52
Cigar City Brewing 150
Citra Double IPA (Kern River) 154
C!tra Double IPA (Liberty Brewing) 280-1
classic IPAs 82-99
Clockwork Beer Company 218
Cloudwater Brew Co 202-3
coke industry 73, 74
Cold Spring Brewery 86
Collective Arts Brewing 235
Commodore Perry IPA 120-1
Concertina Brewery 203
conditioning 18, 25
Coopers Brewery 272, 277
Cornell, Martyn 25, 49
Coronado Brewing Company 299
Craft Beer Kitchen 220
Craft Brew Alliance 156
Craig Allan, Brasserie 248
Crazy IPA 251
Crikey IPA 156
Crow Peak Brewing 150
Curious IPA 202
Cwtch 227

Damme Nation 245
Dark Arches Black IPA 295
Dawn Stealer Noir IPA 296-7
De Koninck 241
De Proef Brewery 248, 269, 270, 271
De Sutter, Brasserie 251
Delicious IPA 143

Delta IPA 240
Denbigh Brewery 224-5
Deschutes Brewery 112-13
Deuchars IPA 16, 51, 217
Dieu du Ciel, Brasserie 300
Disco Soleil 300
Discovery IPAs 230
Dogfish Head Craft Brewery
    114-15
Dolden Sud IPA 264
Dolly India Pale Ale 264
Dominion Brewery Company
    204
Doom Bar 93
Doore, Dick 129
Dorber, Mark 13, 14, 16
Double Dog IPA 117
Double Imperial IPA 267
double IPAs 7, 105, 115, 117,
    127, 131, 137, 146, 149,
    152, 154, 155, 156, 158,
    160, 181, 202, 215, 221,
    223, 226, 233, 236, 243,
    244, 253, 255, 256, 259,
    266, 267, 270, 274, 275,
    277, 279, 280, 286
Double Joker IPA 221
Dreadnaught Imperial IPA 158
Driftwood Brewery 236
dry hopping 67, 78, 84, 306
Duvel Moortgat, Brouwerij
    148, 151, 239, 241, 242

Earl Grey IPA 208-9
Ease Up IPA 165
East Beach India Pale Ale
    190-1
East Coast IPA 191
East India Company 24, 25,
    28, 29, 31, 74, 175
EastBound Imperial India Pale
    Ale 226
Easy IPA 117
ecological breweries 135, 143,
    145, 146, 165, 169, 213,
    224, 255
Edinburgh & Leith Brewery 96
Edwin Tucker's East India Pale
    Ale 210-11
Elland Brewery 212
Empire Pale Ale 16, 166-7
Empress Ale 208
Endeavour IPA 162-3
England 15, 16, 62, 66, 67, 88,
    161-213, 292-3, 295, 296-7,
    298
Epic Brewing Company 279
Ernestine 247
Everards 38, 202
Evil Twin Brewing 293, 303
Extrovert American IPA 128-9

Fabrique Ninkasi 249
Falstaff Brewery 83
Falstaff Double IPA 255
Fat Tug IPA 236
Fawcett, Thomas, & Sons 59
Femme Fatale Noir 293, 303

Feral Brewing Company 274
fermentation 75-8
Firestone Walker Brewing
    Company 151
First Frontier IPA 271
Five Points Brewing Company
    16, 168-9
Five Points IPA 16, 168-9
Fixation Brewing Company
    275
Fixation IPA 10, 274-5
Flagship 11, 207
Florida Beer Company 152
Flying Dog Brewery 117
Foghorn Brewhouse 276
Founders Brewing Company
    118-19
Fountain Brewery 98
Fourpure Brewing Co 204-5
France 9, 16, 103, 246- 51
Frank Jones Brewery 52
Fraoch 221
Freak of Nature Double India
    Pale Ale 160
Friday 262-3
fruit IPAs 7, 291, 298-303
Frye's Leap IPA 157
Fuggles IPA 139
Full Whack 209
Fuller's Brewery 16, 17, 170-1
Fyne Ales 16, 215

Gaina IPA 252-3
Garrison Brewing Company
    236-7
Germany 9, 261-7
Go To IPA 143
Go West! IPA 108-9
Good People Brewing
    Company 101, 152
Goose IPA 153
Goose Island Beer Company 8,
    41, 153
Gotlands Bryggeri 270
Goutte d'Or, Brasserie la 247
Grain Brewery 205
Great Basin Brewing Company
    153
Great Lakes Brewery (Canada)
    233
Great Lakes Brewing Company
    (USA) 120-1
Great Leap Brewing 284
Green Bullet 227
Green Devil IPA 188-9
Green Flash Brewery 244
Green Flash West Coast IPA
    244-5
Greene King 191, 206
Greene King IPA 284
Grolsch 238
Guava Islander 299
gypsy brewers 9, 263, 268, 270,
    271, 282, 293, 295

Hadouken 227
Hammerstone IPA 100, 224
Handwerk 262-3

Hardknott 172-3
Harpoon Brewery 15, 103,
    122-3, 220
Harpoon IPA 122-3
Harvey's Brewery 72
Hawkshead Brewery 206-7
Hawkshead IPA 206-7
Head High IPA 154
Heady Topper 146
Heart & Soul 211
Heineken 98, 125, 228, 238
Hepworth 202
Heriot Brewery 96
history of IPA 21-52
Hodgson, Frederick 29
Hodgson, George 14, 24, 28,
    29, 37, 49, 161, 175
Hodgson, Mark 29
Hogs Back Brewery 161
Holgate Brewhouse 275
Hook Norton Brewery 11, 207
Hop Art 10-11, 256
Hop Devil India Pale Ale 159
Hop Hog 274
Hop Nosh IPA 144-5
Hop Ottin' IPA 146
hop plant 62, 63
hop varieties
    Admiral 207, 221
    Ahtanum 177, 199, 217,
        248
    Alluvial 135
    Amarillo 7, 67, 111, 117,
        119, 133, 137, 146, 147,
        150, 151, 152, 153, 158,
        159, 160, 165, 175, 177,
        181, 221, 227, 234, 235,
        236, 239, 243, 245, 249,
        264, 271, 273, 274, 276,
        294, 296, 298, 300
    Apollo 109, 123, 145, 146,
        294
    Aurora 217
    Azacca 143, 266
    Boadicea 165
    Bramling Cross 202, 210,
        216
    Bravo 109, 113, 145, 300
    Brewers' Gold 86, 205
    Calypso 109, 143
    Cascade 7, 62, 67, 86, 107,
        111, 113, 121, 123, 125,
        131, 133, 139, 145, 146,
        148, 149, 150, 151, 152,
        153, 154, 156, 157, 158,
        159, 160, 169, 173, 183,
        187, 191, 193, 205, 206,
        208, 209, 215, 216, 217,
        218, 219, 224, 227, 229,
        230, 231, 236, 237, 241,
        242, 243, 245, 249, 253,
        255, 264, 267, 270, 274,
        276, 277, 279, 285, 294,
        296, 300
    Celeia 111
    Centennial 107, 111, 113,
        119, 125, 131, 137, 143,
        146, 147, 148, 150, 151,

152, 153, 155, 157, 158,
159, 160, 165, 177, 181,
199, 202, 204, 205, 208,
218, 221, 223, 234, 235,
236, 237, 241, 245, 247,
250, 253, 257, 264, 266,
267, 270, 271, 274, 275,
277, 279, 292, 299
Challenger 93, 167, 220,
221, 224, 240
Chinook 107, 131, 133, 139,
143, 145, 146, 148, 149,
152, 154, 155, 158, 159,
160, 165, 173, 177, 193,
195, 199, 202, 212, 216,
217, 218, 219, 223, 224,
227, 241, 247, 253, 255,
257, 263, 264, 266, 270,
275, 293, 296, 299, 301
Citra 7, 62, 67, 109, 117,
141, 148, 154, 155, 158,
160, 173, 177, 181, 189,
195, 202, 205, 208, 215,
230, 233, 236, 237, 240,
242, 245, 248, 250, 254,
266, 269, 274, 275, 277,
293, 294, 298, 300, 301
Cluster 41
Columbus 86, 127, 133,
146, 148, 149, 150, 152,
154, 155, 157, 160, 165,
175, 177, 181, 191, 206,
208, 212, 223, 226, 227,
233, 236, 247, 248, 254,
255, 257, 267, 271, 277,
279, 292, 299
Comet 129
Crystal 141, 292
CTZ 117, 137, 293
Delta 113
El Dorado 177, 234, 255
Ella 143, 202
Endeavour 67, 161, 163
Equinox 109, 129, 233, 248,
253, 276
Eureka! 109
Falconer's Delight 148
Farnham White Bine 161
First Gold 67, 179, 209,
210, 221
Fuggle 7, 15, 16, 17, 62, 86,
93, 103, 121, 161, 167, 171,
179, 183, 185, 197, 203,
205, 207, 208, 209, 217,
225, 226
Galaxy 165, 169, 173, 177,
212, 272
Galena 212, 249, 296
Golding (English) 7, 13, 14,
16, 17, 18, 41, 62, 98, 111,
133, 161, 165, 171, 183,
185, 197, 202, 207, 208,
210, 221, 230, 244, 273
Golding (Styrian) 62, 98,
165, 167, 203, 206, 217,
220, 244
Green Bullet 208, 220, 227,
250

hedgerow varieties 67, 179
Hersbrucker 98
Jester 67, 161, 187
Magnum 86, 141, 143, 148,
181, 220, 231, 234, 236,
264, 266, 274, 298
Mandarina 219, 265
Millennium 113
Mittelfruh 264
Mosaic 107, 160, 165, 175,
177, 204, 212, 233, 248,
253, 255, 260, 274, 275,
277, 295
Motueka 143, 150, 177,
206, 278, 280, 281
Mount Hood 127
Nelson Sauvin 62, 67, 177,
202, 217, 233, 248, 278,
280, 281, 282, 293
Northdown 93
Northern Brewer 113
Nugget 248, 300
Olicana 212
Pacific Gem 179, 223, 250
Pacific Jade 173, 177, 202
Pacifica 220
Pallisade 237, 249
Perle 216
Pilgrim 153, 202, 264
Pride of Ringwood 272
Progress 13, 16, 201
Rakau 177
Riwaka 278, 281
Saaz 153, 239
Simcoe 107, 117, 121, 137,
146, 149, 150, 151, 152,
155, 158,159, 160, 165, 173,
175, 177, 181, 202, 208,
212, 217, 221, 233, 234,
241, 243, 245, 248, 249,
250, 253, 254, 255, 264,
266, 267, 271, 274, 275,
277, 279, 295, 298
Smaragd 240
Sorachi Ace 255
Southern Cross 273, 280
Spalter 264
Summit 111, 117, 129, 148,
191, 212, 230, 231, 253, 292
Target 171, 201, 203, 204
Tettnang 152, 264
Tomahawk 239
Vic Secret 143, 202, 273
Waimea 224
Wakatu 173, 220
Warrior 117, 147, 152, 155,
160, 271
Willamette 121, 133, 193,
285
Zeus 253
Zythus 145
Hop Zombie 279
Hopinator 275
Hoppiness IPA 187
Hopster New Zealand IPA 282
HopStrosity 100, 212
Hopwired IPA 280
Hot Rye IPA 240

Houblon Chouffe Dobbelen
IPA Tripel 239
Howling Hops 16, 174-5
Human Cannonball Double
IPA 181
Humpty's Fuddle IPA 225
Hürlimann Brewery 258

I Presume Ale IPA 224-5
IBUs see international
bitterness units
Ichthyosaur IPA 153
Icon 2 IPA 276
IIPA 277
Imperial Brewery 24
Imperial IPA (Garrison
Brewing) 236-7
Imperial IPA (Tower) 16
imperial IPAs see double IPAs
Ind Coope 14, 15, 38, 43,
167
Indeed Brewing Company
294
India, exports to 24-9, 32, 37,
43, 77
India Dark Ale 294, 302
India Project Ale 10-11, 248
industrial espionage 45, 96
Industrial Revolution 37, 45,
70, 73, 74, 199
ingredients
adjuncts 72
hops 62-7
malts 55, 58, 62, 84
see also water and yeast
Innis & Gunn IPA 218-19
Innovation IPA 164-5
Intergalactic Space Hopper
172-3
international bitterness units
(IBUs) 68
(20 to 29) 296
(30 to 39) 206, 251, 293
(40 to 49) 15, 93, 107, 119,
123, 153, 156, 171, 183,
197, 239, 240, 247, 274, 301
(50 to 59) 125, 129, 148,
153, 163, 199, 201, 250,
263, 264, 286, 295, 298
(60 to 69) 41, 84, 139, 141,
157, 160, 189, 212, 221,
234, 243, 253, 270, 273,
275, 279, 292, 299
(70 to 79) 84, 87, 121, 129,
143, 146, 147, 148, 150,
151, 154, 155, 159, 191,
204, 249, 254, 277
(80 to 89) 13, 18, 113, 117,
131, 145, 154, 259, 276,
293, 294
(90 to 99) 14, 41, 115, 149,
245, 281, 279, 281, 286
(100 or more) 7, 127, 146,
152, 155, 158, 253, 266,
277, 282
Introvert Session IPA 129
Invasion Farmhouse IPA 269
Inveralmond Brewery 218

Inversion IPA 112-13
IPA! 233
IPA Gold 206
IPA Reserve 206
IPA style 307
IPA West Coast Special No 2 174-5
Ireland 16, 228-31
Irish Craft IPA Rí 230-1
Ironmonger India Pale Ale 11, 231
Italy 8, 9, 16, 103, 252-7, 296

Jackson, Michael 13, 105
Jacques West Coast IPA 264
Jai Alai IPA 150
Jaipur India Pale Ale 198-9, 279
Japan see China and Japan
Jing-A Brewing Company 284
John Smith's Brewery 98
Julius 159

Ka Pai 220
Kane Brewing Company 154
Kelham Island Brewery 181
Kern River Brewing Company 154
The Kernel Brewery 16, 176-7
The Kernel India Pale Ale 16, 176-7
King & Barnes 92
Kingstone Brewery 225
Kirin 273, 278
Kitchen Brew 260, 294, 302
Kompaan, Brouwerij 242-3
Kronenbourg Brewery 246

La Ribalta, Birrificio 255
Labatt's 153
labels 38, 42
see also labels illustrated under brewery entries
lager 43-4, 68, 84, 258, 268
Lagonda IPA 208
Lagunitas Brewing Company 124-5
Lagunitas IPA 124-5
lambic 8, 238, 244, 308
Lambrate, Birrificio 253
Langton Brewery 208
Last Chance IPA 160
Laughing Dog Brewing 126-7
Le Castor, Microbrasserie 237
Le Paradis, Brasserie 250
Leffe 243
Left Hand Brewing Company 128-9
Lerwick Brewery 219
Lerwick IPA 219
Liberty Brewing Company 280-1
Liefmans 241
Lighthouse Brewing 236
Lignum Vitae 205
Lion Nathan Group 273
Little Creatures IPA 273
Little Valley Brewery 178-9

Lloyd George, David 47, 49
Lolipa IPA (BS4.7) 10, 255-6
Long Hammer IPA 156
Lupuloid IPA 298

Magic Rock Brewing 180-1
magnesium sulphate 17, 31, 43, 68, 69
malting 55, 58, 59, 62
malts 55, 58, 62, 84
Manhattan Brewing Company 14
Marble Brewery 202, 208-9
Marjoribanks, Campbell 29, 30, 31
Marston's 14, 15, 16, 68, 76, 77, 161, 182-3, 195
Martin's IPA 244
McEwan's Export 16, 51, 96-9
Meantime Brewing Company 184-5
Meantime India Pale Ale 184-5
Melvin Brewing Company 155
Mericana India Pale Ale 254
Metalman Brewing Company 11, 231
Midnight Ryder 294
Mikkeller 9, 268-9
Miller Brewing Company 83
mineral salts 17, 31, 43, 50, 68, 69, 96
Molson Coors 77, 83, 88, 92-3
Monkey Fist IPA 138-9
Mont Salève, La Brasserie du 248-9
Monty's Brewery 226
Moor Beer Company 186-7
Mosaic IPA 230
Motley Brew 223
Mumbles Brewery 226
Murphy's 228
Murray's Craft Brewing 276
Myrcenary Double IPA 130-1

Nanjing Craft Brewing Company 285
Nanto Brewery 287
National Brewery Centre 28, 92, 93
National Collection of Yeast Cultures 71, 201
Neath Ales 227
Nebraska Brewing Company 155
Nebraska IPA 155
Nebuchadnezzar Imperial India Pale Ale 270-1
Neck Oil Session IPA 298
Netherlands see Belgium and the Netherlands
new IPA styles 7, 105, 290-303
New Zealand 7, 8, 16, 103, 278-82
Newstead Brewing Company 276-7
Ninkasi IPA 249
No. 58 Handlanger Imperial IPA 242-3

Northern Monk Brew Co 295

Oakham Ales 188-9
October beer 21, 24-5, 28
see also stock ale
Odell Brewing Company 130-1
Odeprot IPA 109
O'Hara's Irish Pale Ale 229
Okinawa Sango IPA 287
Old Empire IPA 15, 16, 161, 182-3
Omnipollo 270-1
Oregon IPA 218
organic beers 179, 204, 224, 237, 242, 247, 265, 278, 287, 295
Otley Brewing Company 223
Otus, Birrificio 10, 255-6
Oxymoron 223

Pabst Brewing Company 83, 84, 86
Palate Shifter Imperial IPA 149
Palm 244
Panhead Custom Ales 281
Pasionaria IPA Double 259
Pasteur, Louis 43, 70, 75
Pays Flamand, Brasserie du 250
Peerless Brewing Company 209
Pentland IPA 220
Pike Brewing Company 15, 132-3
Pike IPA 132-3
Pike Place Brewery 103
Pirate Life Brewing 277
Pitfield's 1837 India Pale Ale 204
Pleine Lune, Brasserie de la 250
Pliny the Elder 16, 136-7
Pliny the Younger IPA 137
Poppyland Brewery 190-1
Prohibition 52, 83
Proper Job Cornish IPA 192-3
Proudfoot, Red 277
Punk IPA 100, 216-17
purity laws 261, 263, 266, 267
Python IPA 178-9

Quarantot Double IPA 252-3

Raging Bitch IPA 117
railways 36, 38, 40, 44, 46, 89, 96, 183
Raj IPA 220-1
Rebel IPA 106-7
rebirth of IPA 7, 12-19
Red Racer IPA 234-5
Red Triangle 38, 42
Redhook Ale Brewery 156
Reinheitsgebot 261, 263, 267
Renegade Red 14
Return of the Empire 186-7
Reuben's Brews 156
Riedenburger Brauhaus 264
Rigden's Brewery 197
Ringwood Brewery 139, 195

RoboHop Imperial IPA 233
Rogue Brewing Company 134-5
Rooster's Brewery 62
Route of All Evil Black Ale 297, 302
Royal Brewery 98
Royale Cascade IPA 243
Ruination Double IPA 143, 266
running beers 47
Rurale, Birrificio 11, 256, 296
Russian River Brewing Company 16, 136-7

SABMiller 185
Saccharomyces 71
St Austell Brewery 192-3
Saint Feuillien, Brasserie 244-5
Saint Louis Brewery 301
Saint-Loupoise, Brasserie 250-1
St Pancras Undercroft 44, 46
St Peter's Brewery 210
Saltaire Brewery 212
Salty Kiss 181
Sambrook's Brewery 194-5
Samuel Adams 15, 106-7
Scandinavia 9, 16, 103, 268-71
Scarborough Fair IPA 213
Scarliga European Double India Pale Ale 256
Schlafly Grapefruit IPA 301
Schönram, Braurerei 265
Scotland 214-21
Edinburgh 16, 50-1, 95, 96
Scottish & Newcastle 51, 98
Sculpin India Pale Ale 147
Sebago Brewing Company 157
Session IPA (Kitchen Brew) 260
Session IPA (Mikkeller) 268-9
Shape Shifter West Coast IPA 204-5
Sharp's Brewery 93
Shepherd Neame Brewery 196-7
Shipyard Brewing Company 15, 103, 138-9
SIBA 205, 226
Sierra Nevada Brewing Company 16, 109, 140-1
Single-Wide IPA 148
SinoFortune 284
Siphon Brewing 245
Sitting Bulldog IPA 270
Skizoid American IPA 256-7
Slow Boat Brewery 284
Smith, Garrett & Co 38
Snake Dog IPA 117
Snake Handler Double IPA 101, 152
Snow 283
Spaceman West Coast IPA 254
sparging 75
Spaten Brewery 43
St see under Saint
Staggeringly Good Brewery

296-7
State of Mind Session IPA 235
Steelhead Brewery 14
Steinlager 278
Stewart Brewing 16, 220
stock ales 8, 41, 51
see also October beer
Stone Brewing 9, 16, 51, 142-3, 266
Stone IPA 142-3
Stone & Wood Brewing 274
Summerhall Brewery 216
Superior IPA 215
Suruga Bay Imperial IPA 286, 287
Swamp Ape IPA 152
Switzerland 9, 258-60, 294

't IJ, Brouwerij 242
tannins 66
Teignworthy Brewery 210-11
Teikoku IPA 286, 287
temperance movement 46
Tennent Caledonian 51
Tetley's Brewery 24
Thornbridge Brewery 198-9, 279
Three Floyds Brewing 158
Tierney-Jones, Adrian 216, 291
Timmermans 244
Timothy Taylor Brewery 103
Tiny Rebel Brewing Co 227
Tired Hands Brewing Company 270
Titanic IPA 250-1
To Øl 271
Toccalmatto, Birrificio 256-7
Torpedo Extra IPA 140-1
Tower Brewery 16
trademarks 38, 42
transport costs 46
Tree House Brewing Company 159
Trois Dames, Brasserie 259
Truman's Brewery 15, 38, 41, 72
The Truth Imperial IPA 116-17
Tryst Brewery 220-1
Tsingtao 283
Tuborg 269
Two Hearted Ale American IPA 147
Two Roads Brewing Company 297, 302
Two to the Valley IPA 276-7

UBREW 8, 16-18
Uinta Brewing Company 144-5
Unibroue Brewery 232
Union Jack IPA 151
United States 7, 8, 14, 15, 16, 41, 51-2, 83, 103, 105-60, 291, 292, 293-4, 297, 299, 301
Uprising Treason West Coast IPA 212-13

Vagabund Brauerei 267

Vale la Pena, Birra 257
Valhalla Brewery 219
Vallée du Giffre, Brasserie de la 250
The Vandal New Zealand Pale Ale 281
Vassar Brewery 52
Vedett Extraordinary IPA 241
vegan beers 179, 187, 204, 208, 270, 287, 296
Vesuvio, Birrificio del 257
Viceroy India Pale Ale 200-1
Victory Brewing Company 159
Vocation Brewery 211
Volcano IPA 101, 216

Wales 16, 222-7
Walkers of Warrington 38
Waltham Brothers Brewery 24
water 51, 68-70
Burton-on-Trent 17, 29, 34, 38, 43, 68-9
Edinburgh 50, 96
London 29, 31, 69
Weezledog Brewing Company 282
Westerham Brewery Company 200-1
Weyerbacher Brewing Company 160
Whitbread Brewery 14, 15, 74
White Horse IPA 13, 14, 16
White Shield, Worthington's 16, 40, 88-93, 105
Wicked Weed Brewing Company 160
Wild Childe Brewing Co 11, 212
Williams Brothers Brewing Company 221
Windsor & Eton Brewery 212-13
Wold Top Brewery 213
women brewery workers 71
wort 17
Worthington, William 31, 40, 70, 88
Worthington's White Shield 16, 40, 88-93, 105

Yakima IPA 237
yeast 17, 70-2, 75, 87, 88, 202, 244, 309
Brettanomyces 8, 18, 37, 41, 84, 269, 293, 305
Saccharomyces 71
see also National Collection of Yeast Cultures
Young's 103
Younger, George, & Sons (Alloa) 50, 221
Younger, William, & Co (Edinburgh) 43, 51, 96, 98
Younger's see Younger, William, & Co